Critical Essays on Wallace Stegner

Critical Essays on Wallace Stegner

Anthony Arthur

G. K. Hall & Co. • Boston, Massachusetts

BP452

Copyright © 1982 by Anthony Arthur

Library of Congress Cataloging in Publication Data
Main entry under title:
Critical essays on Wallace Stegner.

(Critical essays on American literature)
Includes bibliographical references and index.

I. Stegner, Wallace Earle, 1909–   —Criticism and
interpretation—Addresses, essays, lectures.   I. Arthur,
Anthony.   II. Series.
PS3537.T316Z63   813'.52   82-963
ISBN 0-8161-8487-9   AACR2

This publication is printed on permanent/durable acid-free paper
MANUFACTURED IN THE UNITED STATES OF AMERICA

CRITICAL ESSAYS ON AMERICAN LITERATURE

This series seeks to publish the most important reprinted criticism on writers and topics in American literature along with, in various volumes, original essays, interviews, bibliographies, letters, manuscript sections, and other materials brought to the public attention for the first time. Anthony Arthur's volume on Wallace Stegner is the first collection of criticism ever published on this important but neglected writer. The book contains, along with early reviews by Howard Mumford Jones, Joseph Warren Beach, Granville Hicks, Malcolm Cowley, and others, eleven reprinted articles by established Stegner scholars, among them David Dillon, Joseph M. Flora, Robert Canzoneri, Kerry Ahearn, and Lois Phillips Hudson. In addition, there are three original essays written specifically for publication in this collection, including William C. Baurecht on *The Big Rock Candy Mountain*, Mary Ellen Williams Walsh on *Angle of Repose*, and Merrill Lewis on *Recapitulation*. We are confident that this volume will make a permanent and significant contribution to American literary study.

JAMES NAGEL, GENERAL EDITOR

Northeastern University

For
Diana Smith

CONTENTS

INTRODUCTION

In the spring of 1978, Wallace Stegner was the principal speaker at a conference in Banff, Canada, called "Crossing Frontiers." Some two hundred writers, historians, and scholars from Canada and the United States had met to discuss the boundaries and the links between the literature and history of the two nations, paying particular attention to their western regions and to the different ways in which literature and history could convey an understanding of them.

Stegner was a strikingly appropriate choice for such a gathering. Born in 1909 to a restless father and a long-suffering, patient mother, he lived in a dozen different places in the American West during his youth; but six of the most important years, from 1914 to 1920, were spent in the tiny farming community of East End, Saskatchewan, which gives Canadians a partial claim on him. When his family moved to Salt Lake City in 1921, a different sort of frontier faced the eleven-year-old boy, as a member of a "Gentile" family in a Mormon community. In 1925 Stegner enrolled at the University of Utah, beginning what turned out to be an illustrious academic career that allowed him to cross the frontiers between teaching and writing and between literature and history; the culmination of his joint careers came when, shortly after he had retired as Director of the Creative Writing Program at Stanford University, where he had taught since 1945, he won the Pulitzer Prize in 1972 for his extraordinary historical novel, *Angle of Repose*.

Through the years Stegner has written on such topics as "History, Myth, and the Western Writer;" on such Western figures as John Wesley Powell, Bernard DeVoto, Mary Hallock Foote, Willa Cather, and Bret Harte; and on such issues as water policy in the West and conservation. Although any one of these would have been appropriate in Banff for his address, the selection Stegner settled on seemed particularly interesting as a personal statement, especially to those who were familiar with his background. The selection came from his most recent novel, entitled *Recapitulation;* the novel is a retrospective gathering of memories by Bruce Mason, who has returned to Salt Lake City, where his early life is recounted in *The Big Rock Candy Mountain*, for the funeral of a distant

1

relative. Now a successful diplomat in his sixties, Mason remembers viv-idly the painful, humiliating, and prolonged hostility between himself and his father, and the widening of the gulf between the two after his mother had died of cancer during his first year at college. As the narrative begins (it is slightly revised from a 1950 story called "The Blue-Winged Teal") Bruce has carried a brace of ducks he has shot into his father's seedy pool hall. The ducks are received by Harry Mason and the various hangers-on with a mixture of pride, scorn, and incredulity that the college boy could be so lucky, and a feast is planned for the next day. Later, Bruce lies in bed after Harry has gone out for an amorous rendezvous, brooding on his father's physical and moral decline, on "the many failures, the schemes that never paid off, the jobs that never worked out, the hopeful starts that had always ended in excuses or flight." When Harry at last stumbles into their shared room, smelling of booze and cheap perfume, Bruce feigns sleep. In "the little prison" of the room the old man's breathing is "obscene—loose and bubbling, undisciplined, animal." Desperately seeking oblivion in sleep, Bruce falls back on an old trick: a mental game of pool:

> Yellow and blue and red, spotted and striped, he shot pool balls into pockets as deep and black and silent as the cellars of his consciousness. He was not now quarry that his mind chased, but an actor, a doer, a willer, a man in command. By an act of will or flight he focused his whole awareness on the game he played. His mind undertook it with intense concentration. He took pride in little two-cushion banks, little triumphs of accuracy, small successes for foresight. When he had finished one game and the green cloth was bare, he dug the balls from the bin under the end of the table and racked them up and began another.
>
> Eventually, he knew, nothing would remain in his mind but the clean green cloth traced with running color and bounded by simple problems, and sometime in the middle of that intricately planned combination he would pale off into sleep.[1]

Stegner's choice of material was not merely poignant, but re-markably appropriate for the theme of "crossing frontiers." Implicit within this passage are, first, the emotional barrier between the boy and his father; second, the temporal frontier between Bruce past and Bruce present, or the callow boy of sixteen and the distinguished diplomat of sixty; and third, the artistic distance between Wallace Stegner the writer and the historical circumstances of his own life and family on which this narrative is based. Equally significant, because his life and character con-stitute the necessary condition in which the previously-noted facts are grounded, is the memorable Harry Mason. For it is the disturbing thesis of *The Big Rock Candy Mountain* (indeed, of the large bulk of Stegner's work, fiction and non-fiction) that the pioneer virtues of a Harry Mason—restlessness, impatience, individual initiative, and an un-shakable certainty that the American Dream means that he must prevail—have become disabling vices in an era which requires cooperation for survival.

Fortunately, George Stegner's son was able to turn his own initiative, independence, and energy to more productive ends. He has written nine novels, including two of special significance, *Angle of Repose* and *The Big Rock Candy Mountain* (1943), and one shorter work, *The Spectator Bird*, for which he won the National Book Award in 1977; two collections of short fiction, *The Women on the Wall* (1950) and *The City of the Dead* (1956); two collections of essays and reminiscences, *Wolf Willow* (1964) and *The Sound of Mountain Water* (1969); a historical study of the Mormons, *The Gathering of Zion* (1954); two biographies, one of John Wesley Powell entitled *Beyond the Hundredth Meridian: The Second Opening of the West* (1954), and one on his old friend, mentor, and colleague Bernard DeVoto, entitled *The Uneasy Chair* (1974), which was followed by an edition of *The Letters of Bernard DeVoto* (1975); and, finally, scores of magazine articles, introductions to texts, and reviews.

Given his personal background and the body of work related to it which he has produced, it is not surprising that Stegner is perfectly willing to define literary art in terms of the so-called "personal heresy."[2] Expanding on this idea, Merrill and Lorene Lewis have suggested that the central theme of Stegner's work has been the quest for identity in the personal, regional, cultural, and artistic senses of that word.[3] In the episode from *Recapitulation*, Bruce Mason has effected, in his own mind, the transformation from a confused, lonely boy into an "actor, a doer, a willer, a man in command"; he is now one who arranges patterns and actions to his own satisfaction, both the subject and the agent of his transformation. In the process of determining his own identity, he creates himself, and thereby creates art.

The adolescent search for identity that Stegner revisits in *Recapitulation* is, of course, a major theme in American literature. Some writers, such as Thomas Wolfe, never went beyond it, and their work now seems rather overwrought. An essential difference between Stegner and a writer like Wolfe, whose compelling account of his childhood and his overwhelming father in *Look Homeward, Angel* is not unlike *The Big Rock Candy Mountain* in emotional appeal, is that Wolfe died young while Stegner has had the opportunity to let his protagonists grow older along with him. They are still searching: the now-mature Bruce Mason; the retired literary agent, Joe Allston, of *All the Little Live Things*, "Field Guide to the Western Birds," and *The Spectator Bird;* and Lyman Ward, the retired history professor in *Angle of Repose*, all share with Stegner's younger characters the need to strike a balance, to find an "angle of repose" from which they can view their lives with understanding. What gives their stories added depth is that all these men had enough experience of life to transcend the youthful ignorance and naivete imposed by the limitations of the initiation theme.

Another reason for the wide appeal of Stegner's books may be that he presents his characters, particularly when he is dealing with the West, in a context larger than their own egos. Defining for us and for himself the regional identity of the inter-mountain West, he shows the connections that exist between the land and those who inhabit it, both past and present.

This concern for the land is one that Stegner shares with most other Western writers, and it means something beyond and above its significance in terms of history and human drama and esthetic beauty. In 1960, well before the environmental movement was widely known or understood, Stegner sent a letter to a government official which has since been reproduced by the Sierra Club and distributed widely throughout the country and abroad. Stegner takes a pardonable pride in that "Wilderness Letter," which is indeed a model of cogent, persuasive prose. It concludes with an appeal not to the mind but to the soul by noting the need for preservation of the wilderness according to some other, and higher, purpose than commercial exploitation or recreation.

> We simply need that wild country available to us, even if we never do more than drive to its edge and look in. For it can be a means of reassuring ourselves of our sanity as creatures, a part of the geography of hope.[4]

It may sound from this passage as though Stegner, because he values the land so highly, is one with such poets and writers as William Everson, Walter van Tillburg Clark, Gary Snyder, Frederick Manfred, and Frank Waters, all of whom have described the western landscape in terms of mystical transcendence, reflecting the principle of "sacrality" that the critic, Max Westbrook, has coined and explained.[5] But there is a critical difference, for Stegner the land is "nothing in itself":

> It has no meaning, it can hardly be said to exist, except in terms of human perception, use, and response. The wealth and resources and usefulness of any region are only inert potential. . . ; and natural beauty is nothing until it comes to the eye of the beholder. The natural world, actually, is the test by which each man proves himself: I see, I feel, I love, I use, I alter, I appropriate, therefore I am. Or the natural world is a screen onto which we project our own images; without our images there, it is as blank as the cold screen of an empty movie house.[6]

In philosophical terms, then, Stegner's world is man-centered, not nature-centered or God-centered. Nature is not a gift but a test, one that is often failed. It is part of the continuing history of the West, Stegner says, that the ignorant eye can be indifferent or hostile to the most magnificent landscape, and the effects can be disastrous, as he notes in a recent article on the resistance of native Utahns to environmental controls that would preserve the beauty of their state.[7]

It is what people do to and with the land, and why, that most interests Stegner; he is intrigued by the culture that gave definition to the

West, and some of his best work deals with what the Lewises have called his search for cultural identity, described in "Born a Square" and other essays. Stegner regrets the lack of a usable intellectual tradition and the necessary provinciality that results from such deprivation. At the same time, as he explains in the interview with David Dillon reprinted in this volume, Stegner also sees the advantages of a nation and a region being able to start fresh, to create its own identity without the burden, as in modern Greece, of a too-glorious past. Characteristically, Stegner occupies the "middle ground," defined by Forrest Robinson and Margaret Robinson in their excellent study, between Clio and Calliope, the muses of literature and history.[8] Like the nineteenth-century English and European novels which he prefers to much contemporary American fiction, all of Stegner's work constitutes a general criticism of his culture.

The recurrent theme in his work, touched on already in connection with Harry Mason, is that the West is in danger of becoming a despoiled oasis, a synecdoche of the American dream defiled. The cause lies in the American myth of the solitary seeker who descends upon the land, uses what he can for personal advantage, discards the residue for someone else to clean up, and moves on further west to repeat the process. Our experience has been a parody of the Turner thesis, which sees in the same pattern the American genius for successful nation-building. Popular literature and popular culture have perpetuated the Western myths until they have become self-fulfilling prophecies, further weakening an already-strained social fabric. Occasional groups and individuals who favor a more harmonious and productive model of social cooperation, such as developed in Canada, are left behind in the dust of the romantic egoists.

Naturally, the issue and its representation in so large and varied a body of work as Stegner's are hardly so simple as this summary implies. Indeed, it is the cluster of paradoxes within Stegner's work that accounts for its compelling nature. Bo (Harry) Mason of *The Big Rock Candy Mountain*, for example, is openly based on Stegner's father, George. In the Robinsons' apt summary, Mason "sacrifices his family, ignores the law, severs his connections with society, and squanders his great potential . . . his life exemplifies the waste of human and national resources that hollow myth and unchecked individualism have meant to the West."[9] But, as the Robinsons also remind us, Mason is, with all his faults, a vividly *alive* character, and his life gives essence and vitality to what remains in many ways Stegner's most affecting novel. Further, Bo Mason is a tragic figure; without George Stegner and the now-challenged ethos that he embodied, we would have been deprived of the art that his misspent life inspired, and perhaps of the writer who grew out of it.

Then too, there is the paradox of the American Dream, of which the title song of Mason's story is a variant. The earlier Spanish-American myths of Eldorado and the Lost Cities of Cibola have now given way to the frontier joke of the mountain made of hard candy, covered with lemonade springs and cigarette trees. But if they had not been possessed by a version of that dream, Mary Hallock Foote and her husband, whose lives are the source for *Angle of Repose,* would not have tried to tap the waters of the Snake River in Idaho in order to make the desert bloom. Arthur Foote's heroic enterprise failed as completely as did Bo Mason's tawdry schemes. In part they both failed simply because they were unlucky—William Mulholland would transform Los Angeles not many years later into a metropolis by piping water 350 miles from the Sierras, and the city itself was to become a mecca for the Bo Mason type of con man/entrepreneur. But Stegner suggests that the major cause for their failures was the absence of a productive social unit to sustain them, and of a social vision to ennoble them.

An alternative did exist, says Stegner, in the form of the Mormons. This "dynamic, dedicated, regimented, group-conscious and Heaven-conscious people"[10] represents a conspicuous rebuttal in particular of Mason's negative model. The dream that sustained the Latter Day Saints in their westward trek was, as the Lewises have said, "the sacred variant of Bo Mason's secular dream";[11] it resulted in harmony and order rather than, as in Mason's case, moral squalor, emotional despair, and suicide.

But another paradox emerges. Stegner has always distrusted zealotry, especially in religion and politics; thus his admiration for the Mormons' social coherence, which is based on the famous symbol of the beehive, is qualified by his skepticism concerning both its sources and the limitations it places on human freedom. The best alternative to Mason, and an improvement over Foote's dependence on commercial interests, is one step beyond the Mormons. It is present in the life of John Wesley Powell, the ideal civil servant, whose career is recounted in *Beyond the Hundredth Meridian.* Bernard DeVoto, later the subject himself of an admirable biography by Stegner, defined the issue lucidly in his introduction to Powell's story. He cites with scorn a review of Stegner's book that remarks on the " 'distinctive traces on the American mind [left by the frontier] through its cult of action, rough individualism, physical freedom, and adventurous romance.' " DeVoto is outraged: "Here are four fixed and indestructible stereotypes about the West," he complains, "all of them meaningless." Powell is valuable, he says,

> precisely because seventy-five years ago he pierced through these misconceptions to the realities. His career was an indomitable effort to substitute knowledge for the misconceptions and to get it acted on. He tried to repair the damage they had done to the people and the land and to prevent them from doing further damage. He tried to shape legal and political and social institutions so that they would accord with the necessities of the West. He tried to conserve the West's natural wealth so that it could play to the full its potential part in the future of the United

States . . . Long ago he accomplished great things and now we are beginning to understand him . . . even out west.[12]

Although DeVoto is occasionally guilty of hyperbole, there can be
little doubt about Powell's importance. But let the reader now count how
many books, movies, or television shows there have been about Powell,
compared with those on Butch and Billy and Wyatt and Bat and the
dozens of other deadly juveniles and thugs who represent the American
West to most Americans, and he will begin to appreciate how different
Stegner's perspective really is from that of our popular culture.

Stegner's search for the best means to convey his views—for his "ar-
tisitic identity"—has involved him in continuing experimentation with
narrative technique and with close study of other writers' methods. A
brief but useful touchstone for considering his approach toward the art of
fiction is provided by his comments on Willa Cather's *My Antonia*. That
novel, Stegner explains, represents a successful attempt to render a
complex subject with "the clean lines and suggestive subtlety of fine architecture." In her earlier novels Cather had reported the action as the
omniscient narrator, "over the protagonist's shoulder." But here the story
is told by Jim Burden, a boyhood friend of Antonia's who now works for
the railroad. "The use of the narrative mask," Stegner explains,

> permits Miss Cather to exercise her sensibility without obvious self-
> indulgence. Burden becomes an instrument of the selectivity that she has
> worked for. He also permits the easy condensation and syncopation of
> time—an indispensible technical tool in a novel that covers more than 30
> years and deals in a complex way with a theme of development. Finally,
> Jim Burden is used constantly as a suggestive parallel to Antonia: he is
> himself an orphan and has been himself transplanted and is himself grop-
> ing for an identity and an affiliation. In the process of understanding and
> commemorating Antonia, he locates himself; we see the essential theme
> from two points, and the space between these points serves as a base line
> for triangulation.[13]

Readers of Stegner's *Big Rock Candy Mountain* may see the connections between this description of Cather's novel and the problems faced by
young Bruce Mason in determining his identity, his need for an "affiliation," his feeling of being rootless and transplanted. Of particular interest
is the idea that an individual life may be "read" as a history of the time
when it was lived. All of this, it seems fair to say, had been perceived in-
tuitively by Stegner when he was still a very young man writing his first
big novel. But by the time he came to write *Angle of Repose*, the intuition
and personal experience that had shaped *The Big Rock Candy Mountain*
had been broadened by 35 years of creative and intellectual labor, and the
later work is accordingly richer in texture and meaning. The following
passage from *Angle of Repose*, in which Lyman Ward, the retired history

professor, talks about his grandmother, shows not only how Stegner's technique resembles Cather's, but also how it is different.

> When frontier historians theorize about the uprooted, the lawless, the purseless, and the socially cut-off who settled the West, they are not talking about people like my grandmother. So much that was cherished and loved, women like her had to give up; and the more they gave it up, the more they carried it helplessly with them. It was a process like ionization: what was subtracted from one pole was added to the other. For that sort of pioneer, the West was not a new country being created, but an old one being reproduced; in that sense our pioneer women were always more realistic than our pioneer men. The moderns, carrying little baggage of the kind that Shelly [Ward's secretary] called "merely cultural," not even living in traditional air, but breathing into their space helmets a scientific mixture of synthetic gases (and polluted at that) are the true pioneers. Their circuitry seems to include no atavistic domestic sentiment, they have suffered emphathectomy, their computers hum no ghostly feedback of Home, Sweet Home. How marvelously free they are! How unutterably deprived! (pp. 246–247).

The main points made by Stegner about *My Antonia*, it will be noted, may also be made about this passage. The historian-narrator is by profession as well as by inclination "an instrument of . . . selectivity," choosing from the vast record of the past those elements that make it meaningful to the present. Similarly, the "easy syncopation" of time that Stegner celebrates in Cather is even more significant in *Angle of Repose*, which attempts to link not merely different generations but different eras. Stegner's third point, that Jim Burden both locates himself and establishes the theme of the novel in the process of "commemorating" Antonia, is vitally important in connection with Lyman Ward as well—the last words of the book have him wondering if he is "man enough to be a bigger man than" his grandfather was, that is, to forgive his wife for injuring him in a way that his grandfather was unable to do (p. 511).

But Stegner does not merely copy Cather's technique; his narrator is a modern man, and the modern sensibility is largely the product of modern science—hence one of the more intriguing aspects of this historical novel is its recurrent use of scientific metaphor, so prominent in the passage above, with its references to physics, chemistry, and cybernetics. This is by no means an isolated pattern of reference, for Ward is obsessed by the ideas of time and perception. Early in the novel, for example, he muses on the so-called Doppler effect (p. 20):

> If Henry Adams, whom you knew slightly, could make a theory of history by applying the second law of thermodynamics to human affairs, I ought to be entitled to base one on the angle of repose, and may yet. There is another physical law that teases me, too: the Doppler Effect. The sound of anything coming at you—a train, say, or the future—has a higher pitch than the sound of the same thing going away. If you have perfect pitch

and a head for mathematics you can compute the speed of the object by the interval between its arriving and departing sounds. I have neither perfect pitch nor a head for mathematics, and anyway who wants to compute the speed of history? Like all falling bodies, it constantly accelerates. But I would like to hear your life [i.e. his grandmother's] as *you* heard it, coming at you, instead of hearing it as I do, a sober sound of expectations reduced, desires blunted, hopes deferred or abandoned, chances lost, defeats accepted, griefs borne. I don't find your life uninteresting, as Rodman [his son] does. I would like to hear it as it sounded while it was passing. Having no future of my own, why shouldn't I look forward to yours?

Later he meets an old acquaintance in a laundry. The man has a speech defect and wears special glasses with quadruple focus.

"Thethe are my working glatheth," he said, "Quadruple focalth."

I looked at them. Four half-moons of magnification were ground into each lens. When I raised them and looked through them, the front of the building swam like hot taffy, and Al became a small crowd. "I thought I had a problem, having to look straight ahead," I said, "What do you use them for?"

Tentatively, delicately, the wart emerged, touched the upper bow of Al's smile, withdrew again. Al stood chuckling, scratching his elbow. "I don't th'pothe a profethor would ever need anything like thethe. But I'm alwayth having to fixth the mathineth. Ever try to thee with your head inthide a Bendixth?"

I get the message. Space being curved, tunnel vision and rigid neck could leave a man focused on the back of his own head. I don't know what the effect of quadruple focals on a historian might be—nausea, maybe—but there might be virtue in trying them on.

Whose head *isn't* inside a Bendix? (p. 65)

Even the title of the book is drawn from science—the angle of repose being a geologist's term for the point at which rocks stop rolling down a slope. If we consider these and other similar references together, it is clear that Ward's retrospective musings on his grandmother's life are less random than they might at first appear. Neither are they simply didactic, though we do learn something from the passage about the course of American history. The proper effect of the passage, finally, is to enlarge the reader's sense of the personality of the narrator—a modern personality indeed, cynical yet sentimental, tough yet vulnerable, independent yet helpless in the face of circumstance.

It is pleasant to note that Wallace Stegner's achievements have been recognized by the literary establishment in both its academic and commercial phases. He has been elected to the American Academy of Arts and Sciences and to the National Academy of Arts and Letters. He has received coveted fellowships from Phi Beta Kappa, the Huntington Library, the Center for Advanced Studies in the Behavioral Sciences, and the Guggenheim, Rockefeller, and Wenner/Gren Foundations. In addition to the

Pulitzer Prize and the National Book Award, he has received the Little, Brown novelette prize (1937), the O. Henry Memorial award (1942, 1948, 1950), the Anisfield-Wolfe and Houghton Mifflin Life-in-America awards (1945) and the Commonwealth Club gold medal (1968).

However, for all his success and recognition, Stegner is less well known than some of his students at Stanford such as Ken Kesey, Larry McMurtry, and Edward Abbey, if one can judge from the attention paid to these writers in the academic journals. One reason might be that, more than these younger writers, Stegner is viewed as "merely" a Western writer, a "regionalist," by influential Eastern critics who fail to perceive the wider appeal of his work. But Stegner is not alone; other excellent novelists of his generation and his realistic mode, including James Gould Cozzens and Thornton Wilder, have received far less attention than such fabulists and ironists as Thomas Pynchon and John Barth. It may be useful at this point to go far afield from American literature and criticism to a European Marxist critic writing in the 1930s who provides a partial explanation for the relative lack of critical attention afforded Stegner. According to George Lukacs, modern European literature had been following two paths: one was that of Thomas Mann, whom he characterized as a realist, and the other was that of Franz Kafka, whose works may be characterized as fantasy. Lukacs was less interested in the particular literary form chosen by his contemporaries than he was in the "personal decision" that each must make: should one accept or reject "angst"—elsewhere characterized as "morbid anxiety"—as the absolute condition of existence? Is angst the determining factor of the human condition? The crucial question, Lukacs says, "is whether a man escapes from the life of his time into a realm of abstraction . . . or confronts modern life determined to fight its evils and support what is good in it." This decision will lead one to the next and central question: "is man the helpless victim of transcendental and inexplicable forces, or is he a member of a human community in which he can play a part, however small, toward its modification or reform?"[14]

Many influential American writers had decided by the 1960s that Philip Roth was right when he argued, in effect, for Kafka's angst as the central condition of mankind. American life, Roth wrote in 1961, "stupefies . . . sickens . . . infuriates and finally . . . is even a kind of embarrassment to one's own meager imagination. The actuality is continually outdoing our talents, and culture tosses up figures almost daily that are the envy of any novelist."[15] Following Roth's lead, it might appear, a generation of American critics in the 1960s wrote studies entitled *Number and Nightmare, The Pursuit of Loneliness, The Absurd Hero in American Fiction, The Dismemberment of Orpheus, A Cheerful Nihilism, The Kafkan Mode in Contemporary Fiction,* and—almost hopefully—*Waiting for the End.*

Stegner was and is emphatically out of sympathy with the attitudes reflected by these titles. His rejection of *angst* is implicit in his work generally, and notably so in the passage cited above from his essay on Willa Cather. His essential premises include the assumption that human development, even the much-maligned notion of "progress," rather than disintegration, is the right and proper subject for art. People do learn, they do grow, beneficial change is possible. A highly significant and characteristic recurring phrase in Stegner's works is "the geography of hope," a phrase which brings us back once again to the importance of place in his thinking. Stegner recognizes his separation from a "literary generation that appears to specialize in despair, hostility, hypersexuality, and disgust," and he credits the "several Wests" which he has identified for helping to perpetuate aspects of "traditional American innocence." These American "Wests," he says, "breed more meliorists than nihilists, and they encourage booster clubs, culture clubs, and reform movements much more commonly than the despair, decadence, masochism, sadism, self-pity, *angst* and the hopeless prick of conscience that are compulsive to many contemporary novelists."[16]

It is not difficult, then, to see how Stegner's works would fail to offer much grist for the mills of critics who see either the past or the present of American life as nightmare. But one final point remains to be made. Stegner's comments on Willa Cather explain the significance of the search for identity, maturity, and competence. The reason for undertaking such a quest, however, is not merely to understand oneself: it is to commemorate someone else. Perhaps Stegner would be amused that so self-evident a proposition should have to be pointed out, but it is no longer self-evident to a generation of Americans whose points of cultural reference are "looking out for number one," assertiveness training, primal screaming, and songs like "My Way."

One is tempted to add, defensively, that there is plenty of violence, sex, and aberrational behavior in Stegner's work, and strong admixtures of fantasy, just so he will not seem unconscionably cheerful or "square." These elements are present because Stegner describes the world as it is, not as he wishes it were. But it is more important to note the elegiac, stoic dignity with which Stegner allows his characters to meet the inevitable defeats of life: not because society is unfair or because the human condition is absurd, though they may well be, but because life is, as Oscar Wilde said, "a tragedy to those who feel," as well as being a "comedy to those who think." Stegner's curmudgeonly Joe Allston, a paradigm of the man who both thinks and feels, may be allowed to have the last words, which I think provide an accurate index to the underlying theses of Stegner's fiction; and to its enduring appeal:

> The truest vision of life I know is that bird in the Venerable Bede that flutters from the dark into a lighted hall, and after a while flutters out again into the dark. But Ruth [his wife] is right. It is something—it can be everything—to have found a fellow bird with whom you can sit among

the rafters while the drinking and boasting and reciting and fighting go on below; a fellow bird whom you can look after and find bugs and seeds for, one who will patch your bruises and straighten your ruffled feathers and mourn over your hurts, when you accidentally fly into something you can't handle.[17]

Wallace Stegner's large volume of work has been reviewed in national publications for nearly four decades; a few representative reviews by such noted writers as Howard Mumford Jones, Malcolm Cowley, and Mari Sandoz are included here to give a sense of Stegner's early promise, his development into a confident professional, and the fulfillment of both the promise and the professionalism.

In contrast, the essays reprinted here represent perhaps half the total criticism done on Stegner, excluding the studies by the Robinsons and the Lewises. Most of them were written fairly recently, by younger critics and scholars, and they have appeared not in such national forums for criticism as *American Literature* but in journals with regional identification such as *Western Humanities Review*, *South Dakota Review*, and *Western American Literature*.

The chief conclusion to be drawn from these contrasts between the reviews and the essays would seem to be that Stegner is a regionalist with a national reputation. This feeling is likely to be reinforced by the strong emphasis in the essays on the historical perspective that informs Stegner's work. David Dillon, who taught English at Southern Methodist University and is now Associate Editor of *D Magazine* in Dallas, captures Stegner's voice, personality, and ideas admirably in the interview which introduces the critical essays. Joseph Flora, Professor of English at the University of North Carolina at Chapel Hill, has worked with both Stegner and Vardis Fisher and points out how the delicate relationship between the two men is developed in an early short story by Stegner. Further analysis of Stegner's shorter work, particularly *Wolf Willow*, is provided by Robert Canzoneri, Director of Creative Writing at Ohio State University; Canzoneri's long essay on Stegner, from which the selection reprinted here is drawn, was one of the first extended critiques of the writer's work. The Robinsons' study is useful in every aspect of Stegner's career; the selections reprinted here on *The Preacher and The Slave*, a novel/biography of Joe Hill, the Wobbly labor leader and martyr, and *A Shooting Star*, a novel about modern California, represent the only extended comments on these neglected works of Stegner's mid-career. Forrest Robinson is a professor of English at the University of California, Santa Cruz, where Margaret Robinson is a librarian.

The central idea of rootlessness in Stegner's work is discussed by Jamie Robertson, Director of Adult and Continuing Education at Oglala Sioux Community College in South Dakota; Robertson considers the relationship between learning and place, and finds an intellectual link between Stegner and Henry Adams, another writer who, oddly enough, felt uprooted from his past.

William Baurecht, Assistant Director of the Honors Program at the University of New Mexico, helps to establish the social context of *The Big Rock Candy Mountain*. Kerry Ahearn, who teaches at Oregon State University in Corvallis, is one of the Stegner's most perceptive and productive critics; he demonstrates the connections between *The Big Rock Candy Mountain* and *Angle of Repose*, and argues that the later book represents an artistic advance. Barnett Singer and Lois Phillips Hudson both provide overviews of Stegner's major work; Singer is a historian at the University of Victoria who admires Stegner's ability to represent history in his fiction. Hudson, a novelist and critic who teaches at the University of Washington, examines Stegner's search for a rooted, stable society in the West.

A broadly-based perspective on Stegner is provided by Richard Etulain in "Western History and Fiction: A Reconsideration." Professor of History at the University of New Mexico and one of the most active and productive scholars presently dealing with the American West, Etulain is currently editing a series of ten conversations he taped with Stegner in 1980 and early 1981; they are scheduled to be published as a book by the University of Utah Press in the fall of 1981.

Sid Jenson, who wrote his doctoral dissertation on Stegner at the University of Utah, here concentrates on providing a "philosophical focus" on Stegner's attitudes and ideas, with an emphasis on *Angle of Repose*. Audrey Peterson, a professor of English at California State University, Long Beach, examines narrative technique in that novel; one of her main points is the distinction between a "chronicle" of the West, such as Mary Hallock Foote provides in her letters and memoirs, and the artistic recreation of the past which Stegner provides through his use of those materials. This distinction is vigorously, if implicitly, challenged by Mary Ellen Williams Walsh, who is Associate Dean of Humanities at Idaho State University and a professor of English. In her detailed examination of Stegner's use of the Foote materials, she argues that Stegner has been less than fair to Foote, both in his use of the materials and in what she regards as a negative portrayal of Susan Ward, the character based on Foote.

Finally, and appropriately, Merrill Lewis provides an essay written especially for this volume on Stegner's latest novel, *Recapitulation*. Lewis, who teaches English at Western Washington State University, has edited several volumes of essays on Western writers and topics, and his book on Stegner with Lorene Lewis for the Western Writers Series laid down the guidelines for future study of the writer's work. In this essay he explains how *Recapitulation* represents a homecoming of sorts for Bruce Mason to Salt Lake City, the locale for much of *Big Rock Candy Mountain*.

Although it is comprehensive, this collection should not represent the final word on Stegner's accomplishments, for much remains to be done. The recent fiction, particularly *The Spectator Bird* and *Recapitulation*, will repay our critical attention; Stegner's role as occasional journalist, especially in connection with the environmental and ecological controversies of recent years, has been perhaps as significant as that of Bernard DeVoto; and he had an as-yet-undetermined effect on a generation of younger writers during his years at Stanford. Wallace Stegner's career, in summary, has been a notably successful one, lacking only the full critical recognition which it deserves. If this volume serves to stimulate further interest in the accomplishments of that career, it will have served its purpose.

ANTHONY ARTHUR

Notes

1. *Recapitulation* (New York: Viking Press, 1979), p. 255.

2. "Fiction: A Lens on Life," *Saturday Review* (Apr. 22, 1950), p. 32. Stegner says in this regard that the reader generally seeks to find himself in fiction, but will settle for "the completely intimate contact which may show us another like ourselves."

3. *Wallace Stegner* (Boise, Idaho: Boise State College Western Writers Series, 1972), p. 3.

4. "Wilderness Letter," in *The Sound of Mountain Water* (Garden City, N.Y.: Doubleday, 1967), p. 155.

5. "Conservative, Liberal, and Western: Three Modes of American Realism," in *The Literature of the American West*, ed. J. Golden Taylor (Boston: Houghton Mifflin, 1971), p. 9.

6. "The Marks of Human Passage," in *This is Dinosaur, Echo Park Country and its Magic Rivers*, ed. Wallace Stegner (New York: Alfred A. Knopf, 1955), p. 16.

7. "Rocky Mountain Country," *Atlantic* (July, 1978), pp. 45–96. Stegner is increasingly concerned that the Western landscape and character are endangered by mining and industrial development, as "church, state, and business cooperate" to promote growth. Thus, Stegner says, "Utah is busy Californicating itself."

8. *Wallace Stegner* (Boston: G. K. Hall, 1977), pp. 51–52.

9. Robinson, p. 114.

10. *Mormon Country* (New York: Duell, Sloan & Pearce, 1942), p. 218.

11. Lewis, p. 22.

12. Introduction, *Beyond the Hundredth Meridian* (Boston: Houghton Mifflin, 1954), p. xvi.

13. "The West Authentic: Willa Cather," in *The Sound of Mountain Water*, p. 241.

14. "Writing American Fiction," *Commentary*, (September, 1961), p. 250.

15. "On Critical Realism," in *The Meaning of Contemporary Realism* (London: Merlin Press, 1963), p. 122.

16. "Born a Square," in *The Sound of Mountain Water*, p. 171.

17. *The Spectator Bird* (Garden City, N.Y.: Doubleday, 1976). p. 213.

REVIEWS

World Out of Nowhere

Howard Mumford Jones*

In a lean year this is a major novel. It would be a major novel even in a rich year, and the reasons lie in the quality of vitality, of generous strength, of something pressed down and running over in the new book by Wallace Stegner, that takes it completely out of the realm of intellectualism into the kingdom of fiction. The kings of fiction—at least the kings of English fiction—have ordinarily been open-handed monarchs, givers of manifold good things and careless about the minor morals of the muse. They have created vast, living, untidy books. "The Big Rock Candy Mountain" is a vast, living, untidy book. Whole sections of it, for example, can be lifted out; in fact, have been lifted out to appear as independent literary units. But the living force of the narrative, the large, loose curve of the story here hold them in embrace, and the reader knows only that a whole world has arisen out of nowhere around him.

"The Big Rock Candy Mountain" is the biography of Bo Mason, who grew up in the West (including western Canada) too late to be a pioneer and too early to be a politician. Trap-shooter, gambler, bootlegger, real estate entrepreneur, and the like, he yet possesses the fascination and the repulsion of something original, elementary, and unpredictable. He is a fool and a hero, a swindler and a god. He marries a Norse wife, who bears him two sons. His profound and masculine egotism compels his wife to follow the adventure of his existence against her judgment, and alternately fascinates and disgusts his sons. We have his complete portrait, a dossier of events from childhood to the grave, a telling revelation of masculinity. But it remains a portrait, it never descends to become a case study. The author is steadily and sympathetically aware that his creation came too late into a world too old.

But to call this the substance of "The Big Rock Candy Mountain" is to do the book some injustice, inasmuch as it suggests that the novel is a conscious piece of psychological analysis, another performance by the fictional advanced guard. Bo Mason's life is, however, the occasion, not the thesis, of the book. The tale is a revelation of life in the contemporary

*Review of The Big Rock Candy Mountain. Reprinted from Saturday Review (October 2, 1943), p. 11.

West, a revelation without illusion and without bitterness and therefore credible and sweet. For Mr. Stegner the visible world exists. He knows the feel of a frozen radiator cap, the smell of baked clay, the look of a dead gopher, the flash of white skin at a necking party, the deadness of a shut-up shack. His boys live in a boy world, not in a projection of their parents' troubled existence. Only occasionally does the gulf open to show us the emotional tensions that slowly force father and children apart. This grasp of the normal and the sane, of what is visible and commonplace keeps the narrative in balance and compels us to accept as true the sudden spurts of cruelty that Bo Mason's impatience with dullness activates.

I have, to be sure, one major fault to find. That point of view should shift and change is, I think, normal in good English fiction, but I do not find Mr. Stegner's occasional use of differing styles quite acceptable. I prefer his direct report of act and thought to his occasional (and innocent) attempts to write like Thomas Wolfe. For example, towards the end of the novel, he drops into a stream-of-consciousness manner in an effort to acquaint us with the values Bruce, the younger son, has acquired, that jars with the geniality and strength of the rest of the narrative. The slow death of the mother, the blindness of the son to what the father feels and of the father to the suffering of the boy—all this is true and poignant in this part of the book, but it is true and poignant in spite of the way it is presented, not because of it.

"The Big Rock Candy Mountain" is not a conscious rediscovery of American values. Mr. Stegner is as amused at small-town cussedness as was Sinclair Lewis, but he knows that satire accomplishes nothing. In a larger sense, however, his book is an extraordinary study in American folkways. The language, the psychology, the customs of his characters are essential and characteristic, largely because, knowing them, he takes them for granted and does not dissect and analyze. His, to be sure, is a masculine world, just as, despite the tenderness with which the wife is treated, this is a masculine book. Possibly it is a study in an epoch that is dead. Reflecting on her husband's incapacity, Mrs. Mason talks to herself:

> What is your husband a slave to, Mrs. Mason? To himself, Mrs. Webb, to himself. To his notion that he has to make a pile, be a big shot, have a hundred thousand dollars in negotiable securities in his safety deposit box, drive a Cadillac car, have seven pairs of shoes with three-dollar trees for each pair, buy three expensive Panamas during a summer and wear a diamond worth fifteen hundred dollars in his tie. He doesn't know, he wouldn't know, what to do with money when he has it. Would he ever think of going to the theater, or reading a good book, or taking a trip somewhere just for the trip?

The worship of the bitch-goddess, Success, troubled Henry Adams. The case of Bo Mason is an object lesson in that cult reduced to the lowest, plainest, most masculine terms.

Life-Size Stegner

Joseph Warren Beach*

Wallace Stegner's latest book shows great advance in power and grasp over the shorter novels for which he is chiefly known, and is a much more satisfying example of regional fiction. Maturity of experience and human insight are brought to the treatment of a serious theme; characters unusually vivid and convincing are involved in a story of deep human interest. An exacting reader may note with surprise that, in spite of all this, he somewhat misses that peculiar pleasure that is to be derived from a work of literary art. He will ask himself how this is possible. And he will reluctantly conclude that Mr. Stegner has yet to find himself a thoroughly distinctive style, an esthetically significant point of view.

Mr. Stegner is exceptionally well equipped by personal experience to stake out his claim in that vast and glamorous country which has not yet found its Faulkner, Wolfe, Glasgow, Caldwell or Rawlings, though it has found its Vardis Fisher and H. L. Davis. Born on an Iowa farm and living successively in Washington, Saskatchewan, Montana, Utah, Nevada and California, Stegner is prepared to give an inside view of the great Northwest as it was passing from the pioneer to the settled agricultural stage. In numerous tales he has faithfully worked this mine, without really striking pay dirt until the present moment. *Remembering Laughter* was a fastidiously fashioned story of Iowa farm life vaguely reminiscent of *Ethan Frome* and *A Lost Lady*, and was rewarded for these merits with a publisher's prize in 1937.

With *The Big Rock Candy Mountain* the author takes real hold on his subject. He starts out with the heroine's background in a Minnesota village, takes her to a "populated locality" in North Dakota where she marries Bo Mason, the keeper of a blind pig, and follows her through a heart-breaking series of moves across the American and Canadian Northwest as her husband tries, one after another, the possible ways of making easy money.

Best justice is done to the homesteading venture in the lonely wheat fields of Canada. Here the author makes of the influenza epidemic of 1918 (featured in his earlier novel, *On a Darkling Plain*) one of the most powerful episodes in this harrowing saga; and it is here that the boy Bruce, with his gopher traps and caged weasel, is made the chief reflector of the shape and color of their life. Mr. Stegner has felt the spell of mountain and prairie, of drought, flood and blizzard; he can write of moving accidents and hairbreadth escapes which give us the feel of frontier life better than phrases about the stars and seasons. Perhaps the most intensely interesting

*Review of *The Big Rock Candy Mountain*. Reprinted from *The New York Times Book Review* (September 20, 1943), p. 4.

passages are those which describe the rum-running drives of Bo Mason through treacherous back roads in peril from weather, law, and hijackers.

Of course the serious novelist will want to give us something more than exciting episodes and local color; and Mr. Stegner's narrative is held together by themes significant on several levels of interest. His title recalls that land of Cockaigne where plenty comes easy for the man who knows how to beat the game. Plenty comes less easy since the closing of the frontier, and Bo Mason leads his family a vagabond underground life in which the satisfactions of home and society are tragically missed.

That is the upper or cultural level of interest, typifying much in our rootless America. At the deeper, psychological level is the still more significant theme of personal relations in a family dominated by a strong-willed he-man, whose imagination is all used up on his buccaneering enterprises, leaving none to guide him in his private life.

Between husband and wife, the day is saved by the courage, loyalty and staying power of Elsa Mason. Between father and sons the Oedipus complex rages furiously; the life of one of the boys is ruined, and the other, hating his father, makes a narrow escape with the help of his speculative intelligence, which enables him to view the family history in long perspective. The real character creations are Elsa and Bo. Bo is a fascinating figure, many-faceted and intensely human, interesting in himself, and doubly interesting as the typical man (or grown-up boy), a little more than life size. Elsa is also rather more than life size, and it is with her that the reader most often identifies himself. If she cloys a little in her sweet and brave long-suffering, blame it on the author's style rather than his substance.

And what of the distinctive pleasure which one takes in a work of art? There is little in the book which has not some pertinence to the theme; yet one might wish to see a more jealous selection of detail for more particular effect. The scrupulous author refrains from using the "distortions" of art, and he does not greatly command the finer tools of irony, suggestion, pathos, fancy, or intellectual abstraction, which variously serve in the masters to give esthetic point to a neutral subject.

The patient, realistic method is adequate to the plain truth of the situation, but the point of view is indeterminant. It is not sharply objective, as in pure naturalism; and at the same time the impressions of the several characters, through which the action is interpreted, are not nicely individualized in tone. They are all presented in a uniform soft middle style, a trifle hesitant and apologetic, and not remarkable for either beauty or precision. The book is full of languid echoes. Bruce, driving west through Dakota (pp. 421–7), is half-hearted Thomas Wolfe. What is here referred to is not something peculiar to Wallace Stegner. It is the average well-bred "sensitive" style of contemporary American "realism" where we do not have the intervention of an artistic individuality that speaks with authority.

Prophet of the Far West

by Mari Sandoz*

One of our magnificent, and neglected, American stories is that of John Wesley Powell, who risked his life and those of nine others to conquer the roaring waters of Grand Canyon, and then spent much of the next twenty-five years trying to trap the lesser waters of the West and tame them to the parched earth. It is a complex story, but no man is better fitted by understanding and artistry to tell it than Wallace Stegner, which he does in "Beyond the Hundredth Meridian."

The son of a peripatetic Wesleyan preacher, Powell was stoned as an abolitionist for his father's sake—good preparation for some later stoning he would need to fend off. As a boy he had met a farmer who worked in the Underground Railway, a self-taught man who owned a museum and a library of scientific works. He instructed any youth who would come to him, and through him Powell's thought found its direction. By the end of the Civil War, Powell was a major with a missing right arm, a homemade education, and an urge toward natural history and the West.

From the start Powell's expeditions were undertrained and underfinanced, yet he inspired confidence in Western pioneers like William N. Byers, the Denver editor, who had tried to climb Long's Peak and failed. Byers made it with Powell's group, the first men to stand on the summit.

In 1869 the great challenge for explorers was the Grand Canyon of the Colorado. After some investigation Powell ordered four boats and braced Congress for a little money, getting a bit, and bits elsewhere, some from the Smithsonian Institution. His expedition down the Colorado was adventure of the highest order and Wallace Stegner makes the most of it, particularly in his discernment of the patterns in character and happenstance that explain so much of the later Powell. With virtually every living soul in the Green River valley watching from the banks, the four boats spun out into the current and around the bend, not to be heard from. Then a report arrived that all but one man had been drowned in the terrible rapids of the Green. Never reached the Colorado at all.

This turned out a typical high-country canard. The inexperienced boatmen could have drowned but didn't. There was Powell's fabulous daring with his one arm, his irksome caution, the recklessness of some of the others, the threatening starvation, heat, canyon fever, the split in the party, and the final desperate run over the angriest of the igneous rapids. When they came out, those who got out, Powell faced ten years of proving, explaining, and justifying the spectacular exploration.

But out of the Government centralization left over from the Civil War various new institutions were growing up to fight the speculation

*Review of *Beyond the Hundredth Meridian*. Reprinted from *Saturday Review* (Sept. 11, 1954), p. 36.

and romance that passed for science, using the West as their laboratory. One of these was the new U.S. Geographical and Geological Survey of the Rocky Mountain Region, with Powell in charge and the leader against the romantics. His new work put him into closer contact with Indians, whom he accepted as human beings with the right to be what they were. His interest resulted in the impressive and vastly important volumes of the Bureau of Ethnology, including the linguistic studies of the tribes, long overdue, all capped by his own "Handbook of American Indians."

Wallace Stegner gives his reader an understanding of the West as a separate entity, and adds much to his understanding of the temper and men of the times, particularly such men as Henry Adams. He discusses the various expeditions and studies, including those of King, Marsh, and of course Hayden, creator of Yellowstone National Park, which set the pattern for the nation's park system. He presents also the work of the conspicuous artists and photographers of the West—Seymour, Stanley, Moran, Jackson, and others, and offers some samples of contrasting portrayals of the Colorado: a fine fold-in gives Holmes's panorama of the Grand Canyon. Mr. Stegner contrasts the mystical fervor of a Gilpin to the realities of the scientific government surveys of natural resources, including water. These findings led directly to the question of proper administration, whether the resources were to be reserved or distributed, protected or exploited. The romantics had no problem, but the realistic Powell saw that the new land acts intended to provide settlement in actuality encouraged a hundred unpleasant possibilities of conflict, spoliation, monopoly, and waste.

In Powell's complex conception of the West there was one universal—drought, aggravated by the limited resistance of the crops then available. In addition, many settlers restless and venturesome enough to move into a wilderness lacked the patience and fortitude for the long taming.

To make existence possible on 160 acres of arid land, Powell suggested irrigation, but as water was the basic wealth of the region, it must be kept out of private hands. In his "Report on the Lands of the Arid Regions," he offered a revolutionary blueprint, with plans for irrigation systems and two sample bills, one for irrigation districts, the other for cooperative pasturage—the group doing what one man could not.

This was heady stuff for the poor man. I recall the impassioned talk of a Chinese graduate student from Cornell in 1931. In America he had discovered Powell and was taking him back to his native Shensi Province. It was heady and alarming stuff in Powell's time, too, and brought scare headlines, demands for Congressional investigations, and charges of fakery. Temporarily the Gilpins won, for Powell was challenging not only the profits of the exploiters but also the myth of universal fruitfulness that had supplanted the myth of the Great American Desert. But they didn't win completely, for the drought of the 1890's underlined the need for irrigation, and eventually Theodore Roosevelt pushed both conservation and reclamation. Powell, however, had resigned from the Geological Survey, though still fortified perhaps by his homemade education against the cynicism that tinged so much of Henry Adams's later life.

Today it is plain that Powell was a prophet. Many of the great river systems he wished controlled are under reclamation; even his Colorado is dammed. As he predicted, reclamation in Montana helped reclamation in the faraway swamps of Mississippi. But neither Stegner nor Bernard DeVoto in his excellent introduction to this book is optimistic about the future. Since 1953 great pressures have been exerted against the Indian reservations, the national forests, forest management, the replanting by lumber companies—on the entire reclamation program. For the moment it seems that John Wesley Powell is finally losing the fight. Watersheds, once denuded, whether in Shensi or in Wyoming, are denuded for a long, long time. Our grandchildren will discover this.

Whitemud Revisited

Robert Harlow*

Mr. Wallace Stegner, now head of the Creative Writing Centre at Stanford University, lived from his sixth to his twelfth year in a place called Whitemud, Saskatchewan. His family lived in the village during the winter and in the summer engaged in what he calls, aptly, "wheat-mining" on a 320-acre homestead that straddled the Saskatchewan-Montana border, perhaps forty miles southwest of the town. He left his family in the spring of 1920 and didn't see Whitemud again until he visited it four decades later. His return to his old home settlement was an experience that yanked at the roots of his memory and chopped through to the heartwood of his emotional and intellectual being. The result is a unique book whose whole cloth is made up of the warp of memory and the woof of history, colored by the sociologist's approach and fashioned with the craft of a very good writer indeed.

Wolf Willow concerns itself first of all with ". . . that block of country between the Milk River and the main line of the Canadian Pacific, and between approximately the Saskatchewan-Alberta line and Wood Mountain. . . ." Second, it is a memory of Mr. Stegner's growing years, his Tom Sawyer years, in the town of Whitemud. Third, it is a study of "the place where the plains, as an ecology, as a native Indian culture, and as a process of white settlement, came to their climax and their end." Fourth, it is a special look at Canadian history with the above three concerns in mind. And fifth, it aims at searching out some of the thousands of reasons

*Review of *Wolf Willow*. Reprinted from *Canadian Journal* (1963), pp. 63–66, with permission of the author.

for Whitemud as a last frontier, as an escape, as a state of mind, as a victim and as a miracle. To gain his objectives, Mr. Stegner uses any and every resource he has discovered out of his long years as a writer, teacher, researcher.

For those of us who have lived in one of the hundreds of Whitemuds scattered throughout the west and near-north, this book will have a special meaning. I know I read it with a real sense of relief. What I thought I had remembered, Mr. Stegner went back and found to be true. He confirms my suspicion that, while history was made in Whitemud, the place existed, and still exists, with no sense of it at all. In Whitemud—all of them—between the turn of the century and the Second World War, there was a mindlessness akin to the calm at the eye of a hurricane, while the physical struggle simply to exist shut out twenty-five centuries of civilized achievement. The word that occurs to me which describes Whitemud the best is Exposed. Are not all small frontier towns too hot, too cold, too dusty and dry, and too near a flooding river? The men who live in Whitemud—are they not exposed too? Nobody is born in Whitemud; he comes there, for whatever reason, and I have often wondered if each man didn't look at his neighbour and hold him in a little contempt for having made such a foolish decision. In my own personal Whitemud, we had a doctor who scaled logs in a local mill, a sergeant-major from the Household Guards who was my father's chief clerk, a scion of one of England's first families who discovered milk, and an extremely literate Irishman who dug our ditches by choice. What were any of them doing there? What, indeed, were the professional men doing there—the doctor, the lawyer, the teachers, the accountants? And so on down the line to the cheerful, often alcoholic drifter who happily played bedrock to the single thin stratum of society above him.

Things were not different in Mr. Stegner's Whitemud. He remembers it well; that it was wild, cruel, elemental, terrifying, unfettered, warping, grasping, unlettered, unbearably cold, hot, dry, flyblown, wet. As a society it was a cultural desert, laughably optimistic (this perhaps above all else: Whitemud lives on dreams of financial glory), insufferably prudish, tell-taleably licentious, soul-shrivelling, and oddly enough, a good place for a boy to grow up in and to have come from because—well, because life is sometimes one or the other of all of these things, and certainly is as unsheltered as Whitemud, and perhaps learning early to run the gauntlet is not a bad thing.

Yet, to go back to Whitemud is painful, and for a writer it is extremely dangerous. Nostalgia is a fact. He cannot escape it. Walk down the main street and see where the poolhall was—above which, in a single, barren stuffy room he first went to school. Walk by the river and see the dam that burst in 1917, remember the swimming and fishing holes. This kind of activity can lead to sentimentality of the worst order. Then seek out the few old-timers left who can remember with him his stay in

Whitemud and listen to the stories they tell. Melodrama. The floods, the storms, the dust drifting, the hopes and fears of a whole town, the winter of 1906–07 that destroyed, in one long incredible killing, the cattle economy of the area and forced it toward the constant disaster of trying to farm the thin land and make wheat the raison d'etre for Whitemud's continued existence. What does a man who wants to write a book about the place and its people do to ward off this triple threat? Like a hardy neo-Confucian who faces rape, he remembers to relax and enjoy it. In *Wolf Willow* you find nostalgia, some sentimentality, and melodrama, but they serve a purpose.

The book is divided into four parts and an epilogue. In the first section we remember with Mr. Stegner as he tours Whitemud after forty years away from it, and almost at once the reader begins to realize that *Wolf Willow* is not going to be simply an historian's aide-memoire. Clots of total recall begin to coagulate under the influence of the dust-dry air of reality. Here now is Whitemud, softer, greener, neater, but really only an echo that has refused to stop; and somehow, too, we sense at once the tragedy of the place: that it was born, lived briefly, died and became fossilized beneath the weight of the prairie sun without ever knowing why. "Our education . . . did not perform its proper function of giving us distance and understanding by focusing on our life from outside. Instead, it focused on outside from inside . . ." Thus, "The one aspect of Whitemud's history, and only one, and a fragmentary one, we knew: the town dump." Only a story-teller with a trained eye could see the implications. "The town dump was our poetry and our history," he says . . . "For a community may well be judged by what it throws away—what it has to throw away and what it chooses to—as by any other evidence. For whole civilizations we sometimes have no more of the poetry and little more of the history than this. It is all *we* had for the civilization we grew up in."

In the following three sections and the epilogue, Mr. Stegner tells of the "why" of the birth, life and death of Whitemud. He begins with the early explorers who did no more than pass the place by, and later who did not come within several hundred miles of Whitemud—Kelsey, Verendrye—until we and that "as late as 1860 . . . the Cypress Hills and the little river they mothered were still lost in an unmapped West as wide as ocean, being saved, perhaps, after all the rehearsals on other frontiers for the staging of one last drama of white settlement." From the Indians, to the Metis, to the Company of Adventurers, to the coming of the R.N.W.M.P. and finally to Whitemud, "the capital of an unremembered past, we follow the mainstream of Canadian history, seeing always with the eyes of the boy who has become a man, a story-teller and a disciplined thinker. It is probably more meaningful history about our frontier west than you can read in any other book.

Once we know why Whitemud was born, we must know why it died. It died in the winter of 1906–07, when the cattle industry was wiped out.

Mr. Stegner tells the story through the eyes of fiction. For a hundred pages we leave off remembrance and history and watch while the spirit and the edge of a frontier are blunted by the hard facts of the climate of the region. It is a good story; it stands well within the bounds of the author's plan for the book. It is meant to loom larger than its telling, and it does. We know from it why men of tremendous strength and purpose gave up and left, and we know, too, a little of why some stayed and turned on the land and plowed it to dust and lived on to watch it blow away.

The final section brings us again, full circle, to the Whitemud that Mr. Stegner knew and left as a boy. Here, the historian turns sociologist as he quietly brings us up to date on Whitemud, whose keynote is now struck in a phrase from Sinclair Lewis' *Main Street:* ". . . the humdrum inevitable tragedy of struggle against inertia." This is the final "why" of Whitemud. "It emphasized the predictability and repetitiousness of the frontier curve from hope to habit, from optimism to a country rut . . ."

Wallace Stegner could have settled for writing another *Main Street* or a *Winesberg Ohio*. Perhaps he could have reaped a kind of *Patterns of Culture* from his notes. I doubt if he thought of writing a straight historical account. But, in fact, there are elements of all three of these approaches, and the result is certainly history as it may very effectively be written.

Fiction That Grows from the Ground

Granville Hicks*

The two novels I am considering this week have little in common, but taken together they raise some interesting questions about the nature of fiction. Although there is a sharp difference in their ages—Wallace Stegner is almost sixty and Joyce Carol Oates under thirty—the authors of both books are experienced writers. Stegner, who is also well known as the head of the Creative Writing Center at Stanford University, has produced more than a dozen books, most of them fiction. But Miss Oates, young as she is, has published two excellent collections of short stories, and *Garden of Earthly Delights* (Vanguard, $5.95) is her second novel. Both writers know what they are doing, and that gives point to the fact that their works stand far apart in theme, style, intention, and achievement.

Miss Oates has usually written about poor or at any rate not very prosperous people living in the country or in small towns. They are likely

*Review of *All the Little Live Things*. Reprinted from *Saturday Review* (Aug. 5, 1967), pp. 23–24.

to be suffering, either through physical affliction or because of some kind of frustration. Their moments of joy, if there are any, are so brief as to have a pathos of their own. Miss Oates's style, subdued and often somber, is appropriate to her themes. The title of her first collection of short stories, *By the North Gate*, was taken from a poem by Rihaku, translated by Ezra Pound, that perfectly expresses her prevailing mood:

> By the North Gate, the wind blows full of sand,
> Lonely from the beginning of time until now!
> Trees fall, the grass grows yellow with autumn.
> I climb the towers to watch out the Barbarous land.

Garden of Earthly Delights is a novel about three generations of Americans. First there is Carleton Walpole, a migratory worker in the desert of the Thirties, moving about the country—Arkansas, Florida, South Carolina, New Jersey—with his wife and children. The important thing about Carleton is that he feels himself to be superior to the circumstances in which he has his meager existence. He is incapable of taking practical steps to better himself, but alcohol and violence nourish his self-esteem.

His daughter Clara runs away at the age of fifteen because he beats her. She has his sense of superiority, but in her it is balanced by a degree of shrewdness. Capable of intense, romantic passion, she is practical enough to attach herself to a wealthy man when she finds she is pregnant, becoming first his mistress and then his wife. The child, Steven or Swan, is brought up in luxury, but he is torn by conflicts, and he ends, as the reader knows he must, in disaster.

Here then are three lives, none of them noteworthy, none of them ending well. But these people are real. They often seem mysterious to us, as, for that matter, they do to themselves; but we accept their existence. They are real to me in exactly the same way as are my neighbors: I don't know all there is to be known about them, but there, for better or worse, they are.

Stegner's *All the Little Live Things* (Viking, $5.95) has a more recognizably timely theme than *Garden of Earthly Delights*, and is more entertainingly written and more skillfully put together. I expect that it will be more popular than Miss Oates's book, but I am not convinced that it is a better novel.

Stegner's primary theme is the conflict, much publicized of late, between generations, and this inevitably leads into consideration of the meaning of life. The narrator is a retired literary agent, Joe Allston, who has settled in California with his wife, Ruth, and who, as the story begins, is taking a qualified but genuine satisfaction in his withdrawal from the world. The Allstons's paradise, however, is invaded by an up-to-date serpent, a bearded, dirty, arrogant beatnik, Jim Peck. The conflict between Allston and Peck, constantly intensifying, is made more painful for the former by his recollections of his failure with his own recalcitrant son, who died at the age of thirty-seven without ever having found himself.

Joe is challenged in another way by the arrival in his neighborhood of a young woman, Marian Catlin, who has a passion for life in all its forms, for "all the little live things," including gophers, poison oak, beggar's-lice, cockleburs, needle grass, and foxtails. Joe, who finds Marian's philosophy ridiculous, nevertheless is greatly attracted to her, wishing she were his daughter, and her affirmativeness, undiscriminating as it seems to him to be, makes him ashamed of his negations. When he learns she is dying of cancer, he is doubly devastated.

Stegner, who does many things well, is especially effective in his creation of the setting—weather, birds, animals, insects, flowers. The novel begins as Allston looks back on the events that he is about to describe:

> A half-hour after I came down here, the rains began. They came without fuss, the thin edge of a circular Pacific storm that is probably dumping buckets on Oregon. One minute I was looking out my study window into the greeny-gold twilight under the live oak, watching a towhee kick up the leaves, and the next I saw that the air beyond the tree was scratched with fine rain. Now the flagstones are shining, the tops of the horizontal oak limbs are dark-wet, there is a growing drip from the dome of the tree above, the towhee's olive back has melted into umber dusk and gone. I sit here watching evening and the winter rains come on together, and I feel as slack and dull as the day or the season.

The novel is full of observations as sharp and evocative as those we find in this passage. But what of the people? As for Joe Allston, Stegner has said that he found it necessary to give him "a comic sense which was like a defensive skill of a boxer with a glass jaw." Stegner's intention was sound, and he is witty enough to have made Joe a formidable wisecracker. But, though I have known men that I think might be rather like Joe, I never feel that I know Joe. Ruth, his wife, scarcely rises above the horizon. Jim Peck, as Stegner's plan demanded, is seen only through Joe's eyes, and though we suppose there is more to Jim than Joe sees we don't know what it is. And Mrs. Catlin is the greatest problem of all. Stegner has said: "If there is an answer both to Peck's lust for kicks and Joe Allston's impulse to flinch away and retire, it is in Marian Catlin's openness to all experience and her affection for all life." I wish I could believe in Marian, but I can't.

Stegner had some currently relevant themes, and he has been able to present them in a piece of fiction that is both entertaining and stimulating. What more can one ask? People, of course, not embodiments of ideas—such people as one finds in *Garden of Earthly Delights*. Stegner's novel is wonderfully well contrived, but Miss Oates's grows out of the ground.

The Sound of Mountain Water

Edward Abbey*

This book is a collection of essays, letters, memoirs and speeches, some of them more than twenty years old. Most were previously printed in various periodicals. Though diverse in form, length and weight, all deal with some aspect of a common subject, the contemporary American West and the problem, for the writer, of how to write about it.

Not any easy matter: as many have observed, our West, the home-land of the essential American myth, is the one clearly definable region of the nation that has yet to produce a literature comparable to the best of New England, the South, the Midwest or (even) California. (California is not part of the West, as Wallace Stegner points out; it is rather "something else"—Erewhon—the specter that haunts our dreams.)

"The Sound of Mountain Water" is divided into two parts, the first a group of essays outlining the appearance of the West, the second dealing with the peculiar difficulties of being a Western writer. (Which is not at all the same thing as being a writer of "Westerns.") In the first part, "the attempt . . . to understand what it is one loves, and how far love will take us," Mr. Stegner retraces the exploration and development of the land, which he sees as being the victim of a succession of economic raids by trappers, miners, ranchers, and more modern varieties of ex-ploiters—such as dam builders.

By and large the history of the American West is the story of rapacity and greed, but all is not lost; in what he calls "the geography of hope" the author foresees a time when through cooperation rather than competi-tion, the West may yet create a society fit to match its landscape.

After this historical and geographic survey come the travel sketches: a car trip through the desert and mountains after the war and the end of gasoline rationing; a ride down into Havasu Canyon, with some reflec-tions on the plight of the Indians, lost between two worlds; Glen Canyon before and after the dam with a plea for preservation of the Escalante wilderness area, the nearest thing to the original Glen Canyon still left; highways and billboards; the title piece, a short prose hymn in celebration of the wonder of mountains as remembered from boyhood; and a public letter to a recreation commission in which Mr. Stegner sums up the con-cept and value of wilderness.

In the second group of these essays from two decades we learn—not for the first time—that Western writers labor under special difficulties. They are, it seems, perhaps even more disadvantaged and underprivi-leged than Navajos. At least the Indians have a home. But the typical Western writer—and Mr. Stegner cites his own life as example—is rootless as a tumbleweed. (Itself not a native but an alien from Mongolia.)

*Reprinted from the *New York Times Book Review* (June 8, 1969), p. 10.

The nearest thing to a hometown for Stegner is Salt Lake City, where he spent much of his boyhood, and in this book he includes a long memoir in praise of that Mormon capital. But he is not, never was, a Mormon.

The Western writer (Stegner, Guthrie, Clark, Morgan, Lea) suffers from a second even more severe handicap; he is likely, as the author says to himself, to have been born a square. By which he also means born lucky—WASP, raised in a clean free rural environ or in cities like Salt Lake where the unspoiled out-of-doors is only a short hike away for any boy with legs. Born lucky, such a writer has an unlucky career, for he is predetermined to believe in honesty, honest work, monogamy and heroism (the two are easily coupled), the heroic past, the flowing future, virtue, health. How can a writer burdened with such a load, "still half believing in the American dream," compete with angry transvestite poets of the Negro persuasion or with sextortured Semites from the big cities making a lifetime literary project out of their Jewishness? It ain't fair.

Mr. Stegner writes of these matters with humor and sense, fully aware of the many ironies involved. His voice is that of a gentle and humane liberalism, which believes that even the life of quiet desperation is still worth living. His fault, it seems to me, as revealed in this assembly of incidental material, is an excess of moderation, an extremity of forbearance.

He can write, for example, of Glen Canyon *submersus* without even suggesting that the proper answer to this typical act of politico-industrial vandalism is not the acceptance of what is now called Lake Powell but rather the demolition of Glen Canyon Dam. He writes of the lack of apparent connection between the West's romantic past and its vulgar present, citing this discontinuity as an obstacle in the creation of a regional literature. Why not consider instead the possibility that this past requires a re-evaluation and that its true character is exposed by the quality of its historical fruits, i.e., by such phenomena as Phoenix, Ariz., or Albuquerque, N.M.?

He refers to the West as a land where the only constant has been and is change—what's so Western about that? Ask any Easterner about the stability of his world.

No sir, Mr. Stegner, there is no West anymore. Only the landscape gives it any distinction; all the rest has long since been overwhelmed by that monstrous tragicomedy (cf., William Eastlake, William Burroughs, William Gaddis, William Gass, William Blake and others) that we call the United States of North America.

The Real Thing

William Abrahams*

It is cause for celebration in this age of pop and plastic—whether in the bookshop, the talking shop in Washington, or the food shop around the corner—to come once in a while upon the real thing. Here, for example, is a long, intricate, deeply rewarding novel by Wallace Stegner. It has been written seriously and deserves to be read seriously, not dynamically or speedily, though whether or not there are enough such readers still around—a form of the real thing in themselves—to assure Mr. Stegner the large audience he ought to have is an open but lesser question. What is important is that he has written a superb novel, with an amplitude of scale and richness of detail altogether uncommon in contemporary fiction.

Mr. Stegner ranges widely: in his settings—California, New York, the Dakotas, Idaho, Mexico; in his time span—from 1870 to the present; and in the number and variety of his characters. Yet what he has written is neither the predictable four-decker family saga, the Forsytes in California, so to speak, from the first sturdy pioneers even unto the fourth and declining generation—though to the superficial eye it may appear that he has done both. For all the breadth and sweep of the novel, it achieves an effect of intimacy, hence of immediacy, and, though much of the material is "historical," an effect of discovery also, of experience newly minted rather than a pageantlike re-creation. Stegner's method is to keep us up very close to his principal characters, close enough to hear, to see, to recognize, to understand and sympathize, as they reveal themselves to each other and to themselves: notably, from the first generation, Susan Burling, in her time a famous writer-illustrator, "some sort of cross between a humming bird and an earth mover," who leaves her genteel artistic circle in New York to marry and go West with Oliver Ward, from one ditched hope to the next, as he, a mining engineer, seeks his fortune; to the third generation, their grandson Lyman Ward, a historian, who is narrator, commentator, and interpreter of the action at one level, and participant in it at another.

It is Lyman Ward's voice we hear first, for the strategy of the novel is to have us believe that we are reading what this middle-aged historian, the victim of a crippling bone disease that keeps him prisoner in a wheelchair, speaks to a tape recorder through the spring and summer of 1970 in the house Oliver and Susan Ward had built in Grass Valley, California, at the turn of the century. Deserted by his wife, patronized by his son, Rodman, a confident sociologist, he spends his time sorting out his dead grandparents' papers (and their lives), feeding them onto the tape—in effect, bringing them and himself back to life. (One is reminded

*Review of *Angle of Repose*. Reprinted from the *Atlantic Monthly* (Apr., 1971), pp. 96–97.

of the *Four Quartets:* "We die with the dying:/See, they depart, and we go with them./We are born with the dead:/See, they return and bring us with them.") All this is quite beyond sociology. Rodman disapproves: If the papers have any value, give them to the Historical Society and "get a fat tax deduction"; as for Pop, he should be sensible (that is, save Rodman tiresome anxiety) and let himself be "led away to the old folks' pasture down in Menlo Park where the care is good and there is so much to keep the inmates busy and happy."

There is no reply Lyman can give to Rodman that that noisy young man would pause to listen to; but the tape recorder listens:

"Fooling around in the papers my grandparents . . . left behind, I get glimpses of lives close to mine, related to mine in ways I recognize but don't completely comprehend. I'd like to live in their clothes awhile, if only so I don't have to live in my own. Actually, as I look down my nose to where my left leg bends and my right leg stops, I realize that it isn't backward I want to go, but downward. I want to touch once more the ground I have been maimed away from.

"In my mind I write letters to the newspapers saying Dear Editor, As a modern man and a one-legged man I can tell you that the conditions are similar. We have been cut off, the past has been ended and the family has broken up and the present is adrift in its wheelchair. . . . The elements have changed, there are whole new orders of magnitude and kind. This present of 1970 is no more an extension of my grandparents' world, this West is no more a development of the West they helped build, than the sea over Santorin is an extension of that once-island of rock and olive."

Implacable and pessimistic, "Nemesis in a wheelchair," Lyman Ward begins his exploration of the past. But however bleak his expectation, he is historian enough to wait and see: he has no predetermined notion of what he will find—that life was different is not to say that it was automatically better—or indeed of what he will make of what he finds—a biography, a monograph, or mere historical doodling. Gradually other voices are heard on the tape: Susan's, in particular, in letters that are a triumph of verisimilitude, perfectly matched to Mr. Stegner's carefully rendered locales and social discriminations. As she and Oliver come into clearer focus—she perhaps the more vulnerable, but finally the more fascinating and memorable of the two—and as more and more of their extraordinary experience is brought into the foreground, the device of the recorder is discreetly modulated: for long stretches nothing is allowed to break the communication that has been established. What is communicated proves to be of a different order than might have been anticipated from Lyman Ward's first bleak estimate. For what we see, what the historian sees, is the essential changelessness of human behavior; the relationship of the Wards, the strains of their marriage, the conflict of their deeply contradictory natures, transcends time and place. "What interests me," their grandson observes, "is not Susan Burling Ward the novelist and illustrator, and not Oliver Ward the engineer, and not the West they spend their lives in. What really interests me is how two such unlike particles clung together, and under what strains, rolling downhill into their future until they reached the angle of repose where I knew them. That's where the interest is. That's where the meaning will be if I find any."

And he does find a meaning—virtually on the final page—which joins, illuminates, and in a sense reverses the two parallel stories that have been deployed. But here let me abandon the conceit that the book of which I have been speaking is *by* Lyman Ward. For he, his grandparents, and all the other figures of the tale are created by Wallace Stegner; we are speaking of a novel, not history; and if Lyman Ward is moved by "a sense of history," his creator is moved by a sense of the past.

It is this dimension of time, an enrichment of the novel from Tolstoy onward, whose absence one notices in much of contemporary fiction, thereby perhaps accounting for its peculiar flat-effect. Characters are deprived of any more biographical past than might emerge in an En-counter Group marathon; a cartoonlike absence of depth is deemed the suitable mode (perhaps it is) for a preposterousness or a minimum of event that in either case is deliberate and expressive of the thinned-out quality of contemporary life. In the passion for the Now, we are told, there is no place for the Past, which merely by being "not-Now" becomes un-interesting. Try, for example, to imagine a prior life for any of the characters in a TV commercial, or the "early experience" of a plastic politician or preacher before he was sold, as in a TV commercial, to his admirers: it is an impossibility—they begin where they are. In the land of Now there is no curiosity about the past, nor the faintest apprehension that Now is in process of becoming Then. "I don't want any leading actors over thirty-five," a Hollywood production boss declares. "The young au-dience can't identify with anyone older." (He, of course, is in his swinging forties, love beads and all.)

"We have been cut off, the past has been ended . . ." So it would seem. But a novel like *Angle of Repose*, admitting the possibility of the past as still a part of fiction, suggests its possibility still as a continuing part of our lives. Between art and life, past and present, the moment and its aftermath, Mr. Stegner reminds us, there are still connections to be made, and we are the richer for them. His novel stands out already; it may prove a landmark.

The Uneasy Chair

Malcolm Cowley*

Let me tell the story in brief and hope that it doesn't spoil your pleasure in reading *The Uneasy Chair*. The book is full of dramatic episodes and offers, from a special point of view, a battlefield panorama of the literary world from 1920 to 1955. As for the story when told in brief, it becomes a fable of sorts and a heartening one, though I'm not sure about the moral of it.

"Once there was a boy—" is the way it should start.

—who was born shortly before the turn of the century in Ogden, Utah, a city then divided on religious lines. The boy's father was a Catholic of Italian descent, an educated, impoverished, bitter man; his mother was the daughter of a Mormon farmer; and the son was accepted by neither community, Mormon or Gentile. "He was precocious, alert, intelligent, brash, challenging, irreverent, literary, self-conscious, insecure, often ostentatiously crude, sometimes insufferable." Those are the words of his biographer, Wallace Stegner, but the sister of a high-school companion had a simpler judgment: "the ugliest, most disagreeable boy you ever saw." His face looked as if a horse had stepped on it and squashed the nose into both cheeks. Neighbors said that he had been hit by a baseball or a baseball bat—they had forgotten which, but they remembered that a doctor had botched the repair work.

Bernard Augustine DeVoto. He was an outsider in Ogden and again an outsider at Harvard, where he arrived in 1915 after a year at the University of Utah. In those days Harvard looked down on high-school boys and ignored the out-of-class students who had transferred themselves from a Western state university. It was the time of the Leyendecker men—see old-time illustrations in the *Saturday Evening Post*—all of whom were football heroes with clean-cut Anglo-Saxon features and inherited money. It was also the time of the Harvard Aesthetes, devoted to esoteric ideals of life and literature. DeVoto abhorred both types, perhaps with a shadow of envy. He dreamed of living in the easy style of the English gentry, preferably in Cambridge, and meanwhile he wanted to confound the Aesthetes by writing more professionally than they did, more common-sensically, more Westernly, and simply more. One imagines him gritting his teeth and saying, "I'll show the bastards."

Show them he did, though it took him a dozen years or more. The wounds he suffered had given him pertinacity and determination. First, after going back to Ogden and falling into an acute depression, he taught for some years at Northwestern, where he rather terrified the administration while exhilarating the students. He married one of these (and would stay married). Then he moved back to Cambridge, where Harvard made

*Reprinted with permission from the *New York Times Book Review* (Feb. 10, 1974), p. 1–2.

him the niggardly offer of a part-time instructorship. He accepted it though, worked hard at teaching, and by 1930 he was also editor of the Harvard Graduates' Magazine, not a post that an outsider might expect to fill. In spite of being aggressively Western, DeVoto had become part of Cambridge life, with warm friends on the faculty, enthusiastic students and bitter antagonists.

He was writing as well as teaching and editing, and was writing much more than others who had nothing else to do. Book reviews, articles, angry editorials, novels (which he thought were his true medium), romantic stories that met the requirements of the best-paying magazines; he tried his hand at almost everything. "I can sell anything I write," he boasted. Except in his recurrent periods of depression, he worked as if Simon Legree were standing behind him with a black-snake whip. He was, however, his own Legree, lashing himself with his own whip.

He had disappointments that would have broken a less persistent man. Perhaps the worst of these, for him, was in 1935, when President Conant refused to give him a post on the Harvard faculty. Soon afterward DeVoto went to New York, where he had been given charge of the money-losing *Saturday Review*, and the experiment ended as another disappointment. Stegner says of him that "he jumped into midtown Manhattan, threw his coonskin on the ground, jumped on it, leaped into the air and cracked his heels three times together three times, and announced himself as half horse, half alligator, ready to take on not only moderates like Carl Van Doren, but all the literary aesthetes and political idealists of a quarter century." He did take them on and won some battles, not without stomping and gouging, but the magazine continued to lose money. DeVoto was not a good administrator and, after 17 months, he went quietly back to Cambridge.

Stegner, by the way, is an ideal biographer for DeVoto. Their careers sometimes crossed—though Stegner was born a dozen years later—and often ran on parallel lines. Both were brought up in Utah, though in different towns, and both, as Stegner says, were "novelists by intention, teachers by necessity, and historians by the sheer compulsion of the region that shaped us." Two differences between them are that Stegner is an immensely better novelist than DeVoto ever could have been and that by nature he is somewhat less given to perpetual indignation. As he says of DeVoto in one of his understanding comments, "Indignation was his style, and the style was the man. There was no more moderation in him than there is in gunpowder."

For a long time the indignation was directed against the writers who dominated the years between two wars and made them a glowing period in American letters. Van Wyck Brooks was DeVoto's favorite target, but he also had bitter things to say about Eliot, Lewis, Dreiser, Sherwood Anderson, and their younger colleagues Hemingway, Fitzgerald, Faulkner, Wolfe, DosPassos and Hart Crane; indeed, about almost everyone except Robert Frost, whose work he admired to the point of adoration. He dismissed not only the writers as individuals but the literature of the whole age in which they flourished. "Seeking for a phrase which will convey the quality of that literature," he said, "history may sum it up as the Age of Ignominy. 'We must begin by thinking of American literature,' the topic sentence may read, 'not as functional in American life but as idle, dilettante, flippant, and intellectually sterile.' The age of literary folly. The age of slapstick."

The judgment is quoted from "The Literary Fallacy" (1944), which is like a surveyor's monument placed at the farthest point to which he allowed pure indignation to carry him. As author of *Exile's Return*, I had been abused by DeVoto in the recent past; I thought he was completely wrong about the 1920's—as about literature in general—and I prepared to review his book without benevolence. Sinclair Lewis rushed in ahead of me. He too had been abused, his wife had been abused, and his riposte was to write an article, "Fools, Liars and Mr. DeVoto," that is still a landmark in literary invective. The article appeared in, of all places, DeVoto's former organ, the *Saturday Review*. Lewis quoted DeVoto's remark, "An uninstructed gentleness toward writers has been the mistake of readers of our time. Words like 'fool' and 'liar' might profitably come back to use." "Very well," Lewis answered, "I denounce Mr. Bernard DeVoto as a fool and a tedious and egotistical fool, as a liar and a pompous and boresome liar." He continued in that tone, using such epithets as "yahoo" and not omitting a reference to DeVoto's "froglike face."

At first I enjoyed the article, human nature being what it is, but then it made me unhappy. I wrote DeVoto saying that my review of his book would be unfavorable, but that I proposed to make it accurate, fair, and free of epithets. DeVoto answered in a frank and reasonable tone. Other letters followed and we even had dinner together—a rather dull dinner, since neither of us was disposed to have an exciting quarrel, but after that we remained friends at a distance. I kept hearing about kind things he had done for distressed people; also I liked almost everything I read of his after "The Literary Fallacy."

I probably wouldn't have liked *Mountain Time*, the novel that was published in January, 1947, after a long delay. It received the same mixed verdict as the four novels that preceded it, and after that DeVoto abandoned fiction, as he had already abandoned anti-literary polemics. For what remained of his life, he was to be partly a historian of the Western frontier and partly a rare sort of public defender. DeVoto's Western histories—*The Year of Decision: 1846* (1943), *Across the Wide Missouri* (1947) and *The Course of Empire* (1952)—deserved the prizes they won: Pulitzer, Bancroft, National Book Award. Everything he had learned as a failed novelist went into them—it seems he had learned a great deal—and they also revealed a historian's passion for getting the facts right, as well as the vigor of a panoramic draftsman. They are probably his lasting contribution to American letters.

It was in his other role of public defender, however, that he made a contribution to his own times. Month after month (from 1935 to 1955) in the department he wrote for *Harper's*, "The Easy Chair," he defended authors against censors, national forests against greedy stockmen and lumbermen, national parks against being neglected and nibbled away, consumers against shoddy products, and most of all, free-minded citizens against the inquisitors who flourished in the early 1950's. Some of the enemies he attacked were men of power—not men of letters this time—but DeVoto was boiling again with indignation and did not count the cost of being frank. He heartened others to resist; he helped to win some victories in Congress; and he lopped off the heads of a few American dragons. Unfortunately most of our dragons belong to the type that grows new heads as soon as our backs are turned. They are here again in the 1970's, breathing fire, destroying the earth itself, and now we have no DeVoto to defend us.

To the end he was his own Legree, driving himself with his own whip, and he died in 1955 when his heart gave out.

And what is the moral of this fable from the first half of the century? Stegner offers none and I'm not sure about the answer myself, as I said at the beginning. Perhaps there are several morals. That, for example, a writer's virtues are intimately connected with his faults and weaknesses and may even grow out of them. That skills acquired by writing spoiled novels may lead to success in another field. That energies mobilized by private resentments may be carried over into public causes. Finally, that "the ugliest, most disagreeable boy," avoided by his neighbors, may end by deserving this long, fascinating biography and even by achieving a sort of heroism.

The Spectator Bird

Thomas N. Walters*

The Spectator Bird is a powerful, important work. Because of its themes of aging and identity, it is destined to become even more influential as we move further into this century.

Wallace Stegner's previous novel, *Angle of Repose*, earned a Pulitzer Prize. He has written some twenty other books, including an influential conservationist, nonfiction work, *The Sound of Mountain Water*. He is perhaps best known still for his monumental novel of an American family

*Reprinted from *Magill's Literary Annual 1977*, ed. Frank N. Magill (Salem Press: Englewood Cliffs, N.J.), II, 769–775.

and its dreams, *The Big Rock Candy Mountain,* or for his accurate depiction of love's pain in the novel, *All the Little Live Things.* Whether in fiction or nonfiction, Stegner has consistently demonstrated craftsmanlike ability to carry large concerns, tell large and difficult stories, make cogent observations on a wide range of life experiences. His importance lies not only in his energetic and unrelenting investigation of human motives and actions, but also in his considerable talent at arresting readers' attentions and telling them spellbinding tales about themselves and their neighbors.

Stegner has never retreated from a tough subject; instead, he has confronted, head-on, the two most difficult decades for fiction writers to grasp in this century. In the 1960's, which many writers found it expedient to slip away from into writing about the past, or biography, or mysticism-fantasy-occultism-escape, he lowered his lance and charged. What he charged, of course, was the tragically distorted emotional landscape of mid-Vietnam War America. The topics were frighteningly complex: the dissolution of the family, accelerating erosion of marital bonds, meaningless sexual permissiveness, political, social, educational and religious chaos, the dying environment. All these he treated, and he worked, too, on a pet theme, the angry, apolcalyptic differences between young and old, black and white, people. There was no escape into the nostalgia of the Depression years for Stegner. The problems of the day were his meat. Some of his conclusions were not modish or popular for the acid-rock, guru-haunted, "if-it-feels-good-do-it" mentality of that period. But Stegner was not blindly attacking the times or youth. In many ways, he stood alone in his equilibrium, excoriating alike the silly balloons of mindlessly, desperately "with-it" kids *and* the repressions longed for by the angrily confused, hurt "over 30's" and "senior citizens." Inexorably, he made those who would read him, young or old, look at how stupid and vain, cruel and wasteful we were being, and his novels offered some leanly won, old-fashioned humanistic remedies for the problems. He depicted characters as having to learn first of tolerance, then of acceptance, then of respect, then, if possible, of love and faith. Along the way, he suggested, it would not hurt to return to and improve upon the out-of-favor skills of listening and of helping, doing both with some modicum of courtesy and empathy. Stegner's novels have all been pleas for good sense, modulation, union. His gift, however, is that he deals *creatively* with the immediate, the important. He converts reality into art by emphasizing and crafting the drama of life itself mainly through strict adherence to accuracy of observation and thoughtful depiction of the natural drama of human problems.

The protagonist in *The Spectator Bird* is one of Stegner's most compelling characters. Joe Allston, a seventy-year-old former literary agent, is not enjoying his well-off California retirement. In what his society considers a kind of twilight Eden, Joe and his wife, Ruth, live supposedly quiet, comfortable lives. But Joe is not quiet or comfortable. He rails and

rages at television, students, land developers, writers, everything
—including himself, and even at times his patient wife. Joe is intelligent
and articulate, has enough insight to make himself convolutedly more
miserable when he realizes he is indulging in self-pity. He knows it, but
finds himself powerless to achieve another form of resistance to two foes
his retirement makes it impossible any longer to avoid: his lack of identity, and his painfully advancing age.

Joe estimates himself to be a nonperson. He feels he has no foundations. He never knew his father. He goads himself with sparse memories
only of the embarrassment his Danish immigrant mother caused him:

> Everything in the New World that she tied her hopes to, including me,
> gave way. I spent my childhood and youth being ashamed of her accent,
> her clumsiness, her squarehead name, her menial jobs. It used to shrivel
> me to put down, in the space marked Mother's Maiden Name, Ingeborg
> Heegaard. I never discovered until she was dead that she was a saint, and
> that realization, with all the self-loathing that came with it, put me into a
> tailspin. . . .

Joe is thus emotionally cut off from his past. Additionally, he tortures
himself with memories of his failure as a father to his own child. He comes
back again and again to the scars of two decades before when he thinks of
his only son:

> . . . Curtis, who had been nothing but anguish from the time he was
> breech-born, fell from or let go of his surfboard on the beach at La Jolla.
> He died an over-age beach bum, evading to the last any obligation to
> become what his mother and I tried to make or help him be, and like my
> mother's, his death lay down accusingly at my door. He was my only
> descendant, as she was my only ancestor, and I failed both.

So, Joe is equally bereft of roots or any extension into the future.
Moreover, Joe realizes that he has had no control whatever over these
events, or any others, in his life. Powerless, it seems to him, except to
make tragic mistakes, he has drifted in a current, ". . . gone downstream
like a stick, getting hung up in eddies and getting flushed out again, only
half understanding what he floated past, and understanding less with
every year." Even the surface good fortune of an employment which has
provided materially well, he now knows required no talent. It ws all luck
and he feels guilt for that. Indeed, he feels tainted to have lived off the
talents of others.

All this painful introspection is compounded again and again by his
growing consciousness of age. Joe will forget himself a moment, sitting,
talking, then stand—thirty years younger in his mind—only to be ar-
thritically, brutally reminded of his irreversibly deteriorating joints. And
the pills his doctor prescribes do not deal with his real pain. Joe is
frightened and disgusted, too, by the increasing frequency of the deaths of
friends. He sees himself surrounded by decay, death, disease. And he is

angry, does "not go gentle." He cannot accept the approaching end of things with the calm and—to him—clichéd sweetness which his wife seems to possess. Joe has found life empty; now he finds the end of it equally devoid of any affirmative point. His only solace is his own sardonic, wise-cracking, kid-it-before-it-kills-you stance. Unfortunately, his wife and friends are even further alienated by this mechanism, and Joe is caught in an untenable position he has no choice but to occupy. Even when he contemplates suicide, he mocks himself: "I have put away a bottle of pills, as who hasn't, but nobody can guarantee that when the time comes he will have the wit to take them, or even remember where he hid them." This, suggests Stegner, is modern man, either cut off from basic realities, or fearful of them, afloat, alone in an ever faster-moving sea, a tide bumping and cluttered with detritus which was supposed to make life wonderful but did not. Even worse, this is modern man grown old without grace or sense of accomplishment. Like the worst aspects of modernity, Joe is not truly part of any flock. He is an isolated observer. Outside the V-shaped flight of ritual, natural direction. Joe envies and despises those in the flight. He despises his envy and sneers at himself now as "the spectator bird."

What brings Joe's frustration to a climactic point is his realization that his advanced age has betrayed him even through its failure to relieve him—through what he calls the "grandfather clause"—of the memory of an old, disruptive passion. He discovers that, at seventy, he can still stump angrily away from Ruth through the dark of a rainy night, his cheeks stinging with tears for a chance at love lost twenty years earlier.

In California, Joe gleans what he can from grumping. He muses, gardens, picks at his past; Ruth visits and entertains "old" people, is caught up in civic affairs. To occupy his time, Ruth encourages Joe to write a book—the sort of things he calls "my life among the literary." To placate her, he thumbs through his journals, knowing he will never write the book. It is all an unspoken charade.

Into this delicately balanced situation comes a postal card out of the past—a note from the Countess Astrid Wredel-Krarup, in whose home Ruth and Joe had lived several months during their journey to get away from the reminders of their son's death. Joe had rationalized their traveling to Denmark by suggesting he might visit there his mother's old village of Bregninge. Typical of Joe, he was cynical about his motives in doing this, since he was not sure he really wanted to find any roots after all. He and Ruth had developed a sincere and touching friendship with their hostess, the Countess Wredel-Krarup, her mysterious problems taking them outside their own sadness for the first time since their son's death.

The first hint of just how powerful an impact on their lives the Countess had is given when Joe keeps the postal card secret from Ruth. Inevitably, however, she senses that what he now reads among his papers is something more disturbing and important than he has encountered there before. Her probing results in his sharing the card with her, and in his confession to her that he had kept, secret from her, a very personal detailed journal during their Denmark stay. Now, because of the card, like lifting the bandage from a wound, he has begun to read that journal. Though it is dark and heavy with remorse, pain, confusion, even horrifying knowledge, Ruth insists that he read it aloud to her—that they share this pain together. Joe reads his journal to her. It becomes *their* journal.

Thus Stegner has provided himself with a remarkably effective framework for his method of rendering and texturing his story. Through this flashback device, we see Joe and Ruth in their present, and we see them in their past. We move back and forth not only in time, but also between cultures. We learn much that is personally linked to Joe and also much that is generally linked to the times and settings which Joe experiences. It is a marvelous device, as Stegner develops it, for giving us one of the most perceptive, brutally honest, and informative profiles of a man, his wife, his country, and his time.

As the story develops on its two levels, Joe and Ruth relive those curiously exhilarating yet puzzling days they spent in Denmark talking, traveling, and learning with their friend, the Countess. They live again, too, the dark turn of the learning, for in a hypnotically complex twist of events, Joe learns that the Countess knew of his mother, indeed knew why and how his mother was able to emigrate alone at age sixteen, penniless. They learn, as well, why no one speaks to the Countess at the opera or on the streets. There is her quisling husband, who has abandoned her, and other sad and sordid truths to be learned about the Countess's family; Ruth and Joe learn them. The sky of their retreat turns dark with Scandinavian night. Horrified, they learn of Astrid's scientist father's eerily objective experiments in incestuous human breeding. She bitterly tells them of her half-siblings who are listed in the family "stud book." They learn that despite both her parents' suicides, resulting from the notoriety of these practices, Astrid's brother, Count Eigil Rodding, actively continues the work of his father. Before he knows all this, Joe, the troubled but relatively naive American, meets the Count, the bored, moody, superbly intelligent and totally autocratic European, in a strange sort of comic-saga tennis match. Joe barely manages to hold his own in this battle between old and new worlds, one combatant with an ancient family line, the other thinking that he needs a heritage.

Through this dark theme of incest, Stegner seems to be suggesting that the many Americans like Joe should not be depressed at their rootlessness, their lack of discernible family line. Rather, they should see their "mongrel" blood lines as more natural, and as certainly more conducive to freedom. The distinction is clear: Count Rodding's incestuous experiments have improved nothing and are emotionally bankrupt. Such a clearly known, coldly controlled heritage as Astrid possesses has only produced evil.

Eventually Joe is attracted to Astrid as much, it seems, by her dignity-within-tragedy as by her beauty. In a powerfully restrained scene, Joe kisses her, though they both know they can never have each other. Joe and Ruth return to America and proceed for the next twenty years to avoid acknowledging what happened to them in Denmark. Significantly, something else more powerful happens to them in the comfortable bedroom of their old age as Joe reads his naked confessions aloud to Ruth. They are both hurt and frightened deeply. They talk of Denmark for the first time. They hurt each other. Then they help each other to heal, are drawn closer together—not in passionate love but in companionship. Joe realizes that he has been more blessed than he knew in the woman who is his wife. And he learns he loves and has loved her more than he knew. It is a harsh lesson, tender knowledge that comes to this white-haired Adam and Eve in their stormy Eden. But the knowledge is not too late; they have each other. For a while longer yet.

Aside from his obvious prowess as a weaver of contemporary plots, Stegner's most striking gifts are his sure grasp of telling details and his ability to create memorable characters with an economy of description. Joe first sees the Countess, for instance, as ". . . sometimes earthy as the stableman's daughter . . . she noticed Ruth's shoes and cried out, 'Oh, those tiny American feet'. . . . She has a smile that would melt glass . . . a true Dane: her cheeks glow in the rain like shined apples." Usually, the details which are so sharply etched on Stegner's pages function first as images, then reflect deeper possibilities. Notice, for instance, these seemingly offhand observations on the first page of *The Spectator Bird:* "From my study I can watch wrens and bush tits in the live oak outside. The wrens are nesting in a hole for the fifth straight year and are very busy. . . . They are surly and aggressive, and I wonder why I, who seem to be as testy as the wrens, much prefer the sociable bush tits." And, in another of Joe's morbid ruminations on death, the images function on two levels: "One of these days the pump will quit, or the sugar in the gas tank will kill the engine in a puff of smelly smoke, or the pipes will burst, or the long undernourished brain will begin to show signs of its starvation." Finally, Joe summarizes his predicament: "I really *am* getting old. It comes as a shock to realize that I am just killing time till time gets around to killing me."

In his methods of characterization, Stegner is peerless. He can detect the exact moment or posture or tone in which to reveal a person. For instance, he shows us Ruth at the moment she surmises Joe is troubled by his papers, asks him what he's reading, sees through his demurrer that the journal is merely dull recollections of their journey. Stegner shows her lying in bed holding the cat, Catarrh, on her stomach as she says in her soft Bryn Mawr whisper, " 'I was watching you while you read it. . . .' The look she was bending on me . . . was troubled and troubling, steady, undisguised by any of the games we play. She wasn't sparring, or joking . . . 'Joe', she said, 'Why *not* aloud? Why not together?' " It is a poignant moment. Ruth's own loneliness and her bravery in beginning the painful process of healing through honest confrontation is a memorable scene and firmly establishes her among Stegner's finest portraits of women, of whom he writes with much admiration and considerable awe.

In a book filled with memorable characters, one who best illustrates Stegner's remarkable love of people—their resilience, their colorations, their subtleties—is Joe's physician, Dr. Ben Alexander. Ben, seventy-nine, who squires pretty women around in a top-down convertible, and is writing a book on old age as a time of liberation, gives "youngster" Joe some advice:

> ". . . For God's sake don't go thinking yourself into any God damned wheel chair!" He reversed his cane and thumped me for emphasis on the breastbone and almost knocked me down."
>
> "What the hell *is* that, a shillelagh?"
>
> "Haven't I shown you that?" He held it up. To the shaft, which looked like cherry wood, had been fastened this big bone, obviously the ball of the ball and socket joint of some large animal. . . .
>
> "That's my hip joint," Ben said, "When I broke my hip, and they had me in the operating room . . . I said to the surgeon . . . "Doctor save me that joint. I want it." I'd walked on it for seventy-nine years and I damn well wanted to go *on* walking on it.

It is a mark of Stegner's ability to establish character economically that Ruth, who speaks less than anyone in the book, and who is shown doing fewer things than practically anyone else, remains vividly in one's mind after the book is finished.

Challenging in its structure, *The Spectator Bird* is a vigorously inventive and restlessly seeking, probing work. It is brave in taking on the life-questioning dilemma of old age. It is ambitious in its themes and philosophy. It is honest in its resolution. Stegner's satisfying ability to limn our times is surely one of our most precious natural resources. We know ourselves better for his looking for us. In this novel he has important things to say, and he says them with stylistic sureness and mature power.

ARTICLES AND ESSAYS

Time's Prisoners:
An Interview with Wallace Stegner

David Dillon*

DILLON: I'd like to begin by reading a passage from the introduction to *The Sound of Mountain Water* and asking you to comment on it.

> No matter how hard I try, I cannot believe in the "liberated" consciousness that is the subject of so much contemporary writing. Though I may enjoy these productions, and may even myself play games with Kronos as a literary exercise, I want a foot on earth, I am forced to believe in Time. I believe we are Time's prisoners, I believe Time is our safety and our strength. One of the deprivations of people in western America is that Time in their country is still not molded by human living into the forms of sanctuary, community and confidence that it is the ambition of all human cultures to create.

This would appear to be a statement about history and also a credo for fiction. Let's talk about history first. Would you say that establishing some kind of conscious continuity with the past, locating oneself in time, is a central concern of most western writers?

STEGNER: I'm not sure about its being a central concern of most western writers, but it certainly is for me. I couldn't deny it. I was talking this morning about that little essay, "The Dump Ground," which is really a symbolic essay on the raw materials of history, the odds and ends out of which we make history, especially when, as I did, you grew up without it. You feel a want or a lack that you can't quite define, as if you had a vitamin deficiency or something. I don't suppose that I missed history until I was at least middle-aged, and then I realized that I didn't have a single place to which I could refer myself. I had no crowd, I had no gang, I had no sociological matrix or context except as I could find it or form it by going back along my life, which I did in *Wolf Willow* and some of the novels. The reason for feeling that lack of history—I don't know. There are plenty of people in the world who have too much history. I remember talking once to the Greek Academy, a bunch of writers from contemporary Greece who have five thousand years of history weighing on their heads. Every time they open their mouths they are measuring themselves

*Reprinted from *Southwest Review* (Summer, 1976), pp. 252–267.

against Aristotle and Aristophanes and Aeschylus. The dead hand of the past can really be a dead hand if you've gone from glory to mediocrity, as Greece has. I would hate to be a Greek. I would rather be an American brought up without history and begin to build history than have to tear it down or ignore it or be oppressed by it.

DILLON: Did growing up partly in Canada and partly in the United States affect your sense of history?

STEGNER: I have always felt a little isolated, a litte out of phase, a little out of time and society. It gives you the sense of the unknown about your own citizenship, your own affiliation. I can remember as a child signing my name with my grandfather's Norwegian name, which was obviously an attempt to be somebody I wasn't quite but wished I were. All of this eventually comes to a head in a book in which you try to create your own history and find your own place in it, which is what I did in *Wolf Willow* and the biographies and so on. As a writer from the West, who knows the West better than he knows anywhere else—whether he knows it or not—I've tried to make the western past, which has been partly obliterated by the mythmakers and the shoot-em-up writers who created a sort of timeless, never-never land where gunfights take place. The real western past has never been adequately built or made. To take that real past and make some continuity between it and the real present is, I suppose, an ambition of mine. If history isn't human continuity and the sense of human continuity, then I don't know what it is. I would like more sense of continuity than the West has shown me or than I have been able to show myself.

DILLON: It occurs to me that most of the major western novelists—yourself, Paul Horgan, Vardis Fisher, A. B. Guthrie—have also tried their hand at history, either straight or fictionalized. It's as though there were a regional compulsion to do both.

STEGNER: I think to become aware of your life, to examine your life in the best Socratic way, is to become aware of history and of how little history is written, formed, and shaped. I also think that writers in a new tradition, in a new country, invariably, by a kind of reverse twist of irony, become hooked on the past, which in effect doesn't exist and therefore has to be created even more than the present needs to be created. Actually, you find that all the way through American literature. Hawthorne was bent upon creating what he called a usable past, and he created all those legends of the customhouse and the charterhouse and the stories about the Puritan past in an attempt to create something which any English writer of his time would have absorbed through his skin and eyes just by walking down the streets and being aware of the architecture. This is a real lack, and Hawthorne and James and all kinds of people have lamented that lack in American life. As we get older it begins to be less and less important, but it was important. In any new society it is particularly important, so that somebody like Edward Eggleston, who in

1870 was writing *The Hoosier Schoolmaster* and being the emergent novelist of Indiana, wound up by writing history. He conforms to a kind of pattern.

DILLON: This turning from fiction to history in later life seems to be another aspect of the pattern, particularly among western writers. Is this because they feel the lack of a usable past so keenly that they feel obligated to add to the stockpile of raw material that the next generation will draw upon?

STEGNER: Partly that. It may also be that their society is thin enough that they run out of material. It's not quite as rich, I don't think, as another kind of society would be unless you have a terribly fecund imagination and a wide experience of your region. Walter Clark is a good example because he is one whose real theme is civilization, not the Wild West. His theme is how cultivation is melded with things about the Wild West, how a culture and a desert topography finally grow together and become a single thing. You see it in pretty windy, overlong terms in *The City of Trembling Leaves*. But when Walt finally got to the end of *The Track of the Cat* he was out of fiction. For years and years he tried to do it and threw it away and finally settled into the long, long journal of a relatively unimportant Nevada miner who happened to record his whole life. Walt edited those journals, which I think the University of Nevada Press has now published. That's a historical job of a quite local, meticulous kind, as if he were taking sanctuary in it. It's too bad, because he was a lovely writer. I would have liked to see more fiction rather than this particular book. But you do what you can do.

DILLON: To return to Hawthorne and James for a moment, how would you compare their attempts at creating a usable past with those writers from the West?

STEGNER: It's more complex, more difficult, because the West is more places than New England, let's say. New England is relatively easy. The South, it seems to me, is relatively easy, and it's been done. You have Yoknapatawpha County in length and depth, all the way from the settlement in the 1830s, or way beyond that back to Ikkemotubbe and the Chickasaws, on up to Montgomery Ward Snopes. The whole business is an intricate, continuing human pattern, overlapping and rolling over itself. That's very hard to do in a country that changes as fast as the West. The South has been essentially an agricultural society that changed little.

DILLON: Is the key distinction then between stable and changing societies, or between small and large societies?

STEGNER: Well, stable because essentially uniform, changing, in the West, because heterogeneous. The West is many regions with many climates and all kinds of topographical, meteorological, and other kinds of differences. You can't talk about western weather in the way you can talk about a hot southern night and get that instantaneous, universal response to it because everybody has experienced it. Somebody who lives in San Francisco knows nothing whatever about Oregon weather or the weather of Southern California, except as a visitor. As far as a regional mystique is concerned, that belief that every region develops a kind of organic voice and that the people who live there for a couple of generations want to express the region and themselves in the region, is much more split and divided in the West than elsewhere.

DILLON: In other words, because the West is the newest region it has not yet developed its own voice.

STEGNER: If you believe that organic theory. I do to some extent, but not entirely. Moreover, the West was not settled at a time when it could develop a couple of generations in relative isolation. It was developed after the railroad and very close to the automobile and the airplane, and it's been in violent motion ever since. And I suppose we're more mobile at the moment than we've ever been, and the kind of organic literature that the regionalists talk about is something which develops in stable societies. Something else is going to come out of the other. I don't know what it will be, but it's not going to be that standard midwestern, or New England, or southern regionalism just transferred to another place.

DILLON: I'd like to talk more specifically about your own methods of writing history. Obviously, you think of history as a branch of literature, not as a science or a narrow academic discipline. You rely heavily on the techniques of fiction, particularly those related to dramatic narrative. What is gained by this approach?

STEGNER: I'm one of these unfortunates who reads with his fingers and his lips, slowly, probably as a result of reading too many freshman themes. I want to hear it as well as see it. I want, in other words, to take pleasure in what I read, and the fact is that most historians don't write very well. It isn't so much a distinction between expository or analytic history and narrative history as it is simply an inability to write, which was one of Benny DeVoto's loud complaints against the profession. He made two or three exceptions, like Henry Commager and Sam Morison, but most of them didn't write well enough to be interesting because, as he said, there was some kind of belief in the profession that historians didn't hit home runs. They just met the ball. Benny's advice was "Swing for the fences." I don't see anything wrong with that because it makes infinitely more interesting reading than some kind of dry expository account. And I don't think it necessarily damages the history. There is no reason it should, unless you invent scenes, unless you not only play the scenes that history gives you to the hilt, with all the freedom that history will allow, but go beyond that freedom and distort. Then you are culpable. You shouldn't call it history. At that point, you are beginning to shade over into fiction, and that is a slippery line.

DILLON: You've tightroped it yourself a few times.

STEGNER: True, but I think it's primarily a matter of intention, of knowing which you want to be held to—to the strictures of what actually happened, as in history, or to some kind of fictional truth of what was likely to happen, what the probability of the situation was. I've played it both ways. I wouldn't want to write history if I couldn't put into it all the excitement that it seems to me to permit.

DILLON: But you're speaking now only of exploiting the authentic drama of the material itself.

STEGNER: Oh, yes. There's nothing more sickening, I think, than an overt attempt to blow up, as if with a bicycle pump, a piece of history so that it looks like more than it is. There is such a thing as making the best of an almost purely expository section, being quite frankly chronological, explicit, detailed in the analysis of point after point in an orderly routine. If you look at *Beyond the Hundredth Meridian* you find both. I chose to start with a hundred and fifty pages or so of adventure story about running the river. But once you get into that you begin to get into the formation of the Powell survey and the geological survey and the bureaucratic finaglings in Washington. That's pretty straight history, and I wasn't trying to dress it up. I think the best thing to do with that is admit that it is information which is useful. You can write as pleasant sentences as you want, but you really can't ornament it. Writing isn't interior decoration, it's architecture, as Hemingway said. You do with the materials and the site what you can do, but you don't erect Rhineland castles in the wrong places.

DILLON: A. B. Guthrie once wrote that the biggest reason for history in fiction is that history offers perspective. Many historical novelists doubt their ability to interpret the present but feel that they can see the past whole and intact. Would you agree?

STEGNER: I think that is probably true, although I also think that if you don't have any more confidence in yourself than that you shouldn't be writing either. You have to stick your neck out. You have to believe that you can interpret both the past and the present, or you shouldn't be writing books. That's the whole function of a book, it seems to me, to give somebody a view of experience through a particular set of eyes which are honestly described so that you are not being conned in any way. I don't think you have to assume you are writing for the ages, however, and that your point of view is going to last indefinitely. History, even though you may think you see it plainly, may suffer some very strange distortions with time.

To take a single example, Benny DeVoto was a kind of Manifest Destinarian. He believed in the dynamism that took over the West, and it so stirred his enthusiasm that he took it on and gave it pretty much his entire approval, which meant that in 1941 or 1942, when he was writing his histories, he was probably unjust, even scoffingly unjust, to certain minorities who got in the road of Manifest Destiny—Indians, Mexicans, various peoples. By and large he didn't write very sympathetically about Indians, though he took more time to study them than most historians did, because he thought of them as manifestations of some kind of dark subconscious savagery, which he equated with his own unconscious. It scared him to death. To read DeVoto now, I think you have to adjust his historical stance to a greater sympathy for those minorities simply because we have learned more about their point of view. So when Bud says you can see history, you can, after a fashion. But you can't see it all, and you are never going to see it so plainly that it won't be subject to change. When he did *The Big Sky* he was seeing the mountain men pretty much in DeVoto's terms, because he was strongly influenced by DeVoto at that time. If you looked at *The Big Sky* from an Indian point of view, I think you would find in it some of that same feeling about Indians, a certain superciliousness and condescension you wouldn't want to accept.

DILLON: You must have learned a great deal from DeVoto about writing narrative history. I'm thinking, for example, about his fondness for synecdoche, a device you use so effectively in *Wolf Willow* and sections of *Beyond the Hundredth Meridian*.

STEGNER: I believe in that remark of Frost's, "All the artist needs is samples." I don't think you have to do Oberholtzer's *History of the United States since the Civil War*, that kind of solid, academic job that tells you everything about everything and results in being a compilation instead of a book. It's better to select, to take an example and develop it fully. I don't do it quite so much as DeVoto, who built whole books on that principle. In *The Year of Decision*, he was taking a series of samples and developing them by what he called simultaneity—you know, keeping every chariot going forward at the same speed, trying to produce, as you really can't in print, the effect of simultaneity. The event you come to second will seem as though it happened after the first one no matter how you try. Still, what Benny's historical method did was to throw the emphasis upon individual figures, which means that character emerges out of his pages as it does in fiction, and upon individual scenes, which means that the writing is active and draws upon the dramatic impact of an action. At the same time, he retains the historian's willingness to judge. He even takes along a rope. A lot of his historical friends objected to his judging boldly or brashly. He takes things that historians don't particularly like to do, or aren't able to do, and almost as if he separated them out, makes a historical method out of those scenic and judgmental aspects. Unquestionably, I learned something of that from him, but I think that would also have been my native bent. I don't think I could have written anything but narrative history, no matter how I tried.

DILLON: Was Frost also an important influence?

STEGNER: As much as DeVoto, because I talked with Frost more about literary techniques and what you do with certain kinds of material in certain circumstances. Frost was always saying that all poetry tends toward the dramatic, which is quite the reverse of the tendency now, in which everything gets more inwardly lyric. He was also saying that the object of fiction is to tell what happened to you as if it happened to someone else, and what happened to someone else as if it happened to you, which is, in effect, to get that air of plausibility and propriety without intruding your own personality. Things like that ring around in my head, and sometimes I can't separate which is Frost and which is DeVoto, because they thought a good deal alike.

DILLON: A moment ago you said that a writer has to believe that he can interpret both the past and the present or he shouldn't be writing books. One of the persistent criticisms of western literature, one you've made yourself, is that it has no present. Writers are preoccupied with the old myths instead of contemporary issues.

STEGNER: To some extent that's a problem of nomenclature and organization, because when a contemporary novel is written about the West it isn't called a western novel. Everbody lists *On the Road* not as a western novel but as a contemporary novel. And yet it does at least concern western affairs, western landscapes, and people who are living in the West in ways that are at least as native to the West as anywhere else. What kind of novel is *The Last Picture Show?* Is it a Western? It is West Texas, and it is authentic life observed at close hand in a characteristic little town. It's a kind of *Winesburg, Ohio*, with a little more explicit sexual aberration, a little more desperation. I don't see any reason why a book like that, or *Horseman, Pass By* or *Leaving Cheyenne* or any of them shouldn't be called western novels, if by that we mean that they are reasonably accurate representations of life in that region or a particular part of that region, the Southwest. We just cut off the contemporary from our considerations of the Western, and that's partly the influence of that sense that the West is a timeless place. It's always Tombstone with guns in each hand. What I really would like to do, what I was trying to do in *Angle of Repose*, what I would try to do in my next novel, is to make that human continuity between a real past and a real present so that there is no danger it will ever slip into the never-never land and no danger that it can be detached from the West the way a lot of western novels can be.

DILLON: Without the old myths to depend on, what will the western writer do for subject matter?

STEGNER: Look at the life around him, not Tombstone, Arizona, which was an aberration in the West. The Tombstone situation, which multiplies violence and drama and walkdowns, is what seems to have taken over the popular western line, the television line, the movie line. I'm a realist, I guess, and what I'm interested in is showing the West as it is and as it has been, not as it might have been and not as imagination has re-created it. *Angle of Repose* is built on quite a lot of historical research. That Leadville is an authentic Leadville. Howard Mumford Jones wrote me a chiding letter, wagging his finger, saying, "Come on, why did you get all those people together in that one log cabin in Leadville? You wanted a scene." The fact is they were all there, and maybe some others that I didn't put in because I couldn't accommodate them. That doesn't justify it. If it didn't persuade him, then it's bad. But the idea itself, that that kind of person would have been in that kind of cabin in Leadville in the 1870s, is perfectly sound. I think when he thinks it isn't he's not remembering the real West. He's remembering a mythic West inhabited only by gunfighters and gambling madams.

DILLON: Which confirms the tremendous appeal of that myth. It must be extremely difficult for a western writer to get the reading public to accept characters and situations other than the traditional ones.

STEGNER: Well, this is partly because the book review media have been reduced so much in number and in variety that you get only one little peep sight view. I doubt that the reviewing journals adequately represent the variety of taste that the reading public represents. All kinds of people can't find in the *New York Times Book Review* or the *New York Review of Books* the kinds of books reviewed that they like to read. That doesn't mean necessarily that those books are beneath notice. It means that they are not within the purview of a particular group of critics or reviewers. It was very much better when there was some competition, when *Saturday Review, Book World,* the *Herald Tribune Books,* and the *New York Times Book Review* reviewed from different slants, and also when there were good regional book pages like Joe Jackson's in the *San Francisco Chronicle.* I think Lon Tinkle has been one of the real forces for reasonable, responsible reporting of books that are of interest to the audience in this region. So has *Southwest Review.* It would be even better if some publishing would get dispersed beyond the east coast to, say, Dallas, Los Angeles, Denver, wherever. It's not likely, but it would be nice.

DILLON: So far we've talked mainly about history, but in the passage from *The Sound of Mountain Water* that I read at the beginning you took issue with two elements of contemporary fiction, the so-called "liberated" consciousness and the idea of experimentation. Could you amplify those

STEGNER: I'm probably going to convict myself out of my own mouth of being an old square and a conservative. My trouble is, I guess, that I find a certain amount of contemporary fiction difficult to read, unrewarding to read. It doesn't say anything to *me,* and this probably means only that the world has gone so many degrees over there and I remain in this place. That happens to almost everybody sooner or later. But I can't read certain contemporary novelists, whom I'd just as soon not name, with pleasure, though I try over and over again because people tell me they're good. Some of them are my former students whom I would very much like to like because I like them. I just don't like their books, partly, I suppose, because they seem to be sociologically at large. They don't seem to be attached to any element of the stable life of society; that's to say, the family is gone from most of them. The characteristic hero is a variant of the one R. W. B. Lewis talks about, the picaresque saint, whom

I would rather define as a wandering stud, generally with a guitar and certainly on the make. The wandering aspect of it is almost compulsory. I suppose *On the Road* is a model for a lot of these. They're one-night stands; the ladies don't interest me that much; the thing they're searching for seems to me pretty vague, ill-defined, and probably chimerical, so that the quest itself is a quest without a grail. My general feeling is that novels about that kind of disintegrating social life, the forming and disforming of communes and all that, are ephemera. They don't seem to me to amount to anything because I don't think society can stay in that state of flux. It seems to me that the real relationships, the things that last in life and that will probably last in fiction as well, are likely to be related to parents, children, courtship, marriage, and children, in turn. In other words, I don't think you can douse the family as contemporary fiction has doused it, dousing the kind of glue that holds society together.

DILLON: What about the matter of technical experimentation?

STEGNER: Some of the most experimental novels seem to me self-conscious to a degree. Again, there are people I like very much, like Jack Barth, who write books that I can't quite like. He knows that, so I can mention his name. He's a very nimble talent, gifted with words, but what he chooses to do, to invert and invert and invert and to make out of the techniques of fiction his subject matter, to get lost in the fun house and to sort of go round and round before distorting mirrors, seems to me tricky and sort of amusing, often quite hilarious, but ultimately not worthy of the highest praise. My prejudice is speaking.

DILLON: And yet you've played some games with Kronos yourself.

STEGNER: Oh sure, with chronology. Where does it come from? It comes from Bergson's theory of time, that all time exists simultaneously, that the past exists in your mind simultaneously with the present. This, of course, is what happens in any impressionistic novel. You move back and forth in time. *The Sound and the Fury* is the classic example. Absolutely defensible and absolutely brilliant, I think. But there, it seems to me, you are accepting a truth and enlarging the techniques of fiction to take advantage of it. Where you are only playing games with typography and so on you probably don't have the truth to back you up.

DILLON: In response to your comment in *Wolf Willow* that you had spent a lifetime catching up with civilization, one critic said, sneeringly I thought, "Yes, and at the moment he's about at the end of the nineteenth century." The sneer excepted, it seemed an apt observation.

STEGNER: It may have been a sneer but it is not inaccurate. I don't think the twentieth century has improved on the nineteenth that much that I'm going to be so very unhappy to be left back there. But there isn't any question at all that growing up without history and having to learn it and getting it late had an effect. I've made a kind of American hegira from essential poverty through the academic world, from real ignorance (my parents never finished the sixth grade) to living in a world where my natural companions are people of real brilliance. As Americans, it seems to me, we are expected to make the whole pilgrimage of civilization in a single lifetime. That's a hell of a thing to ask of anybody. It seems to me an extra hardship. It may also be an extra challenge, and it may be good for us, but you cannot, or not very likely, particularly in the new parts of the United States, and particularly from uncultivated families, be born into a culture and acquire in your first impressionable half-dozen years the kind of cultivation that, let's say, Aldous Huxley acquired from the time he was in diapers. And I've talked with Huxley about this and he kept saying, "Yes, but you might have gotten something else." What he meant was that to be a little sensuous savage on a frontier must have been kind of fun. It was, so he's right. There is something else to it. But I don't mind being in the nineteenth century, being still in the age of develop-ment in the United States. As long as I'm in that fix, in that frame of mind, I don't have to concentrate upon the decline and fall, which I would rather not do.

DILLON: I would imagine that you find the nineteenth-century Rus-sian novelists very congenial. Conrad also.

STEGNER: Oh, yes, more congenial, I suppose, than almost any other group, and Conrad one of the first. Chekhov I suppose likewise. Not so much Dostoevski. That's another tradition. I'll give him to Saul Bellow. But there isn't any question that if I were stuck on a desert island with five books, three of them would have to be Russian or Polish. I was charmed and amused when seeing the reviews of Solzhenitsyn's books—*August 1914, The Cancer Ward, The First Circle*. Universal praise, not necessar-ily because they are anti-Russian or anti-Soviet, though that certainly figures, but because they are such rich novels, particularly *The Cancer Ward*, of human life and disease and recovery and infection and the bonds of brotherhood. I think *The Cancer Ward* is his best novel, and I think it is a great nineteenth-century Russian novel. But if an American wrote a nineteenth-century Russian novel, he would get panned off the boards.

So the habit of admiring abroad what we condemn at home is still with us. That irritates me a little bit and amuses me a little bit because if I had an ambition, it would be to write a Tolstoy or a Solzhenitsyn kind of novel. It would deal with the nineteenth century, at least in part, and I think I'm going to start writing it next week, and I suspect it's going to be long and I suspect it's going to involve the exploration of family relation-ships and social relationships and social change within some area of the West, maybe all over the West. You have to think like Tolstoy to do that kind of a novel. If I were Jack Barth I might think "How can I hit Ameri-can literature when it's off balance?" which is the question Barth asked himself when he began. I think that gets you into capering and doing jigs and mugging and whooping rather than paying attention to the work at hand. But that's my conservative point of view again.

DILLON: When you said that you'd given Dostoevski to Saul Bellow it occurred to me that, generally speaking, defeat, despair, and intense subjective conflict are not prominent in your work.

STEGNER: I don't think I'm a particularly jovial or genial writer. I think a lot of my books are kind of glum, bleak even. And yet I suppose that there is something ultimately self-pitying in a lot of the inward novels, the novels of the examination of your soul and its own private hell, which has been a pattern of the last twenty-five years, that puts me off. That may be the old cowboy morality of Saskatchewan talking; you aren't supposed to bellow and cry. It seems to me that a lot of the novels I object to make a lot of fuss about one's internal woes. There was obviously a trend for a while in which a novel meant nothing sociologically but something which was inward. It was inner space you were exploring, and too often, I thought, with a degree of self-pity, of getting even with the world or with your parents or with someone else who imposed upon you things which you found unpalatable. So it may be that my objection is not literary at all but a moral one, a Puritan moral one. Frost used to say, "Sure, I'm a Puritan, and I'm proud of it." If I'm Frost's disciple, I have to say it too.

DILLON: That attitude carries over into the histories and biographies as well. In *Beyond the Hundredth Meridian*, for example, you say that you are interested in Powell as the personification of an ideal of public service, not in his personality. In *The Uneasy Chair* you stay pretty clear of psychoanalytic speculations.

STEGNER: I don't believe in it, for one thing. As a matter of fact, I have watched too many psychotic personalities being treated with drugs and being healed better than psychoanalysis could heal them. I have a strong suspicion, and a lot of my medical friends express the same suspicion, that as a means of therapy psychoanalysis has never proved itself and is pretty soon going to be in the junkyard. No, I really don't like the psychobiographical approach. I'm fond of Erik Erikson, whom I finally got to know a little while ago. I think he is a brilliant man. He was the one who got up psychobiography and psychohistory with his studies of Freud and Gandhi, and it seems to me to open up what was for a little while nailed down, that is the intrusion into dead minds on very speculative bases by untrained practitioners who are more literary than scientific. I don't believe that the picture of the man I get is anything but distorted when I have seen that method applied, at least by a literary man, to, shall we say, another literary subject—biography. I never did believe Leslie Fiedler on *Huckleberry Finn* or *Moby Dick*, and a lot of this goes in similar directions.

DILLON: Was it your intention in *The Uneasy Chair* to write the kind of factual, empirical, inductive biography that DeVoto himself favored?

STEGNER: Well, I did some psychobiography there, but I did it, when I had to, on the basis of his own self-analysis and also on the basis of the papers and letters which his analysts sent to me. Benny had a million of them. But I think, I hope anyway, that I stuck with the self-analysis I found in his own papers and those of his doctors. To that extent, you see, I was getting very personal. I also had to deal with his fantasy life because it infused itself into his writings so much. His most self-indulgent fantasy was to be a hero, a father figure, to some adoring young thing. He married one, and that whole Kate Sterne business is another example. But the thing I didn't choose to deal with was whether he did or did not have any love life, any affairs and so on. I must say that I get kind of sick listening to the affairs, particularly of notable literary figures who seem to think that the world is just panting to learn. One example of that would be Edmund Wilson's *The Twenties*. Damned if I care about Edmund Wilson's love life, and damned if I don't think it odd that he should spend so much time not only writing it down in the first place but preserving it for posterity and preparing it for publication afterward. He's not alone by any means. He is a symptom of the times.

DILLON: It's been said that living in the West directs one's attention outward rather than inward, toward land and space and away from the dark recesses of the psyche. Is there any truth to that?

STEGNER: I don't know. I would like to see the figures on the incidence of schizophrenia in the Mountain West and in the city. If I'm right that the basis is physiological rather than neurological, it ought to be as prevalent in Salt Lake City or Provo as in New York. I do think there is something in a kind of moral atmosphere which makes it seem almost shameful to look inward. I don't think that the rush to psychiatrists took place in the Mountain West the way it did in New York. In California, on the other hand, which is much more like the other coast, it happened pretty frequently. But whether landscape draws the eye outward and therefore takes it off yourself, or whether the society looks with a slight frown upon that kind of nervous trouble, I don't know. I think the latter but I'm not certain.

DILLON: But surely topography and landscape and weather have some effect on a person's outlook.

STEGNER: Of course, but I suspect that effect takes place before the age of ten. It's a formative kind of business. It's the way you learn to see and so you sort of see that way all the rest of your life. When artists came West with one party after another and tried to paint the West, it turned out in the beginning to be almost all Hudson River School. It was full of little green trees and landscapes which simply weren't there, but which somehow the artists persuaded themselves were there. Think of how Möllhausen and some others painted the Grand Canyon. Because there was an impression of great depth and narrowness they painted it like a slot, whereas it is probably fifteen miles wide. You see what you are trained to see. It took a long while before artists coming West, one after another, added something, as Piercy, for instance, added the business of using a little Chinese white constantly to enhance and brighten the land-scape, which began to make another palette. And a whole other palette is necessary beyond the hundredth meridian simply because it isn't a green country. It's a brown country, a dry country. It's got the color of bleached bones and alkali flats and things like that in it. It takes a generation, maybe two, for an art tradition to adapt itself to a new country that much. What I'm saying is that a westerner who grows up with that palette may see in terms of that palette and those shapes—mesas, buttes, whatever—the way eastern artists always saw with a Hudson River School eye. Whether that ultimately gives him a greater sanity, an out-ward looking and therefore less anxiously self-centered view, I would hesitate to say.

DILLON: I'm not suggesting that people living west of the hundredth meridian are saner than those living east of it, but only that, if they're writers, they'll probably be drawn to a different kind of subject matter.

STEGNER: You may be right about that. A literary tradition is a very complex thing, you know. It's made up of many things, many of them below the level of conscious awareness. The problem there again is com-plicated by the fact that most literary discussion comes out of New York, whereas the confrontation of writer and subject matter is quite separated from that. You can get driven away from your natural subject matter or be persuaded that it is not worthy by a discussion which doesn't under-stand it. At the same time, it is just as possible to get convinced that you are right and the whole rest of the world is wrong. You will find plenty of regional old ladies to persuade you of that. You get praised because you're a local boy, not because you're good. The danger of regionalism is pre-cisely that, that it is terribly self-indulgent at times. And yet I don't know any other way to do what I want to do except to do it in what amount to regional terms. So I find myself supporting regionalism, always with a slight ironic distance. I don't really want to get to be a western writer. I'd rather be a writer.

Vardis Fisher and Wallace Stegner: Teacher and Student

Joseph M. Flora*

An important aspect of Vardis Fisher's autobiographical tetralogy and its revision and expansion as *Orphans in Gethsemane* (1960) is Vridar Hunter's relationships with his teachers and later with his students. Fisher first taught English at the University of Utah as a graduate student. He returned to Utah for three years after he received his Ph.D. from Chicago, and then taught at New York University for three years. He also taught two summers at the University of Montana. Fisher's readers will have little doubt that few of his students could quickly forget their experience with him. His personality seldom—if ever—elicited a neutral judgment.

As far as I have been able to learn from reading the Fisher correspondence at Yale University, from correspondence with Fisher, and from an unforgettable weekend visit in the summer of 1963 with Vardis and Opal Fisher at their Hagerman, Idaho, home, the most famous student to emerge from any of Fisher's classes was Wallace Stegner. Stegner was an undergraduate at Utah enrolled in Fisher's English class; one would naturally expect a person of Stegner's talents to have found Fisher of especial interest—as he did. Our conversation turned to Stegner during the 1963 Hagerman weekend because I detected certain similarities with Vardis Fisher in a character in a Stegner short story I had recently taught. The short story is "The View from the Balcony," a story set in an Indiana college town but which really seemed to me to be based on Iowa City, where Stegner had done his graduate work and where, I knew, Fisher had several friends. Fisher told me that he had not read the story. I promised to send him a copy, which I did. Fisher wrote back, not pleased to find himself reflected in the character of Paul Latour but at the same time describing a fight that he had had with Stegner that left no doubt that my hunch had been correct.

I call the attention of Fisher's readers to Stegner's story not because Paul Latour is Vardis Fisher but because he does reflect a side of Fisher's complex personality. Nor do I mean in any way to limit Stegner's story, which is very fine. It is not a factual account but, like most fiction, uses the stuff of reality and transmutes it into something else. The story stands

*Reprinted from *Western American Literature* (Summer, 1970), pp. 121–28.

in its own right. However, I think Fisher and Stegner readers will find the story of interest in an autobiographical light, for it indicates what one would have expected—Vardis Fisher was an important influence on Stegner. I think that one would also have to conclude that the portrait is also—in part—Stegner's judgment on his former teacher.

"The View from the Balcony" portrays a married graduate student community living in a converted fraternity house just after World War II. The students in their sheltered present look forward to "the assured future."[1] Their confidence is brought into question when Tommy Probst freezes and walks out of his final Ph.D. examination. The group decides to go on with the beer party that was to have been a celebration and to invite Professor Clark Richards, head of the social science department, and Paul Latour, a psychology professor, to come to help straighten Tommy out. Especially through these characters, who were "outsiders, older, with better perspective" (p. 100), Stegner demonstrates that the future is never assured, that even if the students live in a fraternity house, each is "alone, terrified, and at bay, each with his ears attuned to some roar across the woods, some ripple of water, some whisper of a footstep in the dark" (p. 120). When the story ends, Richards' wife, Myra, is off in a canoe with a student and her husband is very upset; Paul Latour—whose profession emphasizes understanding of emotional needs and fears—has fought so savagely with Charley Graham that the student would have been thrown from the balcony had he not also been a good wrestler.

Of special interest here is Paul Latour. Stegner describes him as possessing a "grim but difficult smile" (p. 100). Latour has the strongest, most difficult personality of anyone in the story. He drinks his own hard liquor rather than the offered beer, without ice because it reminds him "that it's poison" (p. 111). Like the hard-drinking Vardis Fisher, Latour chooses rather direct methods. He looks right through people. His physical appearance is like many descriptions of Fisher. This is how Latour looks to Lucy Graham, from whose point of view the story is focused:

> His face was like the face of a predatory bird, beaked, grim-lipped; because of some eye trouble he always wore dark glasses, and his prying, intent, hidden stare was an agony to encounter. His mouth was hooked back in a constant sardonic smile. He not merely undressed her with his eyes; he dissected her most intimate organs, and she knew he was a cruel man, no matter how consistently and amazingly kind he had been to Charley, almost like a father, all the way through school. Charley said he had a mind like a fine watch. But she wished he would not come over, and she trembled, unaccountably emotional, feeling trapped.
>
> Then he was in front of her, big-shouldered for his height, not burly but somehow giving the impression of great strength, and his face like the cold face of a great bird thrust toward her and the hidden stare stabbed into her and the thin smile tightened. (p. 108)

Those who have studied photographs of Fisher and read their Fisher will detect much in the long description of Latour that sounds like Vridar Hunter of *No Villain Need Be* and *Orphans in Gethsemane* as well as like some descriptions of Fisher. Vridar, like Fisher, had serious eye trouble, and Vridar, again like Fisher, felt it the novelist's business to be able to strip away human facades. Both minds were often "like a fine watch" in their analyses of human behavior. Readers are invited to compare this description of Latour *(Latour* is an approximate rhyme with *Fisher)* and the picture of Fisher that occurs in *Time* magazine of August 12, 1946. The *Time* article is also relevant; it is titled "Man with a Temper." It begins by calling Fisher "Hawk-nosed" and emphasizes temper. It is not, of course, a flattering article, and it annoyed Fisher greatly. He had his own ideas about why his nose was frequently an item singled out by his critics. The article summarizes, indeed, the way many saw Fisher. But it is not the whole of Fisher, nor are the unflattering aspects of Paul Latour the only truth about him.

As Stegner's story reveals, Charley is correct in saying that Paul Latour has a fine mind. Even though there is a certain irony involved, it is Latour who gives the incisive analysis of Tommy's difficulty. Tommy is a child, afraid to grow up. The truth is—and the story bears Latour out—Tommy was afraid of passing the exam. Paul Latour not only looks like Vardis Fisher, but he functions in a similarly tough, analytic fashion.

It is also clear that Latour has had a beneficial relationship with Charley; Latour has given a great deal of himself to Charley—he had been "almost like a Father." This will strike the most casual readers as Freudian, but for Fisher's readers the ramifications are indeed even greater. The relationship between fathers and sons is crucial in Fisher's books and becomes more so the further Fisher goes with his *Testament of Man.* As Fisher shows it, one of the tragedies of modern life is that fathers have tended to prevent—and often struggle to prevent—their sons from becoming adult. *Orphana in Gethsemane* is set most pointedly to illustrate this theme. It is an irony that Latour's animal action is really an intellectual favor to Charley and his wife. I think Fisher's own rudeness were often attempts to prevent emotional dependencies. Fisher felt tempted to play the role of Father, but what he tried to say was: You need to be adult. I'll tell you what I know, but don't look for me to be Big Daddy for you. Fisher's main dissatisfaction with American politics was the abundance of Father-figures who were all too eager to play that role. Interestingly, Vridar found college campuses filled with professors eager to play the role of daddy.

Fisher would have wanted Stegner—or any of his students—to go his independent way. Like Latour, he behaved in such a way as to insure it.

One of Fisher's comments to me indicates the depth and complexity of his relationship with Stegner. Fisher felt that Stegner's first novel (really a novelette), *Remembering Laughter* (1937), was importantly indebted to his own *Dark Bridwell* (1931). I think there was some resentment on Fisher's part, since Stegner's book was very popular and won a Little, Brown prize for the year. The success of the novel encouraged Stegner's commitment to creative writing. On the other hand, *Dark Bridwell*, although it had been very well reviewed, did not have a large printing. It gave Fisher some attention, but not what he deserved, and little money. The father might understandably feel resentment at the son—especially, I think, since *Dark Bridwell* (Fisher's second published novel) is very much the better of the two books. *Remembering Laughter* is an interesting first book, full of promise, but it does seem in ways derivative and not always credible.

The major strain on credibility comes in the relationship between Malcolm MacLeod and his mother. Malcolm has been born out of wedlock in a rural Iowa community. Everyone knows who his mother is; in fact, she alone carries him to his christening. But his mother and her sister bring up the boy to think of both of them as aunts. Since they are still living in the same community, it is difficult to imagine that the boy would be sixteen before someone would suggest to him that his parentage was not as he supposed.

The point of interest here, however, is possible influence of *Dark Bridwell* on *Remembering Laughter*. While it is true that Stegner's book might as easily invite comparison with Edith Wharton's *Ethan Frome*, it is not difficult to find what Fisher might have sensed in *Remembering Laughter* as similar to his own work.

Both *Dark Bridwell* and *Remembering Laughter* are emphatically rendered with a sense of finality about the histories related. Both are clearly "rememberings." The sense of distance and finality in each is struck by use of frames—a labeled Prologue and finally an Epilogue. In between is a drama of years—high passions and then their frustration and denial. Both works treat the loss of joy and fulfillment. Tonally, the similarity is striking.

The telescoping of time in passages summarizing certain samenesses mark both *Dark Bridwell* (and much of Fisher's fiction) and *Remembering Laughter*. Typical is this languid passage from Stegner:

> And the years,—the stifling nights of summer, windless and humid, the hot oppressive blackness when the three lay awake in different rooms listening to the petulant discomfort of the child and the curtains hung slack in wide-open windows; the interminable days when clothes clung to perspiring bodies and the oaks drooped under the fierce sun and the darkened parlor was the only passably cool room in the house; the slow ripening of September, the golden fields, the farm alive with strange men, huskers and threshers powdered with the bright dust of harvest, and in full view from the window of the haymow the incredible streak of flame that was the creek bed; and in October also the still wavering fall of leaves,—and in the intervals between labor and labor the wild regret that

was never to die, but was to be hidden in silence and unforgiving and the avoidance of outward feeling until over it grew a shell of habit, so that for days at a time the three forgot the reasons for their watchful silence and the bleakness of their house. . . .[2]

There is much of Fisher's rhythms here and in other passages of indirect discourse and summary. To cite another example:

And Margaret, watching him delightedly pour out a lavish stream of nonsense, watching her young sister with bright eyes and pert disbelieving merriment drink it all in, was contented to sit sedately beside them and let her own questions wait. There was much about Scotland, about their father's death, about friends and relatives, that she wanted to know; but meanwhile Alec was telling about the cannibal eels in the Coon River, which seeing their own tails following them, turned and snapped and ate themselves at a gulp in a swirling eddy of water.[3]

In *Dark Bridwell* Fisher has many passages which compress time and summarize feelings. The following passage is typical:

But though Lela believed, in a simple childlike way, that she had been transported to the loveliest place anywhere, she was sometimes strangely shaken when she looked at the river, washing downward over its path, and at the wild tree-bedded bluffs and peaks around her. She would look at her children and wonder what their education would be. She would look at her home and wonder if she would never have more than boxes for chairs, more than pine boughs for a bed. And upon her, even during these first weeks, there would fall a melancholy, a deep and nameless unhappiness, that was to grow with the years, that was to sleep in her heart and await its tremendous hour. Because under her earnestness, deeper than the birdlike joy which she often felt, there was a dark heritage of adolescent doubt and pain. There were memories of childhood years, half-crazed and altogether lonely, when she had been an orphan, dragged from place to place, cuffed and abused. And there was in her, too, a lively ambition, a wish to toil and build, and hoard savings against her old age. But all this in her Charley never understood. In her blue eyes, he saw an infrequent madness, and it troubled him. It made his love for her unreasoning, a desperate greedy devotion, and it made of his jealousy in later years an inner storm of delirium. It stampeded his thoughts, churned his emotions into whey, and left him white and helpless with his own wrath.[4]

There is something of the poet in Fisher's naturalism as he empathizes with his people.

Fisher's *Dark Bridwell* and Stegner's *Remembering Laughter* are strongly regional. Stegner's region is rural and remote Iowa; Fisher's—of course—the Antelope country of Idaho, a setting that emphasizes even more the relationship of the characters with the forces of nature. *Dark Bridwell* relates the history of a family which lives in an isolated area where they often see no other persons for months. When the action starts, they are making their way to this wild home. *Remembering Laughter* starts with the arrival of Elspeth MacLeod from Scotland at the Iowa farm of her sister and brother-in-law. Eventually both works counterpoint a strong Puritan heritage against the force of a joyous embracing of life. In both works the Puritanism is triumphant; everyone loses, but especially the man of the house.

It is probably the great similarity between these two men that most arrested Fisher's attention when he read *Remembering Laughter*. They are not twins, by any means, but they are cast in the same mold. Both are the yea-sayers to life. They have the ability to merge into nature; they have a kind of basic pagan affirmation to have to fight to keep it intact, for civilized life would deprive them of this joy. Alec Stuart's wife can understand her husband even less perfectly than Charley Bridwell's understands him. Alec likes to joke, swim in the nude, and even take a drink now and then. His way—like Charley's—is essentially the way of laughter. He imitates all sorts of animals and loves to invent fantastic stories. For example, he tells Elspeth of Mississippi Valley angleworms so long that a hen worked a whole day to eat one:

> The hen . . . would get hold of one end of the worm and start backing away, to pull it from its hole. If it was a really grown worm, that hen would back away from eight in the morning till three in the afternoon, with an hour's rest at noon. When the tailend finally came loose from the hole the worm, snapping together after its long stretch, would knock down trees for miles; and if it happened to slip around a house or a barn, would snap that off its foundations slick as a whistle. Then the hen, if she recovered from the elastic backlash, would start eating her way back toward home, arriving there generally after nine in the evening, dusty and footsore and completely spent, and so gorged with angleworm that she couldn't get in the door of the henhouse.[5]

Elspeth loves Alec for such tales and laughter—as later her and Alec's son loves him for it.

Like Alec, an extraordinary fund of nonsense is one of Charley Bridwell's chief traits. Charley, too, can do remarkable imitations. Once he imitates a bear so convincingly that he makes a life-time enemy of Adolph Buck. But Charley's motives are not usually malicious, and children love him for his talents. For instance, on his way to his new home Charley explains to the Tompkins boy that he will make "my halter-ropes out of rattlesnakes. I'll use a rattlesnake for a quirt. And if my kids won't be good, I'll blister their hinders with a live snake. How's that suit you?" The lad looks at his father and snickers. Charley continues to elaborate: "And as for wolves and bears and lions . . . I'll carry them little beasts around in my pockets. I'll eat a whole bear for my breakfast, teeth and backbones and toenails. How's that, now?"[6] As we learn in *In Tragic Life* and *Orphans in Gethsemane*, Vridar Hunter is one of Charley's most ardent admirers. Charley is wilder than Alec Stuart, but I think it likely that his portrait more than anything else caused Fisher's reaction.

In any event, Fisher and Stegner scholars may find reading *Remembering Laughter* with *Dark Bridwell* in mind of more than passing interest. It may be that Stegner's "The View from the Balcony" reflects rather than announces Stegner's adieu to the direct influence of his important teacher. In ways, it is a tribute to both Stegner and Fisher.

Notes

1. "The View from the Balcony" in *The Women on the Wall* (Boston: Houghton, Mifflin, 1950), p. 100. Stegner's story first appeared in *Mademoiselle*. Pagination is to *The Women on the Wall* and will be hereafter included in the text.

2. *Remembering Laughter* (Boston: Little, Brown and Co., 1937), pp. 124–25.

3. Stegner, p. 18.

4. Vardis Fisher, *Dark Bridwell* (Boston: Houghton, Mifflin, 1931), pp. 41–42.

5. Stegner, *Remembering Laughter*, pp. 16–17.

6. Fisher, p. 27.

Wallace Stegner:
Trial by Existence [The Shorter Works]

Robert Canzoneri*

Wolf Willow is a remarkable book which has not received the recognition it deserves partly because nobody knows how to label it. The publisher added a subtitle with which Stegner himself was not satisfied: *A History, a Story, and a Memory of the Last Plains Frontier*. Part of the problem is in the repeated indefinite article. The book is in fact divided into three sections, but the first is memory as well as history, and the history is comprehended in terms of what is remembered upon Stegner's return to Saskatchewan. The second part is "a memory" as well as a novella and a short story. The third part is memory, some history, and contemplation—a coming to terms. Even so qualified, the subtitle is misleading. Although what is memory, what is history, what is fiction, and what is speculation are all clearly delineated; they are used in their relationship to a central quest by a central intelligence.

Almost any attempt to describe the book is likely to give the false impression that it is not a single, unified whole. Perhaps if it had appeared after Truman Capote made such a stir over the "nonfiction novel," *Wolf Willow* could have adopted that label, different as it is from *In Cold Blood*. Malcolm Cowley has said that he wrote *Exile's Return*—a nonfictional account—deliberately as a novel. Like *Exile's Return, Wolf Willow* is a search into the past in an effort to understand and assimilate it whole. The basic difference—other than the fact that one book is concerned mostly with Americans in France in the twenties, and the other with a frontier child in Saskatchewan some fifteen years earlier—is in Stegner's use of the novella and short story in the middle of his nonfictional account. Yet even though the voice changes from that of Stegner himself to third person narrative—the point of view is that of a young cowboy in the novella, "Genesis"—the fictional portion of the book is fully integrated in tone, structure, and development with the nonfictional.

The sequence works so well that the reader feels no need to justify it in theory; yet one major reason for the use of fiction is readily apparent—in keeping with Stegner's general approach, it is in fact, virtually

*Reprinted and excerpted by permission of the author from "Wallace Stegner: Trial by Existence," *Southern Review*, 9 (1973), 796–827.

stated. The book begins with an account by Stegner of the Saskatchewan he knew as a child in comparison with its appearance as he revisits it; the account—without changing point of view—moves into history of the place as he did not know it when he lived there, but wishes he had; then it focuses upon one specific crucial time in that history, the winter of 1906–07, about which he had "heard some stories . . . but . . . never heard enough," and later read about "in the middens where historians customarily dig."[1] It is at this point that observed fact and researched fact become blended by the imagination into a fictional experience which Stegner introduces directly:

> If we want to know what it was like on the Whitemud River range during that winter when the hopes of a cattle empire died, we had better see it through the eyes of some tenderfoot, perhaps someone fresh from the old country, a boy without the wonder rubbed off him and with something to prove about himself. If in inventing this individual I put into him a little of Corky Jones, and some of the boy Rusty whose mouth organ used to sweeten the dusty summer shade of the Lazy-S bunkhouse, let it be admitted that I have also put into him something of myself. . . . (p. 138)

I suspect that only a realist of the particular brand I consider Stegner to be could so skillfully and so rightly join the fiction and nonfiction, both clearly identified, into so coherent and unified a whole. Not only is the evocation of the remembered (nonfictional) scene as vivid as I have ever read, and the history as interesting and pertinent, but the mind apparent in the selection and contemplation of fact is as clear, as strong, as profound as any I have run across. It is impossible to separate the inherent quality of mind from what it has disciplined itself to become, but *Wolf Willow* is obviously the product of a talent, an intelligence which has trained itself to see and speak clearly and which takes the validity of the relationship between fact and fiction fully as seriously as that between fact and nonfiction. Both are written "in order to reflect or illuminate life."[2]

The novella, "Genesis," taken alone may well stand as the classic cowboy story. It has all the qualities I have attributed to Stegner's nonfiction prose, and at the same time that it has the clean lines and artistic inevitability of a Greek play, it proceeds with so convincing a sense of reality that—as in *The Big Rock Candy Mountain*—the concept of "rites of passage" is verified in the flesh. When at the end the tenderfoot English boy has proved himself it has been through cold and hardship so palpable that they cannot be doubted, and it is by men whom we know and respect as men that he is accepted. He learns through the test of experience what it means to be "a man" in terms that have validity in the circumstances, limited but real, of a cowboy rounding up cattle in the worst winter imaginable. In that respect, he is closely related to the larger movement of the book: the search of Stegner himself to find what he is and what the circumstances of his environment helped make of him.

* * *

"There may be a number of kinds of short stories," Wallace Stegner
has said, "but all demand an intense concision and economy, and all must
somehow achieve a satisfying sense of finality. Beyond that I don't think
we should define or prescribe. We should only give thanks when we strike
a good one."[3] In *The Women on the Wall* and *The City of the Living* we
strike as many good ones as we do in the works of any short story writer I
know. There is not an unsuccessful story in either volume; the large majority are truly outstanding; a number represent the short story at its very
best. . . .

Several of the stories in *The Women on the Wall* were written prior
to *The Big Rock Candy Mountain* and later became part of the novel. Of
these, "Buglesong," "Goin' to Town," "Two Rivers," "Butcher Bird," and
"The Colt" are crucial points in Bruce's boyhood in the novel, yet each of
them stands as a completely unified separate entity. Another story, "In
the Twilight"—although not included in the novel—is comparable in excellence and shares as well the same characters and setting. All of these
are from Bruce's point of view, have the same quality of realism as does
the novel, and involve the kinds of incidents which are important in making Bruce the man he becomes in the novel. The importance is not stated,
of course; we experience only the shock, the jolt, the slow realization of
the moment.

One of the stories, "Two Rivers," includes the incident Bruce recalls
in the novel when he says, "It was good to have been along and shared it"[4]
—specifically his father's killing a snake from which he pulls a half-
swallowed gopher "coated with slime and twice as long as he ought to
have been."[5] The ambivalence of the rather unappetizing death scene as
representative of a rare good time is in keeping with the duality of the
"two rivers" theme which unobtrusively permeates the story. Bruce wakes
in the "flatness of light" (p. 130) of early morning on the Saskatchewan
plain to go into the mountains and trees. He begins the day sullenly,
hating his father for having hit him the day before when, in an excruciating scene fleshed out in "Goin' to Town," the old Ford refused to
start and they missed the Fourth of July celebration in town. The story
ends with Bruce—"everything wonderful, the day a swell day"—ducking
"when his father pretended he was going to swat him one" (p. 145). Even
more subtle opposites work together throughout the story: the car makes
it up into the mountains only by taking the steepest slope in reverse; Elsa
puts the stem of a maple leaf in her mouth and makes "a half-pleased face
at the bitter taste" (p. 142). Throughout there is "the reflection of ecstasy
and the shadow of tears" (p. 141).

The "two rivers" are a mountain stream and a valley stream which
flowed together where Brucie, at the first rim of memory, was once on
another outing with his parents. Like the cold and warm rivers, Brucie's
and his parents' concurrent recollections of the time are not the same; like

the rivers, too, Brucie's own memory flows ambivalently through the story.

It is when he recognizes that he will always remember his father's killing the snake that the memory first springs in him undefined: "something bothersome and a little scary, and it hurt his head the way it hurt his head sometimes to do arithmetic sums without pencil and paper" (p. 137). Later, as he sits among the trees near the "cold water running from the rock . . . over the whole canyon, like a haze in the clear air, was that other thing, that memory or ghost of a memory, a swing he had fallen out of, a feel of his hands sticky with crushed blackberries, his skin drinking cool shade, and his father's anger . . ." (p. 141). Then he drinks from the spring and pours "a little of it on his arm, and something jumped in his skin. It was his skin that remembered. Something numbingly cold, and then warm. He felt it now, the way you waded in it" (p. 142).

I have lifted out elements of the story to show something of its intricacy; it is, however, an experience much like Brucie's realized with the skin. The same is true of the other "Big Rock Candy Mountain" stories. It is true, too, that although they are different in theme from "Two Rivers," "Buglesong" and "In the Twilight" have similarly ambivalent elements. In the first, Brucie becomes enraptured with life and "literature" ("The splendor falls on castle walls" and the Sears, Roebuck catalog) to the same extent that he is enraptured with death as he feeds a live gopher to a weasel. In the second he comes to a sense of life and power through his weakness and nausea over the killing of an old sow. The other stories have their dualities as well: in "The Colt" he realizes not only the fact of death through seeing the skinned colt he thought had been left to be cared for, but the fact of his father's perfidy. And in "Butcher Bird" he is caught between his "civilized" mother and his "natural" father, asking in effect, "Ma, what'll I do with it?" (p. 185).

Although most of Stegner's stories in the two volumes do not involve Bruce in Saskatchewan, many of them in one way or another do involve the life-death and the civilized-natural themes, and they often end not so much with a solution as with the question of what to do with what has been revealed. "The Double Corner," like all the others I shall mention, is far more complex and real than so narrow an analysis implies, but it may be seen as a complication of the civilized-natural idea. Janet insists on bringing her husband's senile mother to live "naturally" with them instead of in an institution; she discovers, however, that "natural" love is not enough, that the "nature" of the old woman requires "unnatural" restriction: Janet sees her "looking into the open door of the boys' room. Her head was sunk between her shoulders with the intensity of her stare, and her mouth moved on some secret malevolence" (p. 211).

"The Women on the Wall" and "The View from the Balcony" are equally chilling stories which involve the revelation of the "natural" in somewhat the same sense as it is used in "Butcher Bird," where it is related to Bo as killer, as butcher bird. The first of these is about women during the Second World War waiting for their men to return. Gradually, with Mr. Palmer, who observes them benignly at first as "quiet, peaceful, faithful to the times and seasons of their vigil" (p. 29), we learn about them one by one. Soon he becomes aware that within the group there is a groundswell of antipathy and spite in addition to grave problems: Mrs. Corson is on dope; the pregnant girl's husband has been dead three years; plain prim Mrs. Kendall has an adopted son, whom she refers to as a "love child," tied to her apron strings (p. 40). The eruption and confrontation is fierce, and when quiet settles again we realize that the "civilized" scene is inseparable from the "natural," just as to the peaceful beach "the tides leaned in all the way from Iwo and Okinawa"

On a hot Indiana night, "civilized" university people demonstrate much the same thing in "The View from the Balcony." This story, set after the war, is from the point of view of an English girl, Lucy, married to an American graduate student. At a beer party on the balcony of the makeshift apartment house, tensions come to the surface with painful inevitability. When Lucy is finally left alone, she realizes that their "common experience and . . . this common belief in the future, were as friable as walls of cane, as vulnerable as grass huts, and . . . that in their hearts they were alone, terrified, and at bay, each with his ear attuned to some roar across the woods, some ripple of the water, some whisper of a footstep in the dark" (p. 120).

Two other excellent stories in *The Women on the Wall* are similar to those in *The City of the Living* in that they involve realizations on the part of the protagonists about themselves as much as revelations about the nature of existence. In "Balance His, Swing Yours," a middle-aged westerner comes to recognize and accept his greater kinship with a posturing Englishman than with the tanned, assured young men of a Gulf resort. In "Beyond the Glass Mountain," a successful scientist, revisiting an alcoholic college friend, is left just at the point of realizing that his basic certainties about life are not necessarily founded upon knowledge. The two protagonists are kin to that of the story "Maiden in a Tower" in the later volume. After twenty-five years, Harris returns to the tower room where the girl Holly had entertained in the "sophisticated" twenties style, adored by all. The house is now a mortuary, and he sits in the remembered room with a dead woman who is "presentable" but not yet made up as she will be.[6] There he realizes that Holly was "innocence" pretending (p. 81), that the one moment when she became real and begged him to take her away he had kept up the pretense, that he has not changed. He admires the "natural" look of the dead woman more than the artificial, but she is after all dead. In life he has chosen the "civilized" in the sense of its removal from the "natural," and as he leaves he hears "almost with panic, the four quick raps his heels made on the bare floor before they found the consoling softness of the stairs" (p. 83).

Except for "The Double Corner," the stories I have mentioned in *The Women on the Wall* deal with love, when they do at all, not only in terms of family, but from a child's point of view. There are others, two set in New England: "The Berry Patch," an idyllic moment between a man and wife while he is home on furlough during the war, and "The Sweetness of Twisted Apples," in which a skinny, wizened girl far back in the woods is pleased to have for a brief while "gone out." There is implication, too, in "Beyond the Glass Mountain," that the love relationship between the alcoholic friend and his wife, who had slept around before and apparently after their marriage, may be something of more value to them than the protagonist imagines. In their delineation of life these stories go far beyond the kiss-and-go-to-bed routine which has become all too often the substitute for lived-happily-ever-after.

By and large, however, the stories in *The City of the Living* involve both the life-death and civilized-natural themes while dealing with a variety of adult experiences. In "Maiden in a Tower," as I have indicated, part of the point is inability to love. The other stories have to do with the love of men and women (a very important aspect of *The Big Rock Candy Mountain*) only peripherally; they range from a father's hopeless desire that his daughter be happy, in "Impasse," to a social worker's refusal to give up on an incorrigible: "You could not put limits on love—if love was what you chose to live by" (p. 66).

"The Blue-winged Teal" parallels Bruce's relationship with his father in *The Big Rock Candy Mountain*. Through a "duck feed" in the poolroom of his father, whom he despises, a college boy comes to an understanding of their shared humanity. When he tells the father he'll be leaving, "he did not say it in anger, or with the cold command of himself that he had imagined in advance. He said it like a cry, and with the feeling he might have had on letting go the hand of a friend too weak and too exhausted to cling any longer to their inadequate shared driftwood in a wide cold sea" (p. 22). "The City of the Living" works just the other way in that it is from the point of view of a father, Robert Chapman, who comes to realize something about his own involvement in humanity as he watches over his son, wracked with typhoid, in a foreign hotel room. While the feverish boy lies in the darkness, his father, in the "harsh light of the bathroom," clings "to his separateness and identity" (p. 27). Later he feels exposed before the windows, but he does not "get up and pull the shutters and close himself in" (p. 33). As morning comes and the boy's fever subsides, Chapman looks out across the Nile to "the City of the Dead, where the light had been last night and where he had half imagined ghouls. . . . It was innocent and clean now . . ." (p. 36). Through binoculars he watches the river come to life "from his little cell of sanitary plumbing, and on his hands . . . he smelled the persistent odor of antiseptic" (p. 37). A skinny one-eyed Egyptian boy comes into the garden below him, strips, washes himself, prays.

His every move was assured, completely natural. His touching of the earth with his forehead made Chapman want somehow to lay a hand on his bent back.

They have more death than we do, Chapman thought. Whatever he is praying to has more death in it than anything we know.

Maybe it had more life too. Suppose he had sent up a prayer of thanksgiving . . . when he found his son out of danger . . . , where would he have directed his prayer? Not to God, not to Allah, nor to the Nile or any of its creature-gods or the deities of light. . . . To the Antibiotic God. For the first time it occurred to him what the word antibiotic really meant. (p. 39)

As he watches, the "first of the morning buzzards . . . planed across the motionless palm tops. . . . They eyed each other with a kind of recognition . . ." (p. 39–40).

"At its best," Stegner has said, "the miracle that we call the short story can present us with a segment of life. . . . so arranged that it *acts* its own meaning as it moves. . . . At its very best, as in Chekhov, the light it casts on one man or woman in one brief fragment of experience can seem to illuminate the world."[8] He might well be speaking, in the first instance, of all the stories in his own two volumes, and in the second instance—"at its very best"—of well over half. No one I can think of has done better.

*   *   *

Of the twenty-five short stories Stegner has collected, only two are in the first person; each of these is told by a man looking back upon a boyhood incident; each is—in terms of setting and general reference—apparently autobiographical much as is *The Big Rock Candy Mountain*. The stories—"The Chink" and "The Volunteer"—work well enough, but not quite as well, in my opinion, as the related stories of boyhood told in the third person, nor quite as well as Stegner's nonfiction account of his boyhood in *Wolf Willow*. It is in the novella "Field Guide to the Western Birds," included in *The City of the Living*, that Stegner first uses as narrator a sophisticated adult concerned with adult experience. "Field Guide" is told by Joe Allston, a literary agent retired to California. The same Joe Allston is the narrator of *All the Little Live Things*, and historian Lyman Ward, equally sophisticated, narrates *Angle of Repose*. The device is neither better nor worse than the third person narrative of the fiction already discussed, but it allows for a voice interesting in itself and able to make commentary, it tends to send speculation even further into the unknown, and it gives a tone and quality of irony particularly suited to the materials of the three works.

In each case, the narrator is an observer who prefers (or thinks he prefers) to be only that. Joe Allston in "Field Guide" watches the human birds much as he watches the feathered kind, but he not only by his very presence precipitates action, he sees himself in what he observes. The two kinds of birds play off against each other well—far less obviously than my brief analysis may seem to imply. At the beginning of the story Allston tells of a bird he cannot fully identify:

> . . . about ten times a day I see him alight on the terrace and challenge his reflection in the plate glass. He springs at himself like a fighting cock . . . until he wears himself out and squats on the bricks panting and glaring at his hated image. . . . Struggling with himself like Jacob with his angel. . . , old Joe Allston with his memoirs. (p. 127)

The human birds Allston observes at a party given by the very wealthy Casements for Sue Casement's musical protege, a "Glandular Genius" to whom Allston takes an immediate dislike. When the pianist, Arnold Kaminski, humiliates Sue publicly, Allston bursts out to his wife, "Did it ever strike you how much attention a difficult cross-grained bastard gets, just by being difficult?" "It strikes me all the time," his wife murmurs. "Hasn't it ever struck you before?" (p. 153).

Kaminski, it turns out has talent, but it is perhaps flawed. Through the evening Allston remains crusty, disapproving, curious about Kaminski, who is a kind of bird he is unable to identify. As most of the crowd leaves, Kaminski—drunk by now—insults a prim music teacher, partly because Allston is watching. Soon he proclaims the fact: "If I didn't insult people like that I couldn't keep my self-respect. . . . That is why nobody likes me" (p. 184). He then launches into an orgy of self-abuse confessing that he wants failure, that he plans it cunningly. He accuses Allston of having watched him all night because he saw through him, knew that he was not the "Pole from Egypt" he claimed to be. Drunkenly "falling all over Sue," Kaminski says that he lied his way into his confession and can lie his way out, that they all hate him and won't come through on the offer to set up a concert in Carnegie Hall (p. 188).

> "Is that what you *want*, Arnold?" Sue says bitterly. She looks ready to burst into tears.
> "Tol' you I wanted to fail," he says—and even now, so help me, even out of his sodden and doughy wreckage, there looks that bright, mean, calculating little gleam of intelligence. (p. 189)

He continues his abuse, telling them that they don't know yet whether he's lying or telling the truth, until Bill Casement takes the direct approach and tosses him into the pool.

As Joe Allston and Ruth drive home, the questions still remain: "Was he lying first, lying later, or lying all the time?" They creep

> up the last steep pitch . . . with the brown bank just off one fender and the gully's treetops fingering the fog like seaweed on the left. All blind, all difficult and blind. I taste the stale bourbon in my mouth and know myself for a frivolous old man.

In the morning, probably, the unidentifiable bird, towhee or whatever he is, will come around for another bout against the plate glass, hypnotized by the insane hostility of his double. I tell myself that if he wakes me again at dawn tomorrow with his flapping and pecking I will borrow a shotgun and scatter his feathers over my whole six acres.

Of course I will not. I know what I will do. I will watch the fool thing as long as I can stand it, and ruminate on the insanities of men and birds, and try to convince myself that as a local idiocy, an individual aberration, this behaviour is not significant. And then when I cannot put up with the sight of this towhee any longer I will retire to my study and sit looking out of the window. . . . But even there I may sometimes hear the banging and thrashing of this dismal towhee trying to fight his way past himself. . . . (p. 193)

Joe Allston knows and recognizes a great deal about himself, but he is able to face part of it only indirectly. His kinship with Kaminski—the kinship of them all with Kaminski—is stated in terms of birds, but it reverberates through the entire novella. Finally, he looks at his wife and is "filled with gratitude for the forty years during which she has stood between me and myself" (p. 194).

"Field Guide" is radically different in tone, method, setting, characters, movement—what have you—from the straight clean line of "Genesis," but the two novella are equally real and important, one about a young cowboy's proving himself and being accepted as a man, the other about an aging man, where no one knows what "a man" is, "trying to fight his way past himself."

Notes

1. Wallace Stegner, *Wolf Willow* (New York: Viking, 1962), p. 138.

2. Wallace Stegner, *The Writer in America* (Kanda, Japan: The Hokuseido Press, 1952), p. 6.

3. Wallace Stegner, *Teaching the Short Story*, Davis Publications in English, No. 2 (Davis: University of California, Fall 1965), p. 11.

4. Wallace Stegner, *The Big Rock Candy Mountain* (New York: Doubleday, 1973), p. 611.

5. Wallace Stegner, "Two Rivers", in *The Women on the Wall* (New York: Viking, 1962), p. 136.

6. Wallace Stegner, "Maiden in a Tower", in *The City of the Living* (Cambridge, Mass.: Riverside Press, 1956), p. 73.

Wallace Stegner: *The Preacher and the Slave* and *A Shooting Star*

Forrest Robinson and Margaret Robinson*

I *THE PREACHER AND THE SLAVE*

Before turning to Wallace Stegner's partially fictional treatment of him as a character in *The Preacher and the Slave*, let us consider a few facts and questions relating to Joe Hill.[1] Born in Sweden in 1879, Joel Hägglund was a quiet, musical child. Shortly after the death of his mother, he emigrated to the United States in 1902. He came expecting to find gold in the streets. Accounts vary, but it seems clear that his first few years in this country were disillusioning ones. At first young Hägglund worked at odd jobs in New York; sometime later he was fired and put on a blacklist for trying to organize laborers in Chicago; he changed his name to Joe Hill (he was also referred to as Joseph Hillstrom) and moved West to Washington, California, Hawaii, possibly to Mexico; he appears to have joined the Industrial Workers of the World (Wobblies) in San Pedro, California, in 1910. During the next few years he became well known for such union songs as "The Preacher and the Slave," "Casey Jones—the Union Scab," "Workers of the World, Awaken!" and many others which appeared in the Wobblies' "Little Red Song Book."

But the troubadour of a singing union did not begin to achieve international fame until he was arrested on January 13, 1914, in Salt Lake City. Found wounded in a boardinghouse, Joe Hill was charged with the murder of a grocer and his son. His alleged accomplice, Otto Applequist, was never found. The litigations over the next two years were extremely complicated. Hill claimed that he was shot in a quarrel over a woman. Arguing that it was the state's task to establish his guilt, he refused to identify her, and she failed to come forward. He was executed on November 19, 1915.

The case of Joe Hill was an international *cause célèbre*. Appeals came from such notables as President Wilson, Helen Keller, Samuel Gompers, and W. A. F. Ekengren, the Swedish Minister to the United States. The Wobblies, who rallied to his defense, were convinced that their songster

*Reprinted from *Wallace Stegner* (Boston: G. K. Hall, 1977), pp. 123–40.

was the innocent victim of Mormon capitalists hostile to their organization's agitation. The union lost the legal battle, but they elevated their hero to martyrdom after his death. "Joe Hill's Last Will," written the day before his execution, is a masterpiece of artless simplicity and a key element in his legend.

> My will is easy to decide,
> For there is nothing to divide.
> My kin don't need to fuss and moan—
> "Moss does not cling to a rolling stone."
>
> My body? Ah, if I could choose,
> I would do ashes it reduce,
> And let the merry breezes blow
> My dust to where some flowers grow.
>
> Perhaps some fading flower then
> Would come to life and bloom again.
> This is my last and final will.
> Good luck to all of you.
>
> Joe Hill

But legends simplify; they persist only because certain questions are forgotten or overlooked. "The question of Joe Hill's guilt or innocence," concludes Gibbs M. Smith, "is no more certain today than it was in 1915. After reviewing all available records, however, there is considerable reason to believe that Hill was denied justice in the courts of Utah, and that there was still reasonable doubt as to his guilt after the district court and the supreme court had consigned him to the firing squad."[2] He may have been a double murderer, but most observers agree that he was convicted on inadequate circumstantial evidence. A clear motive was never established; the "why" remains unclear; the problem is reduced to what one makes of the man himself. Taciturn, solitary, was Joe Hill the noble soul that the Wobblies have made him? Or was he the killer that the courts of Utah sent to the firing squad? Double murderer or martyr, that is the issue.

In retrospect, it is not difficult to explain Wallace Stegner's interest in this controversial figure. Joe Hill was a Scandinavian, an immigrant from Sweden; he was a songster with a cause; he made his mark in the West; he was executed in Salt Lake City. In the first of two essays about Joe Hill which appeared before the publication of *The Preacher and the Slave* (1950), Stegner describes the famous Wobbly in terms that apply equally well to Bo Mason: he was "a certain type of Western badman, with a pleasant manner, an immaculate exterior, and a lot of cool nerve."[3] To be sure, there are important differences between the two men—for example, Joe was a loner who avoided women, liquor, and tobacco—but the similarities are much more striking. They were both dreamers; both had a knack for lyrics; both (according to Stegner) were prone to violence; both operated outside of the law; both struggled against things as they are; both died frustrated in the city of the Saints.

In the second and longer of his essays, published in the *New Republic* in 1948, Stegner addresses himself both to the Industrial Workers of the World and to their martyr. Marxist and militant, advocates of class warfare and the abolition of the wage system, the Wobblies were bent on revolution. In the light of Stegner's previous pronouncements on radical movements, his hostility comes as no surprise. Never sympathetic to labor agitation—an attitude he shared with Bernard DeVoto—he condemns the Wobblies as "a direct-action movement, believing in sabotage and violence."[4] The context established, he turns to Joe Hill: "What is actually known of him, what can be found out? Who was he, what was he, and how accurate is his legend?"[5] The questions were rhetorical, for Stegner had done plenty of homework.

Stegner's analysis is grounded on interviews and extensive correspondence with old Wobblies, several of whom knew Joe Hill, and on careful study of the records of the trial.[6] Conclusions follow in rapid order: "As for Joe Hill, I think he was probably guilty of the crime the state of Utah executed him for, though I think the state of Utah hardly proved his guilt beyond a reasonable doubt." He argues that the state's failure to establish a motive is not "a sure sign that no motive existed." Rejecting Joe Hill's story that he was protecting a woman, he goes on to relate that "every old-timer I have found who knew Joe Hill admits that he was a stick-up man." Violent crook that he was, however, the Wobbly troubadour was easy "to blow up to martyrdom because he had the poet's knack of self-dramatization." Especially in his "Last Will," and in the many telegrams that he composed during the final days of his life, Joe Hill laid the foundation of his own fame and martyrdom. "These are the words and acts of a great natural showman, the infallible raw materials of legend, and they are in themselves almost sufficient explanation of how an obscure dock worker and sailor, a nameless stiff, a crude poet and mushy writer of sentimental songs could also be the François Villon of American labor."

In the midst of this damning assessment of Joe Hill, we come upon a most startling assertion: "It doesn't really matter what he was."[7] In view of Stegner's questions about the man, and more especially in view of his answers, the statement appears to be a contradiction. Somewhat in spite of himself, however, Stegner the essayist elects to emphasize the important fact of a persistent legend rather than the complicated personality of the man behind it. This much notwithstanding, the reader cannot fail to recognize that what Joe Hill did and why are the issues that caught the novelist's imagination. He confronts those issues, the "what" and "why" of the Wobbly martyr, in *The Preacher and the Slave*.

The obstacles to success in Stegner's seventh novel were enormous.

That he was sensitive to the difficulty of the task is clear enough in the foreword to *The Preacher and the Slave*, for Stegner insists that his novel "is not history, though it deals here and there with historical episodes and sometimes incorporates historical documents; and it is not biography, though it deals with a life. It is fiction, with fiction's prerogatives and none of history's limiting obligations. I hope and believe it is after a kind of truth, but a different kind from that which historians follow." Glancing at the "ambiguous personality" of his protagonist, Stegner concludes that "Joe Hill as he appears here—let me repeat it—is an act of the imagination."[8]

There can be no doubt that Stegner was wise to disclaim any pretense to historical or biographical accuracy. The facts about Joe Hill are too scarce, and the accounts of his activities too contradictory, to permit a definitive analysis of his personality. It follows—as Stegner appears to acknowledge—that any sharp portrait of the martyr (or murderer) will amount to a fictional extrapolation based on a careful, even partisan, sifting of the evidence. Stegner's essays about Joe Hill reveal that he came to the novel with clear ideas and settled opinions about his subject. As some of his earlier works indicate, however, strong prepossessions sometimes lead Stegner into thematic overemphasis, simplification, and jarring authorial intrusions. His principal problem in the novel, therefore, was to apply imagination to a strong and controversial interpretation of Joe Hill without appearing to intrude upon the narrative and without allowing the weight of his prepossessions to flatten character into caricature. In short, to succeed in *The Preacher and the Slave*, Stegner had to overcome his own greatest artistic weaknesses.

In almost all respects he was successful. Joe Hill, as Stegner represents him, is the violent, at times sentimental, self-dramatizing personality we meet in the essays. According to Stegner, he carries a gun; he is a thief; and his thoughts and actions, most of them the creations of Stegner's interpretive imagination, are permeated with violence. "I want to die a martyr" (p. 323), he tells the Pardon Board, and another crucial element in Stegner's interpretation of the man takes fictional confirmation. But, if imagination constructs an irascible felon and a self-generated martyr, it also envisions a talented, intelligent, sometimes gentle man whose human potential is blocked by vague fears and by a crippling sense of personal inadequacy. Joe Hill, we feel, is basically a good man whose background and circumstances combine to bring out what is weakest in his nature.

Moreover, Stegner's potent descriptions of unemployed workmen struggling for survival in a San Pedro slum, or of grossly underpaid migrant workers living in squalor outside of Sacramento, go far to account for Joe's hatred of "the system." True, the Wobblies emerge as an organization that "really liked a fight better than it liked planning, negotiations, politicking" (p. ix). True again, Joe's capacity for self-deception and his inclination to violence are given much greater emphasis than his more positive qualities. But even those who disagree with Stegner's interpretation of the man and the movement will concede that his fictional reconstruction is a plausible, extremely well written, compelling "act of the imagination." Since the truth of the case is beyond recovery, no fictional treatment of the subject can do more.

The key to the success of *The Preacher and the Slave* resides in Stegner's skillful handling of four distinct points of view. The novel is famed in two brief sections narrated by an eloquent, occasionally ironic Wobbly. Looking back on the period of Joe Hill's execution, the narrator, a nostalgic believer, reflects, "We were rich in martyrs then" (p. 1). Distilled and softened by time, vague as a cloud, his Joe Hill is myth pure and simple. The omniscient narrator is heard second. His principal function is to set scenes, to introduce characters, and to relate the larger human movements (strikes, riots, public reactions) surrounding Joe's life. This voice is at once absolutely necessary to the novel and potentially its greatest weakness: necessary because it provides "objective" descriptions of Stegner's acts of imagination; potentially a weakness because Stegner might have violated the illusion of neutrality essential to this voice by using it as a mouthpiece for his own interpretation of Joe Hill. Generally, the omniscient narrator is detached; he describes from the "outside." Occasionally he intrudes. Joe Hill, he tells us, "a man who never led with his tongue; a counter-puncher strictly. . . . A singleton, a loner, a man with a hot temper and no really close friends. But a rebel from his skin inwards, with an absolute faith in the One Big Union and nerve enough for five. . . . What called him, speaking a language he understood perfectly, was trouble. Where trouble brewed, he appeared" (p. 107). Such moments, when Stegner speaks too directly and when the reader feels the pressure of judgments not adequately accounted for by his experience of the narrative, are relatively few.

If the omniscient narrator provides fictional resolution to the "what" questions of a martyr's life, then those portions of the novel which present Joe Hill's point of view address themselves to the "why." From beginning to end, Stegner's treatment of his protagonist's thoughts, motives, and fantasies is impressive because it records a consistent, organic, and therefore plausible development. At the outset Joe is a quiet, lonely man whose anger has not yet found an outlet or a specific object. Later, thanks to his songs, he is welcomed into the union, which provides both. But his involvement in union agitation is disillusioning; he discovers that "every strike and brawl and revolution and mass meeting ended the same way, in a choice between being a willing sacrifice for no real purpose, and running like a scared animal when the law moved in" (p. 152).

More angry and violent than ever, but also more alone and penniless, Joe arrives in Salt Lake City "without a clear destination or a clear purpose except the restless and never-satisfied purpose of striking a blow, keeping a promise, exacting a partial vengeance" (p. 193). Blind lust for revenge and the need for money are the motives which make him vulnerable to Otto Applequist's suggestion that they rob a local merchant. In thus resolving the "why" question, the novel provides fictional justification for the clear implication that Joe Hill was a double murderer. The concluding chapters trace the sequence of rationalizations and seemingly willful self-deceptions which persuade the killer that he is actually cut out for martyrdom.

Finally, there is Gustave Lund, a benevolent Lutheran minister who runs the Scandinavian Seamen's Mission in San Pedro.[9] Lund's role in the novel is manifold. A pacifist, a skeptic resigned to things as they are but ever hopeful of gradual change, at the thematic level Lund represents the Christian alternative to Joe's militancy. At another level, and to the degree that his observations duplicate those to be found in the novelist's essays about Joe Hill, he seems to function as Stegner's alter ego. "The Wobbly movement," he muses, "what made it attractive to men like Joe Hillstrom, was that it was no program at all. It was as reflexive as a poke in the nose, and about as constructive" (p. 187). Later, he raises strong objections to "the story Joe told about the woman: anyone who knew Joe Hillstrom would instantly doubt it" (p. 255). Such speculations would strike us as authorial intrusions were it not for the fact that they are perfectly natural in a man of Lund's background and character. Moreover, although Lund raises intelligent questions about Joe, he is much less ready with answers than Stegner the essayist. Lund is completely undecided; indeed, he is the only nonpartisan observer in the novel. Patiently, with all the objectivity he can muster, Lund searches for the truth about Joe Hill. His questions go unanswered. At the execution we find him still puzzled over his enigmatic friend. "As the white-haired doctor bent forward with his stethoscope to his ears to examine the heart of Joe Hill, workman and singer and rebel, hero now in a hundred IWW halls, either a martyr to law's blindness or a double murderer, Lund examined that heart in another way, and could not find the answer he searched for" (p. 401).

At the conclusion of *The Preacher and the Slave* Lund moralizes about the Wobblies who roar like "an angered animal" outside the prison walls. "For them, at least, there were no complications, no querying of the demands of vengeance, and justice, and love" (p. 402). In the absence of clear answers to the "what" and "why" of Joe Hill, the preacher refuses to take a final position. The reader, it appears, is being invited to join Lund in his rejection of partisanship and in his resignation to ambiguity. In short, the preacher's moral seems to bear the stamp of Stegner's approval. Paradoxically, however, while Lund's ultimate uncertainty is justified, the reader's is not. As we have indicated, the narrative of *The Preacher and the Slave* bears the crystal clear implication that Joe Hill assisted Otto Applequist in the robbery and homicide for which he was tried, convicted, and executed. Lund has no access to this information; therefore his uncertainty is warranted and just. For the reader, however, there is neither uncertainty nor ambiguity. Joe Hill, according to the interpretation presented in Wallace Stegner's novel, is guilty as charged.

Can we account for this curious inconsistency? Is there any way to square Lund's seemingly definitive moral observations with the contradictory evidence provided by the preceding narrative? Probably not. Apparently Stegner nodded. On the other hand, it may be that the lapse is not without its special significance. Perhaps it brings us back to a point that we made at the beginning of this chapter: that in our analysis of human motivation we must settle for uncertainties. Or, perhaps the inconsistency is a reminder that the assignment of guilt, even when it is established beyond a reasonable legal doubt, is a pragmatic judgment made by men, of other men. It does nothing to explain or alter the mysterious human capacity for evil. Perhaps, too, it is Wallace Stegner's inadvertent admission that he was not as sure about Joe Hill as he thought he was.

II CHANGE AND CONTINUITY

The bibliography of Stegner's publications at the back of this volume is a heterogeneous document, but at least one pattern immediately strikes the eye. After the publication of *The Preacher and the Slave* in 1950, the Stegner record is bare of novels for well over a decade. The reasons for this lacuna are not difficult to uncover. An unusual hybrid of history and literature, *The Preacher and the Slave* met with a mixed critical reception. Predictably, the radical press flayed it for daring to debunk one of labor's holy martyrs. The few more moderate publications that noticed the novel generally praised it; but, for the most part, Joe Hill's fictionalized biography was resolutely ignored by the critics. Silence, we are told, is more painful than criticism. Not surprisingly, sales were poor. As a writer used to commercial and critical acclaim, Stegner found the silence and slim sales extremely discouraging. His discouragement ran deeper for the fact that he considered *The Preacher and the Slave* is second attempt at a full-length novel, the only major work on the shelf beside *The Big Rock Candy Mountain*. As the result, Stegner devoted the next decade to other varieties of literary endeavor. He nurtured the Stanford Writing Program, turned out some first-rate journalism, published his Japanese literary lectures, the Powell biography, and a dozen short stories. But between 1950 and 1961 he avoided the critical gauntlet that he was bound to run if he brought another novel before the reading public.

The 1961 publication of *A Shooting Star* marks Stegner's return to the major novel; happily, it was also a return to commercial triumph and to a qualified but tolerable critical success. As a Literary Guild selection,

A Shooting Star quickly reached sales of more than one hundred and fifty thousand volumes—figures which doubtless did much to salve the bruises suffered with the poor reception of *The Preacher and the Slave*. It was followed by *All the Little Live Things*, which appeared in 1967, and the Pulitzer prize winning *Angle of Repose* four years later. No doubt additional novels will follow. For the purposes of critical argument, however, we are forced to ignore the fact that the Stegner canon is still growing. In this final chapter we will proceed as though *A Shooting Star* and its two successors were Stegner's final works of fiction.

Chronologically, these three works are separated from Stegner's previous novels by a chasm of eleven years; in the areas of subject, setting, and narrative voice, they represent an equally significant departure. Apparently pleased with the technical success of "Field Guide to the Western Birds," Stegner continued to make good use of first person narration. All three of his latest novels deal to a greater or lesser extent with life in California, Stegner's ultimate home—with its remarkable landscape, its indigenous character types, and unique forms of social organization. On the other hand, all of the volumes refer to values and life-styles characteristic of other parts of this country, occasionally to evoke an ideal, more often to establish a measure for cultural comparison. In the same vein, each of the novels is firmly rooted in the contemporary world; yet in two of the books vivid recreations of the American past functions as background to, and as a yardstick for, present-day life. This balancing of past and present is not a new feature in Stegner's writing. Rather, it is the clearest possible evidence that he has persisted in his idealization of "the middle ground." Because these novels represent regional and technical variations on familiar themes, they are as important a series of stops along the trail to "the middle ground" as *The Big Rock Candy Mountain* and *The Preacher and the Slave*. Indeed, the final member of this trio, *Angle of Repose*, marks its creator's arrival at the very center of that elusive territory.

III   *A SHOOTING STAR*

A Shooting Star has roots in both nineteenth-century New England and contemporary California. It is when these roots are most intricately intertwined that the book is at its best. Stegner found the material for his eighth novel in a most uncharacteristic margin of California—on the Gardner Hammond estate, an exquisite reproduction of a New England mansion, situated in Montecito, just outside of Santa Barbara. The Stegners were intermittent guests in Montecito from the fall of 1944 to the spring of 1945, the peripatetic academic year which preceded their permanent settlement at Stanford. From this privileged vantage, Stegner had ample opportunity to observe the behavior of California's "idle" rich; and, thanks to Mrs. Hammond, he also had access to more unusual and less contemporary data—the history of this curiously anachronistic estate, its present inhabitants, and their forebears.

The rather complex action of A Shooting Star brings both aspects of Stegner's Montecito experience to fictionalized fruition. Personal acquaintance with the dissatisfied socialites of Santa Barbara (and, later, with their unhappy equivalents in Palo Alto) results in the portraits of Sabrina Castro, her society physician husband, and other denizens of their glamorous but empty world. On the other hand, Stegner's more or less historical acquaintance with Mrs. Hammond and her departed forebears gives rise to Sabrina's mother, Deborah Hutchens, and to other twisted branches of her family tree. As we have indicated, the interaction between the several Hutchens generations, living and dead, is the key to what is successful in the novel.

Sabrina Castro, the central character in A Shooting Star, is an attractive, wealthy young California aristocrat. To any unbiased observer, she appears to enjoy the best of several different worlds. The only female descendant of an old and at least financially distinguished New England family, the Wolcotts, she is the present possessor more dollars than she knows what to do with and heiress to many millions more. She is also the wife of one of the last of the "Californios," the original, native-born Californians of Spanish-speaking descent. Finally, Sabrina is a beauty, and a beauty of an especially memorable kind. Long, lean, fine-boned, and graced with extraordinarily mobile and expressive features, she is instinctively feminine, irresistible, a charmer. But despite, or perhaps because of, her advantages, Sabrina is deeply, even desperately unhappy. Sterile, and therefore deprived of the loving labors of child rearing, she sees herself as no more than an ornament to her husband Burke's fancy Pasadena medical practice. In Sabrina's eyes, Burke is not a healer. Rather, somewhat unjustly, she regards him as chief handholder and pill-dispenser to a flock of wealthy female hypochondriacs. Sabrina subjects her New England ancestors to similarly harsh and reductive scrutiny. From her point of view they appear to have been the stunted progeny of American puritanism; among other things, they were acquisitive, self-righteous, uncharitable, and self-absorbed.

Despite an expensive education and a fast-paced, sophisticated youth, Sabrina has achieved neither self-knowledge nor a clear sense of what she wants from life. Her story is dominated by two images: the mirror and the mask—images which are inversely related. The mirror implies an obsession with self, the mask, real uncertainty as to what that self may be. When she is (all too frequently) alone, Sabrina spends an inordinate amount of time looking at her own image in some reflective surface: mirror, car window, picture window, silver teapot. Even Burke's proposal, as she remembers it, is framed within the borders of an old pier glass. On the other hand, every time we find Sabrina in company, we catch her playing a part: virgin or vamp, sin-struck adultress or existential heroine, anybody but the complex mixture of qualities that she really is. In short, fifteen years past adolescence, this discontented beauty is finally beginning to experience what psychologist Erik Erikson has called the "identity crisis."

The first half of *A Shooting Star* is the record of Sabrina's moral disintegration. In Stegner's suspenseful opening chapter, we gradually discover that Sabrina has jeopardized her enviable personal advantages by indulging in a sordid and unsatisfying affair.[10] Even after she recognizes the limitations of her lover, she resists reconciliation with Burke and continues to confront him with new and increasingly painful humiliations. It all culminates in a classically "lost" weekend which she spends slumming among the bars and barflies of Carson City, Nevada. Having hit bottom, Sabrina recognizes her severely limited options: she can go up or out. The rest of the novel chronicles her slow return to psychological stability and personal integrity.

After the collapse of her marriage, Sabrina has no recourse but to take refuge on her mother's luxurious old estate, her childhood home. Living there, she naturally encounters some of the figures influential in her early years: mother, brother, best friend, favorite family retainer. Each of these individuals has, in his own way, confronted the problem of personal identity. Each illustrates a different response to the questions that Sabrina has been asking herself: what is personal identity? and what does one do with one's life? As soon as Sabrina stops looking at herself long enough to observe those around her, she discovers that some of her childhood fellows have created a satisfying life for themselves, and that others have not. If the difference between the two groups is clear, so is the bearing of the situation on Sabrina's own future. She can be happy and useful only if she is willing to abjure both the sybaritic self-indulgence and unrealistic expectations that Stegner calls "ecstacy,"[1] and settle instead for the limited gratifications of "a halfway decent life" (p. 422).

The wasted lives of her departed Wolcott relations provide Sabrina with another important set of moral *exempla*. The Wolcotts have traditionally resolved the identity crisis in the simplest and least satisfactory manner: by ignoring it. In some respects, it was unfortunate for his descendants that great-grandfather Cornelius was a natural born money-maker. Thanks to his prodigious financial exploits, by the end of the nineteenth century the Wolcotts had amassed a considerable fortune. However, none of them had learned how to deal with the opportunities and responsibilities of affluence. The family failed to develop a tradition of community service; neither philanthropists nor artists nor promoters of culture, they found no socially or personally productive outlet for their money. In the lives of Cornelius' children and only grandchild, Deborah Hutchens, wealth operated as a shield against the larger world and, paradoxically, as an obstacle to personal growth.

Nevertheless, at the beginning of the novel Sabrina's mother is proudly aware of her background: she is a Wolcott of Beacon Street. Family history is Mrs. Hutchens' consuming passion. Her Hillsborough home is a perfect replica of the old Wolcott retreat at Nahant; her conversation is a self-conscious pastiche of reminiscenses and hoary anecdotes. Sabrina feels that her psychological development was hopelessly perverted by growing up in this atmosphere of oppressive reverence for the past; her Wolcott aunts and uncles siphoned off the uncritical and unqualified affection that she herself deserved as Deborah Hutchens' only daughter. Absorbed by memories of rejection, Sabrina has never examined her mother's life carefully enough to resolve the obvious contradiction: if the old lady loved and identified with her Wolcott relatives, why did she leave them?

Newly sensitized by her personal difficulties, and living at home again, this time as an adult, Sabrina begins to unravel the mystery. Her mother's "ancestor worship" is not the single-minded enterprise that it had seemed. Deborah Hutchens loved her husband Howard, in spite of, or perhaps because of, the "vulgar" vitality that offended the rest of the family. When he committed some infraction of their marriage bond, she hewed to the Wolcott line and left him, but with deep and deeply buried feelings of resentment. The separation accomplished, she retreated to the West Coast, ostensibly to avoid scandal, actually to avoid further confrontation with dubious family mores. Having allied herself irrevocably with their values, she was also able to see those values for what they were: small-minded, self-righteous, and pharisaical. Finally enlightened, Deborah was also helpless to change. Despite her fabulous fortune, the opening of *A Shooting Star* finds her a lonely and defeated old woman. Her daughter sees her as a psychological adversary; to her son, she is the chief obstacle to the profitable operation of the Wolcott estate. In the absence of her children's forebearance, Deborah takes consolation in the prepaid affection of her secretary-companion, Helen Kretchmer.

It would be unfair to describe Oliver Hutchens, Deborah's son, as a malicious man; he is simply morally incomplete. Sabrina rightly calls him a "somatotonic" (p. 139)—a purely physical human type. Despite a total lack of planning, Oliver's life has been as orderly as Sabrina's has been chaotic. He succeeds at each stage in his development because his objectives are clear and simple and unchanging: to compete and win, to accumulate material goods and enjoy them, to keep himself moving for the sheer pleasure of watching his muscles work. His current economic campaign against his own mother is a case in point. In his peculiar way, Oliver loves Deborah Hutchens and wants nothing but the best for her; unfortunately, he has his own terribly limited definition of "the best." To be brief, Oliver is prepared to have his mother declared incompetent in order to gain control of the estate and make her, as he puts it, "a hell of a lot richer" (p. 336). Fortunately for Mrs. Hutchens, an unexpected ally enters her life and opposes Oliver. Leonard MacDonald, the husband of

Sabrina's best friend, suggests a entirely novel plan for the disposition of the Hutchens property: why not set aside some of the acreage as a public park?

The example of the MacDonalds represents an instructive contrast to traditional Hutchens values. Strong, competent, tough-minded, Leonard has worked his way up from the slums to an instructorship in English at the local high school. With three small children to support, he is forced to live in Greenwood Acres, the quintessential mass-produced American tract; but, like Joe Allston, he makes the best of "middle-class civilization." Leonard's dedication to cooperative community betterment exemplifies the only hopeful alternative to suburban individualism. If any Americans ever learn to sacrifice present profit for the benefit of posterity, it will undoubtedly be the inhabitants of Greenwood Acres. In Leonard's words, "we're already living in the overcrowded future and we know how it feels" (p. 102).

The MacDonalds have planned their own future with unusual foresight and wisdom. Leonard enjoys the rewards of excellence in his professional career; nevertheless, he does not expect individual achievement to satisfy all of his inner needs. Two other types of activity—activities notably missing in Sabrina's life—are equally important. First, there is participation in the ancient, repetitive, mysteriously fulfilling cycle of procreation and child rearing. Second, there is participation in the slow but steady course of community improvement. As Leonard tells Sabrina, "It's funny how many different kinds of things you can make a halfway decent life out of if you believe in them and work at them. Likewise it's funny how no combination really turns out to be exactly the Kingdom of Heaven" (p. 422). This measured compromise between optimism and pessimism, a familiar element in Stegner's work, is at the core of the MacDonald philosophy.

In the final chapters of A *Shooting Star*, with Leonard as her guide, Sabrina begins the transition from hollow "ecstacy" to "a halfway decent life." First, she acknowledges that she is as much to blame as Burke for the disintegration of their marriage. Recognizing the extent of her own conjugal errors, she considers returning to Pasadena and resuming the role of the society physician's wife. But this rather improbable scheme dissolves when she discovers that she is pregnant with an illegitimate child. Dismayed, but unwilling to admit defeat, Sabrina has at least learned that cooperation and compromise with others are essential to personal happiness. Accordingly, as the second stage in her program for self-improvement, she focuses her attention on her mother and on her own unborn offspring.

Helen Kretchmer, Sabrina realizes, can never provide the filial affection and support that her mother so clearly requires. Nor can Helen protect Mrs. Hutchens from Oliver's insensitive designs. Sabrina resolves to supplant Helen, to become the daughter that her mother desires, and to thwart her brother whenever possible. At the same time, she will try to raise her fatherless child according to the somewhat smug MacDonald formula for family happiness: "love but not too much love, and not the wrong kind" (p. 422). It is a challenging objective, but not an unrealistic one, especially if pursued on a steady, day-to-day basis. Together, grandmother, mother and child may be able to break the twin chains of guilt and resentment that have shackled the Wolcotts and replace them with ties of understanding and love. Then, reaching outward from a secure base in familial affection, they will readily develop the sense of civic responsibility that their inherited fortune demands. In Stegner's view—a view explicit in the MacDonald philosophy, and implicit in Sabrina's conversion—family support and cooperation are the essential first steps toward participation in the larger human community.

A *Shooting Star* closes with Mrs. Hutchens' moving memory of childhood disappointment—what we may call the parable of the pink balloon. Walking one day in the Boboli Gardens, six-year-old Deborah accidentally loses her grip on the most beautiful balloon in the city of Florence. Her mother sternly refuses to replace it. "If there is one day in my whole life I would not . . . want to live over! If there is . . . one day that sums up everything!" (p. 430) she exclaims in a voice resonant with seven decades of imperfect resignation. A trivial loss by all accounts, but with that balloon went the ecstacy in Deborah Hutchens' life. Sabrina listens, understands, recognizes what she shares with her mother and, through that sense of common loss, finds consolation and resolve. Thus the novel's final affirmation arises from the discovery of historical continuities: Sabrina gains a future by uncovering a usable past.

Most readers will agree that the contemporary characters in *A Shooting Star*—most notably Leonard and Oliver—come a little too close to allegory for comfort. They strike us as "thesis" characters—as embodied ideas that walk into Sabrina's experience at appropriate intervals. The novel, as a result, seems too direct and insistent in making its point. A rather contrived plot is also partly to blame. As Stegner put in an interview with us, "there's a soap opera problem in *A Shooting Star*." Finally, the novel is marred by awkward inconsistencies in narrative point of view. At various junctures each of the contemporary characters assumes the mantle of omniscience just long enough to summarize the moral and thematic significance of one of his fellows. Leonard explains Sabrina, Sabrina explains Oliver, and so on.

It is also worth noting that this sort of thematic overstatement never occurs when Stegner is dealing with the ancestors of his characters. Our information about the Wolcotts is always secondhand; it is filtered through Deborah Hutchens' misguided idealization of the past, her daughter's neurotic contempt for it, or Leonard MacDonald's more moderate appraisal of things past. Glimpsed through several imperfect lenses, the background to the action possesses the essential complexity and ambiguity which the foreground lacks. At the end, the reader is left with the final responsibility; he must reach his own conclusions about the Wolcotts.

Notes

1. We rely here on Gibbs M. Smith's compendious *Joe Hill* (Salt Lake City, 1969).

2. Smith, p. 113.

3. "I Dreamed I Saw Joe Hill Last Night," *Pacific Spectator* 1 (Spring, 1947), 186.

4. "Joe Hill: The Wobblies' Troubadour," *New Republic* 118 (January 5, 1948), 20. Stegner's remarks on Joe Hill and the International Workers of the World did not go unanswered. See *New Republic* 118 (February 9, 1948), 38–39. *Time* reported (51 [April 19, 1948], 26) that IWW sympathizers picketed the *New Republic* office in protest over Stegner's "slur on their hero." Many historians of American labor would insist that the Wobblies were no more violent than the Pinkerton thugs and vigilantes who opposed them, and that Wobbly tactics were justified given the failure of political reform and the impoverished impotence of working men during the first decades of this century.

5. "Joe Hill: The Wobblies' Troubadour," p. 20.

6. Stegner reveals the extent of his research in a letter to the *New Republic* 118 (February 9, 1948), 38:

> I have talked and corresponded with several dozen old-time Wobblies who were active in Joe Hill's time. Seven of them knew him personally; three of them knew him well. . . . I have photostatic copies of the only remaining volume of the trial transcript, plus complete files of the Deseret *News* and the Salt Lake *Tribune* from the time of Hill's arrest until his execution. I have the records of the Utah State Penitentiary, the statements of the Supreme Court and the Utah Pardon Board, the coverage of the case in the New York *Times* and various news magazines. I have checked the police records of San Pedro and Los Angeles and files of the Los Angeles papers, and I have consulted with the sheriff who executed Hill, jailers and law-enforcement officers who knew him, a member of his Defense Committee, the Swedish vice-consul who investigated the case for the Swedish Minister, the AP reporter who covered the case and witnessed the execution, the son of the man Joe Hill was supposed to have killed.

> For excerpts from Stegner's correspondence concerning Joe Hill, see the text and notes in Smith, *Joe Hill.*

7. "Joe Hill: The Wobblies' Troubadour," p. 24.

8. *The Preacher and the Slave* (Boston, 1950), p. ix–x. Hereafter the pagination of quotations from this volume is indicated in the text. The novel was reissued as *Joe Hill* by Doubleday in 1969. Readers may wish to consult Stegner's comments on *The Preacher and the Slave* in *The Sound of Mountain Water*, pp. 206–7.

9. Gibbs M. Smith observes in *Joe Hill* (201): "Taking his cue from a letter Hill wrote to an unidentified preacher known only as Gus, Stegner created Gustave Lund, friend and confidant of Joe Hill."

10. *A Shooting Star* (New York, 1961), p. 15. Hereafter the pagination of quotations from this volume is indicated in the text.

Henry Adams, Wallace Stegner, and the Search for a Sense of Place in the West

Jamie Robertson*

> The Rough Rock Demonstration School strives to fit its students for life in a modern world while, at the same time, keeping the best of Navajo tradition and culture.
>
> *Grandfather Stories of the Navajo*
> (Phoenix: Navajo Curriculum Center Press)

This quotation is taken from a preface to a collection of traditional stories of the Navajo whose purpose is to keep in memory the tradition that conveys a people's identity. It presents a central problem of education in the modern world: Can we preserve the best of our cultural traditions and still fit ourselves for life in the modern world? Henry Adams defined the problem in *The Education,* and Wallace Stegner continues Adams' inquiry in *Wolf Willow.*[1] Adams and Stegner view education as the human process of resolving the problem. Both authors understand education in the broadest metaphorical sense as an active, imaginative process of establishing a human connection to the landscape and to the life that is lived in it. For Adams and Stegner, education is the activity of making a coherent symbolic statement about our cultural traditions and how those traditions explain our relationship to, or sense of, place.

In the early years of the 20th century, when Henry Adams began to write his *Education,* there was a fantastic increase in the quantity of knowledge that it was a student's duty to learn. While the educational system did an efficient job of requiring students to assimilate these facts, it had made little effort to teach them how to make sense of those facts in the light of their cultural heritage. Henry Adams found himself a victim of this failure of education. In *The Education* he creates the embodiment of such a failure in the persona of Henry Adams, a personality of fragmented sensibility disconnected from the World and from the traditions of the past by the forces of the 20th century.

The technological forces of progress cut Adams off from the traditions of the past, a separation that, from his viewpoint, fragmented the world:

*Reprinted from *The Westering Experience in American Literature,* ed. Merrill Lewis and L. L. Lee (Western Washington State University, 1977), 135–43.

No such accident had ever happened before in human experience. For him, alone, the old universe was thrown into the ash-heap and a new one created. He and his eighteenth-century, troglodytic Boston were suddenly cut apart—separated forever—in act if not in sentiment, by the opening of the Boston and Albany Railroad; the appearance of the first Cunard steamers in the bay; and the telegraphic messages which carried from Baltimore to Washington the news that Henry Clay and James K. Polk were nominated for the Presidency. This was in May, 1844; he was six years old; his new world was ready for use, and only fragments of the old met his eyes (p. 5).

Education is for Adams the process of putting the pieces back together. Adams' effort in *The Education* is to offer a coherent symbolic representation of the meaning of the technological forces of the 20th century, but the symbol that he creates is the dynamo, paradoxically one not of order but of chaos and fragmentation. Indeed, in Adams' view, the forces of progress seem to have ended the possibility of seeing the world, humankind and nature, whole again. Adams' concern is that the artistic or life process of bringing order to the chaos that confronts humanity is becoming an impossibility in the modern world. The force of the faith of the past that created Chartres Cathedral, he argues, has been lost in the 20th century, and the force of the power of coal has become the sole human reality. And this force is technological rather than cultural. Its force has shaped human beings to its image rather than the other way around.

The 18th-century American dreamed that technology would provide access to the natural world where all might live as artificers who could transform the world into a realized ideal, into a new Garden of Eden that would be both democratic and popular. But that dream became impossible for Adams to maintain. The farms that St. John de Crèvecoeur had envisioned lining the banks of the Ohio were now obscured by coal smoke, the emblem of the industrial revolution. For Adams and his contemporaries there remained only one landscape where the 18th-century dream of Crèvecoeur could be realized. The West offered at least the potentiality for a successful education, for a temporary escape from the power of technology to fragment and destroy humankind's poetic sensibility. Perhaps here in an unspoiled landscape, Adams mused, education might still be possible:

In the year 1871, the West was still fresh, and the Union Pacific was young. Beyond the Missouri River, one felt the atmosphere of Indians and buffaloes. One saw the last vestiges of an old education, worth studying if one would; but it was not that which Adams sought; rather, he came out to spy on the land of the future. The Survey occasionally borrowed troopers from the nearest station in case of happening on hostile Indians, but otherwise the topographers and geologists thought more about minerals than about Sioux. They held under their hammers a thousand miles of mineral country with all its riddles to solve, and its stores of possible wealth to mark. They felt the future in their hands (p. 309).

Topographers and geologists, Adams notes, went west not with the out-dated intention of creating cultural visions such as the Virgin, but with the dream of building more railroads and mining the landscape. One of these men of the future was Clarence King, a man who Adams thought had educated himself in a way to deal effectively with the forces of the 20th century:

> . . . King had moulded and directed his life logically, scientifically, as Adams thought life should be directed. He had given himself education all of a piece, yet broad (p. 312).

If anyone could exert any degree of control over his future, Clarence King could. For Adams, Clarence King was the embodiment of the myth of the perfect American, a man of Eastern talent and social grace and of Western will and energy. This was in 1871, and Adams was at his most optimistic point. Twenty years later he no longer held any illusions of King's success:

> Thus, in 1892, neither Hay, King, nor Adams knew whether they had at-tained success, or how to estimate it, or what to call it; and the American people seemed to have no clearer idea than they. Indeed, the American people had no idea at all; they were wandering in a wilderness much more sandy than the Hebrews had ever trodden about Sinai; they had neither serpents nor golden calves to worship. . . . The American mind . . . shunned, distrusted, disliked, the dangerous attraction of ideals, and stood alone in history for its ignorance of the past (p. 328).

The Anglo adventure in the West was soon over. The hope it had briefly provided for the fulfillment of the dream was lost. Not even King was able to unify the forces of technology which Adams saw gathered together at the Chicago exposition in 1893. That exposition asked the question, "Did the American People know where they were driving?" Adams' conclusion was that they did not, and neither did he. It was unquestionable that we were moving, but whether it was progress or change, directed movement or passive response to uncontrollable forces, was uncertain.

The power of modern America was a different kind from that em-bodied in art. As Adams argued, "All the steam in the world could not, like the Virgin, build Chartres." Adams' failure as he perceived it was that he could not resolve the dilemma of education. He could not bridge the gap between the 18th and 20th centuries, between tradition and technology, and his identity, like the world, remained fragmented:

> His identity, if one could call a bundle of disconnected memories an iden-tity, seemed to remain; but his life was once more broken into separate pieces; he was a spider and had to spin a new web in some place with a new attachment (p. 209).

But what to attach the web to? How to connect the pieces? Adams re-mained far less optimistic about such a possibility than the transcenden-talists of 19th-century America had been.

Wallace Stegner's *Wolf Willow: A History, a Story, and a Memory of the Last Plains Frontier* is a contemporary western-American version of Adams' *Education*. Stegner sees his education—at least the institutionalized part of it—as hopelessly inadequate to the needs of a person growing up in his boyhood home of Whitemud, Saskatchewan, and *Wolf Willow* is, at least in part, intended to redress that inadequacy.

> Far more than Henry Adams, I have felt myself entitled to ask whether my needs and my education were not ludicrously out of phase. Not because I was educated for the past instead of the future . . . but because I was educated for the wrong place. Education tried inadequately and hopelessly to make a European out of me (p. 24).

While Adams thought himself irrevocably separated from the traditions of the European past, Stegner laments the inadequacy of that same European tradition taught in a place rich in regional history. Education in this last plains frontier, Stegner writes, tied "us into Western civilization, if it taught us little about who we were, it taught us something of what we had been" (p. 291). The assumption made by Stegner as he grew up was the assumption handed to him by his teachers. He was told this land was an untouched wilderness, a place of no history or tradition out of which the activities of the people in the landscape grew. Stegner's world "had neither location nor time, geography nor history" (pp. 28–29). The people of Whitemud acted naively on the assumption that they were completely separate from the influence of the tradition of their home place; but *Wolf Willow* repudiates the belief that they were living in such a cultural vacuum.

Stegner argues that, whether people are aware of them or not, the historical traditions of a place affect their lives:

> . . . history is a pontoon bridge. Every man walks and works at its building end, and has come as far as he has over the pontoons laid by others he may never have heard of. The history of the Cypress Hills had almost as definite effects on me as did their geography and weather, though I never knew a scrap of that history until a quarter-century after I left the place. However it may have seemed to the people who founded it, Whitemud was not a beginning, not a new thing, but a stage in a long historical process (p. 29).

But what does education matter if the outcome of a people's actions is the same whether they know their history or not? The implicit argument of Stegner's *Wolf Willow* is that their actions might very well not have been the same had they known and understood the cultural traditions from which they came. Stegner's book is one attempt to provide a coherent statement about the cultural traditions of his home place. It is a symbolic attempt to connect himself and others, spider-like, to the traditions that grow from that place.

Once Henry Adams realized the inadequacy of the 18th-century

European tradition which had been his education, he sought a new beginning in the landscape of the West, an enterprise that he later understood was also doomed to failure. Writing half a century later, Stegner, with a very different idea of history, sought to reestablish connections between himself and a place. Like Adams, he was presented with fragments out of which to construct a new whole. In Stegner's childhood, the site of those fragments was the town dump, the only source of history and poetry Whitemud had. Stegner worked as an amateur archeologist to discover the meaning of his place in the town dump, but it was only years later, after he and his family had left Whitemud for good, that he was able to tie together the history and fiction that would recreate the union of self and landscape he knew as a child. *Wolf Willow*, the result of that at least partially successful activity, conveys in history and fiction the meaning of the Cypress Hills present interpreted by the light of its regional past. As such, it is a symbolic reenactment of a state of human connection to the world.

The book covers a sixty-year span from the first European intrusion of Lewis and Clark in 1805, to the Métis (French and Indian) settlements of the 1860's, to the survey of the 1870's that politically divided a unified geographical area, to the brief reign of the cowboy from 1882 to 1906–07, the end of the plains frontier. What is most interesting about *Wolf Willow*'s mixture of history, autobiography, and fiction is the philosophical statement it implies about the truth of a people's connection to a place. Stegner argues implicitly through such a mixture of fact and fiction that a sense of place is a poetic creation, both real and imaginary, that explains our relationship to a place and to its past. It is the task of the artist-historian to convey the memory, to teach the tradition. The Cypress Hills country of Stegner's boyhood as recreated in *Wolf Willow* is not a dead material fact of the world but a symbolic cultural expression. That is, it reveals an ordered expression of the dynamic interplay between nature and the human imagination, and so overcomes the alienation of humanity from the world that Adams perceived to be our technological inheritance.

The railroad was the symbol of Adams' alienation from the world. For Stegner, the imposition of the 49th parallel on a unified landscape is symbolic of the same sort of separation. This artificial line "split a country that was topographically and climatically one" (p. 84), and did not follow the natural line of the Cypress Hills divide that "had been established by tradition, topography, and a balance of tribal force" (p. 85). The Medicine Line was one of the most significant manifestations of the civilizing forces of the modern world acting to fragment the natural order of the Cypress Hills country and to separate the human world from it. Stegner writes that

> While I lived on it [49th parallel], I accepted it as I accepted Orion in the winter sky. I did not know that this line of iron posts was one outward evidence of the coming of history to the unhistoried plains, one of the strings by which dead men and the unguessed past directed our lives. In

actual fact, the boundary which Joseph Kinsey Howard has called artificial and ridiculous was more potent in the lives of people like us than
the natural divide of the Cypress Hills had ever been upon the tribes it
held apart. For the 49th parallel was an agreement, a rule, a limitation, a
fiction perhaps but a legal one, acknowledged by both sides; and the coming of law, even such limited law as this, was the beginning of civilization
in what had been a lawless wilderness. Civilization is built on a tripod of
geography, history, and law, and it is made up largely of limitations
(p. 85).

Wolf Willow is Stegner's means of transcending the limitations of civilization for it unifies the human and natural landscape that was divided by
the artificial boundary of the 49th parallel.

As a boy in Whitemud Stegner was able to realize Emerson's direc-
tive to establish an original relation to the universe. He feels

how the world still reduces me to a point and then measures itself from
me. Perhaps the meadowlark singing from a fence post—a meadowlark
whose dialect I recognize—feels the same way. All points on the cir-
cumference are equidistant from his; in him all radii begin; all diameters
run through him; if he moves, a new geometry creates itself around him
(p. 19)

Wolf Willow is a reenactment of this human connectedness to the earth
that Stegner knew as a boy. The Cypress Hills become for Stegner and the
reader the symbolic center of the world they had been before the divisions
and limitations of civilization. Stegner makes us aware of the natural cen-
trality of the Cypress Hills which are the watershed not only of the Atlantic and Pacific slopes of the continental divide, but the division of the
north and south slopes as well. Stegner's symbolic landscape is real in a
cultural sense, for it is the creation of the human imagination interacting
with the natural world. The Cypress Hills become once again a place
where "For a moment, reality is made equivalent with memory, and a
hunger is satisfied" (p. 19).

Though it is a poetic creation, *Wolf Willow*'s vision of reality is not a
solipsistic dream. When Stegner returns to his boyhood home, he relates
that he is afraid to visit his family's homestead for fear that all trace of
their contact with the land will have been erased. If his family's mark on
the land is gone, he fears, he will be convinced that his vision is only a
dream disconnected from reality. But the small shrub named Wolf
Willow allays that fear. Its smell, like the odor of *madeleine* and tea to
Proust, convinces him immediately of the reality of the vision. Stegner's
family's impact on the Saskatchewan landscape had been puny and little
evidence of their struggle on the Plains is left. His proof that they had
truly been there, and that *Wolf Willow* is history as well as fiction, is the
smell of this small shrub.

Stegner implies that that is all the proof of meaningful human activity that we should need. The chief argument of Stegner's poetic vision of

place is that the result of human impact on the land ought to be short-lived. Our transient imprint on the world should define our tragic and frail humanity. For Stegner as for Adams, the modern technological world keeps us from learning this lesson. The simple notion of wearing paths in the earth's surface, Stegner's metaphor for meaningful human activity, is banished forever in the modern world:

> Wearing any such path in the earth's rind is an intimate act, an act like love, and it is denied to the dweller in cities. He lacks the proper mana for it, he is out of touch with the earth of which he is made. . . . So we had an opportunity that few any longer can have: we printed an earth that seemed creation-new with the marks of our identity. And then the earth wiped them out again (p. 273).

Stegner's childhood experience was acted out in a landscape that "seemed creation-new" not because there had been no one before him, but because the impact of civilization had not ended the possibility of making tracks in the earth.

In the words of Ray Henry in *Wolf Willow*'s chapter-story "Carrion Spring," we engage in a heroic human activity when we attempt to make the country say "uncle," not by pouring concrete over it, but by wearing transient footpaths in it. In "Carrion Spring," Molly and Ray are heroic in this sense. After the most severe winter in Saskatchewan history they see the wreckage and death which the birth of spring reveals. The meaning of this experience is discovered along with the discovery of a Crocus growing amongst the carnage:

> "Crocus?" Ray said, bending. "Don't take long, once the snow goes."
> It lay in her palm, a thing lucky as a four-leaf clover, and as if it had had some effect in clearing her sight, Molly looked down the south-facing slope and saw it tinged with faintest green. She put the Crocus to her nose, but smelled only a mild freshness, an odor no more showy than that of grass. But maybe enough to cover the scent of carrion (p. 237).

This passage does not indicate Ray and Molly's escape from the reality of their experience, but brings us to the tragic realization of their puny human effort to wrest control of the landscape from nature. This is a fictional experience, but it is one that might well have occurred in this region after the winter of 1906–07, a winter that marked the death of the open range and the cowboy. Though fictional, it is as much a part of the symbolic historical tradition of southern Saskatchewan as the survey that separated Canada and the United States.

The symbolic statement of Stegner's book is important, but there is still something unsatisfactory in the education that *Wolf Willow* affords those who read it. *Wolf Willow* becomes, likes Henry Adams' *Education*, a statement about the failure of education. Stegner's book teaches us that the European experience in the Garden of the West contained the seeds of its own destruction, and the cultural vision expressed in *Wolf Willow* is one that few, if any of us, can experience in our own lives today:

> One who has lived the dream, the temporary fulfillment, and the disappointment has had the full course. He may lack a thousand things that the rest of the world takes for granted, and because his experience is belated he may feel like an anachronism all his life. But he will know one thing about what it means to be an American, because he has known the raw continent, and not as tourist but as denizen. Some of the beauty, the innocence, and the callousness must stick to him, and some of the regret. The vein of melancholy in the North American mind may be owing to many causes, but it is surely not weakened by the perception that the fulfillment of the American Dream means inevitably the death of the noble savagery and freedom of the wild. Anyone who has lived on a frontier knows the inescapable ambivalence of the old-fashioned American conscience, for he has first renewed himself in Eden and then set about converting it into the lamentable modern world. And that is true even if the Eden is, as mine was, almost unmitigated discomfort and deprivation (p. 282).

Like *The Education*, *Wolf Willow* conveys the triumph of the technological dream over the poetic vision of place even as it recreates that poetic vision of an earlier time. But Adams' *Education* and Stegner's *Wolf Willow* are not simply nostalgic remembrances of a lost golden world. Stegner's work makes us aware of the historical tradition of this American place. Too few of those who lived on the edge of the frontier had such an awareness, and too few of us even today have it. By connecting us to the cultural tradition of the Cypress Hills country Stegner does not solve the dilemma of education, but he illuminates the problem. The historical memory that *Wolf Willow* brings to the reader should provide what the town dump provided Stegner as a boy: "an aesthetic distance from which to know ourselves" (p. 35).

Note

1. Page references in the text are made to the following editions: Henry Adams, *The Education of Henry Adams* (Boston: Houghton Mifflin Company, Sentry Edition, 1961) and Wallace Stegner, *Wolf Willow* (New York: The Viking Press, 1966).

Within a Continuous Frame:
Stegner's Family Album in
The Big Rock Candy Mountain

William C. Baurecht*

I

In *The Big Rock Candy Mountain* (1943) Wallace Stegner wrote about a "genuine West," a West of the past but not of the distant past. The novel covers the first three decades of the twentieth century. It closes in 1932, eleven years before publication of *The Big Rock Candy Mountain*, which Stegner composed between 1937 and 1940.[1] Stegner encloses the frame of his fiction by writing accurately of history within a western milieu. The novel is an ambitious, sprawling survey of American folkways and a critique of the expansive promises of the American Dream. Consequently, it surpasses regional categorization, a fate of too many good novels about the West.

Bruce Mason's memories and images from youth and early adulthood are a composite of his evolution within the vast and dry western landscape, time (within the history of the modern West), and family. In this essay I shall examine the latter two influences. Bruce Mason is the protagonist who brings together all of the thematic elements and characters of Stegner's novel. A lifetime of mostly painful memories and experiences provide him with the knowledge of the meaning of his existence. His experiences are framed by the role of his family. The principal agent of psychic continuity for all of the Masons is, as well, the family; the family is, in fact, the die that forms and indelibly stamps the consciousness of each.

The Big Rock Candy Mountain culminates in Bruce Mason's discovery of his manhood. Bruce makes this discovery by realizing that his identity is fixed within the continuous frame of his family's past, which is in turn, molded by American history. The Masons' rootlessness is caused by Harry's obsession with the Big Rock Candy Mountain, and although they are atypical as a middle-class family, their experience is representative in many ways both of the American experience and the impact of the American Dream upon the family. In the novel's final two scenes (the focus of analysis in this essay), examining Bo Mason's "remains," the rem-

*This essay was written especially for this volume and appears here for the first time with the permission of the author.

nants of the man's squandered life, and attending the funeral, Bruce Mason becomes enlightened.

Consequently, section two of this essay examines the convoluted background of the Masons within the history of the modern West. Section three examines, in detail, the final two scenes in which Bruce becomes his own man.

II

Even though Harry "Bo" Mason's and Elsa Norgaard's brief family histories draw one back into the late nineteenth century, Stegner wrote about their family of four growing and changing within the modern West. The novel's action takes place between 1905, when Elsa flees her father's home for the plains of Hardinger, North Dakota, and 1932, when Bo commits suicide after his wife's death. Between 1914 and 1920 the Mason family lived on the last open North American frontier. Drawn to the prairie by the soaring price of wheat, they homesteaded a section near the Montana-Saskatchewan border during late spring and summer, and lived the rest of the year in the frontier town of Whitemud, Saskatchewan. After their pioneering labors, typical of thousands of families which hopefully farmed the arid plains, the family began its hegira outside the law and respectability and without the solace of community friendships; they were led on by Bo Mason's obsession with parlaying wits into fortune—the great American entrepreneurial dream that Stegner mythicized as *The Big Rock Candy Mountain.*

The Mason family, plagued by recurrent frustrations that were caused by repeated moves to new homes and by the stigma of Bo's failure to earn bread by respectable means, remained always socially isolated. The open road is both a metaphor and the means of the family's rootless discontinuity, but the family unit, as fragile and fraught with pain as it is, provides the only solidarity and stability that its members experience. In the 1930s, as Stegner wrote the novel, literally millions driven from the land took to the open road in a colossal human exodus of migrants, either as families or as displaced individuals, exiled in search of a living. In an interview published in January, 1980, Stegner commented on the central role of the American family in his fiction, pointing out that, unlike the mythic masculine West, people "generally" came West as families. This central fact of westering underlies Stegner's thematic focus in *The Big Rock Candy Mountain.* That is to say, the individual's identity, even though forged and stamped by the landscape and the expansive sense of freedom in the West, is rooted most deeply in the family. Speaking of the nineteenth-century West and the early decades of this century, Stegner stated that for most migrants the West had been "a social disruption," but families cohered because they were "the last line of defense against anarchy."[2] The Mason family experienced representative social disruption, but its similar defensive solidarity was not in response to the threat of anarchy but to the fear of exposure to the law through contact with neighbors. Consequently, their exile was atypical only vis-à-vis middle-class respectability, the community to which Elsa, Bruce, and Chet so yearned to belong.

The Mason family situation can be seen as representative of American experience. For example, in his classic study of American immigration, *The Uprooted*, Oscar Handlin succinctly compared immigrant family experience with other American families who journeyed into new country in search of a better life during the nineteenth and early twentieth centuries. Both the immigrant and the typical "native born" family on the move shared mobility, rootlessness, and the loss of assurance that comes from reliable, habitual behavior and permanent residence. These shared experiences had become an American way of life as society continually changed and older, less complex, more intimate mores disintegrated. Both the immigrant and the established American "had to toil painfully from crisis to crisis, as . . . individual[s] alone"; both had to surmount "the discontinuous obstacles of a strange world."[3] Both learned bitter lessons from their lives of motion. "To earn their bread in novel fashion, to adjust their views of the universe to a new world's sights, to learn to live with each other in unaccustomed surroundings, to discover the uses of power, and to uncover beneath the inherited family patterns intimate personal relationships, these were the adventures all people in motion shared with the immigrants."[4] Clearly, these are the lessons we see dramatized in the Mason family's sojourn across the modern West. The Masons' experience in exile outside the communities in which they lived threw the family together into a greater intimacy, although fraught with tensions and explosions of animosity. Handlin argues that the immigrant family experience was remade in the American landscape, in which each member could discover the uniqueness of the others. Similarly, Bruce Mason realizes, though too late to live together in harmony, that his mother, father, brother, and he are partners in a family. In Handlin's precise words: "The family then became a network of connections, exposing to each within the circle the uniqueness of each one among the several."[5]

The dream of upward mobility has been a principal factor in making Americans an uprooted people, and *The Big Rock Candy Mountain* closely examines this theme in Bruce Mason's search for identity. The influence of the American Dream of self-made prosperity is Stegner's central theme. A man who grew to consciousness on the last North American frontier, Stegner rejected the Edenic dream that so possessed his father.[6] Bruce Mason's repudiation of his father's obsession to "make it big" parallels Stegner's own censure of his father's seduction by the "folklore of hope" that the homestead laws represented, and which brought the Stegners to the Saskatchewan frontier in a "blind and ignorant lemming-impulse."[7] As a law student Bruce examines the disparity between the myth and the degradation of growing numbers of Americans as the Great Depression deepens and spreads. At the same time, he resents his father's betrayal of the family because of his desperate loyalty to a futile dream. "So what did you do, if you didn't want to get caught as Bo Mason had been caught, pumped full of the dream and the expectation and the feeling that the world owed you something for nothing, and then thrown into a world where expectations didn't pay off?"[8] Seeking answers to this question and a second equally complex query (where is home?) led Bruce to discover who he is.

As the novel ends, the Mason history becomes the key to Bruce's sense of continuity. "Even if the thing itself was paltry and dull, the history of the thing was not. . . . It was not permanence alone that made what the Anglo-Saxons called home, he thought. It was continuity, the flux of fashion and decoration moving in and out again as minds and purses altered, but always within the framework of the established and recognizable outline" (p. 423). Contemplating the influence of the growing Great Depression upon his family, Bruce admits that they are insignificant in the pattern of the nation's historic events. But he also realizes that his family's identity is molded by American history—that, although isolated, the family and each of its members are expressions of forces which have resulted in making the modern West.

The links between the larger Mason and Norgaard families have dissolved because both Bo and Elsa ran away from their homes to seek freedom, she because her home had become a prison after her father married her best friend, and he because his father expressed only hatred and violence toward him. Bruce has no knowledge of contemporary members of his father's family from Illinois, and although he lived near the maternal side while attending law school in Minnesota, no close network existed between them. The history of his ancestors from Pennsylvania was completely lost, back to the time when "the first great or great-great grandfather broke loose from his Amish fireside and started moving rootless around the continent" (p. 517). Trying to discover where his home is, Bruce yearned for inclusion in a clan: "To see the family vices and virtues in a dozen avatars instead of in two or three" (p. 519).

Next, Bruce wondered what it would be like "to love and know a single place" (p. 519). He understood that his family was not unique in its rootlessness. "The whole nation had been footloose too long, Heaven had been just over the next range for too many generations. Why remain in one dull plot of earth when Heaven was reachable, was touchable, was just over there?" (p. 519). "He had a notion where home would turn out to be, for himself as for his father—over the next range, on the Big Rock Candy Mountain, that place of impossible loveliness that had pulled the whole nation westward. . ." (p. 520). Bruce sees clearly that the great dream that possessed his father was viable only "If you don't recognize limits" (p. 521). In the early 1930s the American Dream of continual progress, let alone its corollary, the illusion of striking it rich, seemed obvious shams. "We are all fighting for the trough, and the healing fiction is fading like a dream" (p. 522). Finally, although Bruce did not know where home was, he knew (because he was a westerner) where he felt at home, in the arid "brown country where the raw earth showed" (p. 524). The western landscape, then, is an integral part of Bruce Mason's sense of being. He yearns, though, for a more tangible sense of his family as he seeks his identity in an America that had lost confidence, was full of dread for its own survival, and was locked in despair during the worst years of the Great Depression.

III

In the latter chapters of *The Big Rock Candy Mountain*, Stegner condenses Bruce Mason's experiences during his high school and early adult years as a student, focusing only upon key incidents that reveal his self-discovery and masculinity. Bruce's self-realization results from his growing adult experiences, most of which Stegner never shows,[9] but most important is his understanding of his father from the "remains," personal possessions, which Bo Mason leaves behind.

In contrast to the romantic cult of action and the masculine mystique, Wallace Stegner realistically portrays Bruce Mason's awakening to manhood. As the protagonist who conveys Stegner's poignant commentary about the compulsive lure of the masculine West upon his father, Bo Mason, Bruce is the younger son who realizes that he must learn who he is in order to become a man; thus, he must look to history as it is embodied in his family, not to myths of gender embodied in American culture. In his journal, Bruce writes: "A man is movement, motion, a continuum. There is no beginning to him" (p. 493). He understands that his identity is inseparable from his family's history, that he is not a severed "self" adrift in space and time, as is the archetypal American Adam.[10]

Bruce understands that "Memory was a trap, a labyrinth. . . . If you could look back through many funneling memories instead of one or two, you might be able to escape the incommunicable identity in which you lay hidden" (p. 563). The "incommunicable identity" is both Bruce's consciousness of "self," and it is also his *family*, from which the self cannot be subtracted if one is to know who one is. Hence, Stegner has Bruce wish for some tangible documentation of his family in the form of a photograph album (an album that does not exist) in order to trace, after the fact, its history (p. 520). Bruce's desire to know and belong to a family is in distinct contrast to the male mystique in which the unattached, orphan protagonist is perpetually on the road among other men, fighting evil, defending justice, and maintaining his inviolable freedom. Examples of this archetypal male are Boone Caudill (A. B. Guthrie's the *Big Sky*,

1947), Shane (Jack Shaefer's *Shane*, 1949), Hugh Glass (Frederick Man-fred's *Lord Grizzly*, 1954), the buffalo hunters of John Williams' *Butcher's Crossing* (1960), and Samson John Minard, patterned after the legend of John Johnston, the "Crow-killer" (Vardis Fisher's *Mountain Man*, 1965).

On the contrary, Bruce learns that nurturance and responsibility to the family are essential to being manly, lessons he absorbs primarily from his mother. Suffering, sacrifice, frustration with repeated failures, and perseverance, not heroism through scenarios of traditional success, are man's destiny. Yet, these tribulations may create an admirable but silent heroism, such as Elsa's and even Bo's, as expressed in the creation and maintenance of their family.

Manhood may both be discovered and asserted through reflection, rather than expressed exclusively through the actions required by the for-mula of the masculine mystique. Bruce knows that his family's history contains tension between men and women, and that he and his brother learned to be manly first through their father and second, but as impor-tantly, through their mother. However, the full significance of this insight is not evident to Bruce until the novel's final scene, his father's funeral, in which he admits the truth about his family. Stegner counterpoints Bruce's thoughts with the hollow platitudes uttered over the "remains" in the minister's perfunctory ceremony, and the novel ends with the hearse door "closing quietly upon the casket and the flowers." To fully understand Bruce's recognition of the necessity of androgyny in the expression of manhood, Stegner dramatizes his shock of recognition of the interde-pendence of father and son and of a profound love neither ever expressed.

Before Bruce leaves to return to Salt Lake City for his father's funeral, he realizes that he is temporarily returning home for the "next to last" time because a part of him is buried in the graves of his mother and brother, and he admits that another part will soon be buried in a third grave. On the drive home he struggles with disbelief in the manner of his father's death, and he knows that Bo, for the first time in his life, looked down the road and saw nothing to escape to. Bruce arrives in Salt Lake in the evening, but despite his exhaustion, his eagerness to resolve the mystery of his father's final hours and the reasons for the murder-suicide draw him to the hotel in which his father died. There he discovers his father's "remains." A newspaper account of the sordid, explosive events yields no insight, except that Bruce discovers his father had purchased a gun only days before his death. The novel's climax occurs in the penul-timate scene in Bo Mason's hotel room.

No single place contains the memories of Bruce's growing and being, and the possessions and memorabilia that remain of his family are a devastating commentary on his loss. He received the paltry possessions of his "inheritance," the accumulated remnants that testify to his pariah-father's earthly achievement, in an envelope inscribed with his name, propped up behind his father's silver shaving mug. This is convincing evidence that Bo had rationally planned his suicide. Without comment Stegner presents a meticulous summary of Bo's meager possessions, conveying Bruce's devastation as he begins to understand his father, although he is not yet prepared to honor or forgive. Bo left no note explaining the murder of his mistress or his suicide. Bruce has no final letter to ponder and interpret, to document that his father had felt at peace at the very end. What remains for Bruce to examine in his father's room, however, does explain much to a young man who is beginning to value the uniqueness of each person in his family as an extension of himself.

Bruce examines the contents of the envelope, an episode that Stegner again dramatizes with Bruce as protagonist under similar circumstances in *Recapitulation*. The room's closet contains a pair of his father's black shoes, a suit, and a bundle of neckties, some never worn. On the dresser sits a silver shaving mug, tarnished and dented, that Bo had won in a trap shoot, inscribed with "Champion of North Dakota, Single Traps, 1905." The mug symbolizes a masculine trait, accurate shooting, once of considerable importance on the frontier, which, in civilized society, is useless except in sport. Opening the envelope Bruce feels sick. It contains an insurance policy for $500, a receipt book proving that all premiums had been paid, five pawn tickets (for an overcoat, a watch, and three suitcases), a map marked with the location of Bo's worthless Della Mine, three letters Bruce had written to his father, a certificate of ownership of a cemetery plot, a sexton's receipt, and "a receipt showing that perpetual care had been bought and paid for" (p. 626). Rereading his letters Bruce loaths the advice he had submitted to his father condescendingly along with "bread-and-butter checks and a lot of smug free advice. Take a brace, keep your chin up, you're not licked yet, why not get a job at something, any kind of job, till you get a stake again, instead of waiting and depending on this mine?" (p. 626).

Bo Mason's key remnant is the receipt for payment of perpetual care of his family's graves. This indicates his implicit doubt that Bruce will honor the memory of his family by caring for their graves, but it also demonstrates that to Bo Mason his family was his greatest comfort and happiness. The purchase of perpetual care may be interpreted as sentimentality, but this sentiment is especially poignant in its authenticity. In light of Mason's financial failure, seamy schemes that depression times necessitated, emotional alienation, the murder, and suicide, the perpetual care receipt makes Bruce see that a man's final spiritual declaration is that his family shall reside together, beside him even in death. This declaration explains that Bo had lived not by the letter but by the spirit of paternalism because he truly did cherish and protect his wife, whom he profoundly loved, and his sons; it proclaims that he will carry on in death symbolically as the patriarch, even though in life he was neither a traditional husband nor father.

That was the final sum, the final outcome, of the skill and talents and strengths his father had started with. One dented silver mug, almost thirty years old. One pair of worn shoes, one worn suit, a dozen spotted neckties, a third interest in a worthless mine, a cemetery lot with perpetual care. A few pawn tickets, a few debts, a few papers, an insurance policy to bury him and a cemetery lot to bury him in, that last small resource hoarded jealous [sic] even while the larger and hopeful resources were squandered. (pp. 626–27)

This revelation does not itself overwhelm Bruce because he does not yet feel its emotional intensity. He believes that his father was making a statement about being manly, but its link to his own awakening is not yet welded in his consciousness.

In the next moment, Mrs. Winter, a sensitive friend of his father, provides the evidence that Bo Mason loved his son, because to his dying day he carried a photograph of Bruce in his wallet. This shocks Bruce, especially because his father had shared, "perhaps with pride," the photograph with a person whom he cared about and trusted. This revelation together with Bo's implied doubt that Bruce will honor the family's graves shame him. "Everything in this bare, cheap little room shamed him" (p. 627). Mrs. Winter (an ironic name for such an important messenger of truth) also tells Bruce that his father had found peace in the last few days before his death. Suicide had been on his mind for a month.

Bruce had hated and misunderstood his father all of his life, but at the end of this scene in the man's room, brilliantly symbolizing both Mason's pathetic emotional squalor and his faith in his life's single covenant to love his family, the knowledge of the multiple revelations cause Bruce to break down.

The novel focuses finally upon manhood within the family and the responsibility that that manliness incurs. Harry Mason's funeral is the novel's dénouement. He was both a child and a man, "a completely masculine being." "He would always have been an underdeveloped human being, an immature social animal, and the further the nation goes the less room there is for that kind of man" (p. 633). Before the funeral Bruce admits: "His qualities were the raw material for a notable man. Though I have hated him, and though I neither honor nor respect him now, I can not deny him that" (p. 633). The anachronism of the popular hero of American masculine mythology was evident to Wallace Stegner as he wrote his novel in the closing years of the Depression. Like most American writers of the period, Stegner focused attention upon man as a social being with responsibilities, although not in the fashionable proletarian style of the 1930s. Of Bo Mason, Bruce eventually understands that "His father had wasted himself in a thousand ways, but he had never been an incompetent" (p. 627).

The Freudian overtones of the father-son rivalry, although never explicit in Stegner's novel, emerge implicitly in his use of the perpetual *testing syndrome* in characterizing the struggle of the father and sons. A small, unathletic, intellectual boy, Bruce knows that he is excluded from the vigorous, athletic world of action of his father and brother, Chet. But Bruce comes to realize the role of intellect in modern manliness, while he simultaneously becomes aware of his father's potential qualities of greatness. Bruce no longer feels compelled to test himself against his father when, as a young man, he goes to law school in the East.

Bruce is convinced that as he becomes "his own man," ultimately alone, he must choose to accept and incorporate many qualities from his once-abhorred father, as well as honor the gentler qualities that he learned from his mother. "There is the making of a man in that family, and more of it than I ever thought will have to come out of the tissues of my father" (p. 633). This is his final lesson. A "proper man," according to Stegner's characterization of Bruce, is created over generations and is not an immature social being like Bo Mason, seduced by and totally committed to the illusion of success. To become whole a man must accept and nurture androgynous characteristics in his psyche. " . . . Perhaps it took several combinations and re-creations of his mother's gentleness and resilience, his father's enormous energy and appetite for the new, a subtle blending of masculine and feminine, selfish and selfless, stubborn and yielding, before a proper man could be fashioned" (p. 634).

In Bruce Mason's attempt to forge his manhood, he had decided to become exactly opposite of his father. As Stegner has said, Bruce's choice of law as a way of life is a rational, logical decision to become a respectable insider.[11] Unlike the outlaw, Harry Mason, his son is the respectable bourgeoisie of American society. Stegner recently characterized the "boomer" Harry Mason as a strong, dominant man, a "deluded man," in many ways a "dangerous man," and finally, a "frontiersman manqué."[12] Of Stegner's world view in the writings through the 1940s, a critic wrote: "He believes in man, whose will and mortality, he thinks, are operative in our culture. He is at his best when he affirms the goodness of life even though his characters know it is latent with horror."[13] Bruce concludes that he must look to the future, not to the past as did his father, and he is hopeful. Having traveled east instead of west to stake out his claim upon the future, Bruce, the last survivor of his cellular family, has become a man; no longer bewildered, he can now strike out on his own. In his opening manhood he will attempt to justify his parents' mistakes and their sacrifices. Despite the grief and suffering of his family life, he had experienced much goodness and pleasure, especially as a boy awakening to consciousness on the Saskatchewan frontier. His hope of success as a man lies in his adjustment to change, and acceptance of the realities of a limited modern period in the West—something that Bo Mason, frozen in an eternal present without a sense of history, a "frontiersman manqué," was unable to do.[14] Within a continuous frame of American and family history, Bruce becomes a man, free from the delusions of the masculine mystique and the Big Rock Candy Mountain that contributed so much to his father's suffering.

Notes

1. Stegner relates that he began work on the novel during Christmas vacation 1937, and he recalls finishing the writing around Christmas 1940. The composition period may have taken somewhat longer because the novel was not published until 1943. Here and elsewhere in this essay I am indebted to Richard W. Etulain for permitting me to listen to several tapes of conversations he had earlier this year with Wallace Stegner.

2. Peggy Fletcher and John L. Lewis, "An Interview with Wallace Stegner," *Sunstone*, January/February 1980, p. 9. For additional commentary by Stegner about the importance of family relationships as subject matter and social context in literature, see David Dillon, "Time's Prisoners: An Interview with Wallace Stegner," *Southwest Review*, 61 (Summer 1976), 252–267. Criticizing the atomistic and jaded view of vagabond protagonists created by many contemporary novelists, Stegner said: "It seems to me that the real relationships, the things that last in life and that will probably last in fiction as well, are likely to be related to parents, children, courtship, marriage, and children, in turn. In other words, I don't think you can douse the family as contemporary fiction has doused it, dousing the kind of glue that holds society together" (pp. 261–62). About the Masons in *The Big Rock Candy Mountain*, Stegner has said: the novel deals essentially with the "tight, internal, intramural war of the family." (Etulain taped interview with Wallace Stegner, 1980).

3. Oscar Handlin, *The Uprooted: The Epic Story of the Great Migrations that Made the American People*, 2nd ed. (Boston: Little, Brown, 1973), p. 271.

4. Handlin, p. 272.

5. Handlin, p. 282.

6. Like other later pioneers of America's last frontier, Stegner's father lamented that he had just missed his opportunity, and in this way Bo Mason lamented that he had been born too late. But as early as 1844 economist Henry Demarest Lloyd wrote of the disparity between the myth of going west and the reality: "Our young men can no longer go west: they must go up or down." Quoted in Robert H. Bremner, *From the Depths: The Discovery of Poverty in the United States* (New York: New York University Press, 1956), p. 21.

7. Wallace Stegner, *Wolf Willow: A History, a Story, and a Memory of the Last Plains Frontier* (New York: Viking Press, 1966), p. 281.

8. Wallace Stegner, *The Big Rock Candy Mountain* (New York: Pocket Books, 1977), p. 522. Hereafter all references to the novel are from this edition and will appear in parentheses within the text.

9. In his most recent novel *Recapitulation* (New York: Fawcett, 1979), Stegner returns to the Mason history in, what he calls, a "trailer" to *The Big Rock Candy Mountain* (Etulain interview, 1980). Stegner again writes of the father-son conflict, returning Bruce to Salt Lake City forty-five years after his father's funeral in 1932. In his "trailer" novel Stegner shows Bruce Mason's reconciliation with his memory of his stern, feckless, and vacillating father. Stegner makes explicit, what had been implicit in the earlier novel, Bruce's understanding of and empathy with his father, bringing full circle, and enclosing the continuous frame of, the Mason history. In his interview with Richard W. Etulain, Stegner says that in *The Big Rock Candy Mountain* Bruce had judged his father "too harshly and too early" in his life. Consequently, haunted by his unburied "twin" ghosts of his father and of his youth, Bruce lays both to rest. Stegner underscores this theme of family solidarity by authorially commenting in *Recapitulation* upon the meaning of the Masons to each other. "Unlikely as it seemed, they were a close family. The internal strains that tore them apart also forced them together. Because they lived outside law and community, they had no one but themselves to share

themselves with" (p. 96). Toward the end of the book, Bruce recalls the key experience in Harry Mason's barroom, shortly after his mother's death, where Bruce instantly recognized in Harry's eyes the depth of genuine love for Elsa and his excruciating suffering of her loss. "He thought of the many failures, the self-deceptions, the schemes that never paid off, the jobs that never worked out, the hopeful starts that had always ended in excuses or flight. He thought of the eyes that had once filled him with fear, but that now could never quite meet, never quite hold, the eyes of his cold son. Thinking of all this, and remembering when they were a family and when his mother was alive to hold them together, he felt pity, and he cried" (p. 263).

As a retired diplomat Bruce set his father's ghost to rest by ordering a headstone for Harry Mason's grave, an act that Stegner admits he has never done nor will ever do for his own father. (Etulain interview, 1980) "Even if the trumpet never blew, the grave at least granted memory its illusions" (p. 279). Through the eyes of a venerable and worldly-wise retired servant of U.S. foreign policy who never married and called the place of his temporary assignment his home, Stegner states the primal meaning of family solidarity in a man's life and for a man's sense of manhood and self: "Yet Harry Mason's only definition, was given him by the relationships he lay beside. Without them he would merge with the universal grass. In his life it was the same. The family that he created and bungled and abused and betrayed was his only accomplishment" (p. 280).

10. R. W. B. Lewis, *The American Adam: Innocence, Tragedy and Tradition in the Nineteenth Century* (Chicago: University of Chicago Press, 1967).

11. Etulain taped interview with Wallace Stegner, 1980.

12. Etulain, interview.

13. Chester E. Eisinger, *Fiction of the Forties* (Chicago: University of Chicago Press, 1963), p. 325.

14. Etulain, interview.

The Big Rock Candy Mountain and Angle of Repose: Trial and Culmination

Kerry Ahearn*

The hallmark of literature in the first half of our century has been stylistic innovation as a means of rendering the complexities of human psychology, and if this were really the only significant method of approaching the raw material of art, then Joyce's notion that *Ulysses* brought us to a culmination and made further fiction unnecessary might be undeniable. Yet I think myth and stylistic one-upmanship and the various permutations of the "dark" tradition of American letters have been overemphasized by critics, and this has in part explained why Wallace Stegner has not received the recognition he deserves. When *Angle of Repose* won a Pulitzer Prize in 1972, skeptics pointed out that the committee has always seemed on the watch for the Great American Novel from the West, and that in the past, such as *The Travels of Jamie McPheeters* or *Honey in the Horn* have unaccountably profited. The National Book Award committee for 1972 ignored Stegner.

Of course, book awards themselves are no reliable index to the state of our nation's literary tastes, but in Stegner's case, the different responses of the "nationalistic" Pulitzer and the "Brahmin" National Book Award judgments hint at what a survey of Stegner criticism would show: an unwillingness by the nation's highest arbiters to admit him to the front rank of American novelists. As Robert Canzoneri noted in his excellent essay,

> Since in Stegner's work neither style, method, nor form is exotic, doctrinaire, distorted, violent, or romantic, and since none of his fiction depends upon myth, symbol, current psychology, or neo-theology, what is there to write about, teach about, or talk about? These characteristics . . . have tended to leave him invisible to cults and coteries.[1]

Many critics, I think, are lukewarm toward Stegner for reasons not easily dealt with in a review of conventional length: stylistic matters. They find his prose correct but not inspired. He seems to them too much in the realistic stream of American fiction, controlled and rational. True, Stegner cannot be called an innovative stylist like Faulkner or Nabokov (though I find his prose, on the whole, every bit as fresh and vivid as that

*Reprinted from *Western American Literature* (Spring, 1975), 11–27.

109

of Bellow, Malamud, Updike, or Barth). There are times when I wish his ear had been listening harder for repetition; too many phrases like "a painful mouthful," "a kind of giggling liking by teasing her," or well-intended but postured attempts like "the receding reach of the room," and "special sin of sensation and excitement" impede the prose and upset its norm, though they are notably absent in his essays and in the fiction dealing with the interior West, his congenial material. Style is often mentioned in reviews, but never at length. In Stegner's case, its importance can easily be exaggerated; he once wrote, in what sounds like self-defense, that

> Serious fiction is not necessarily great and not even necessarily literature because the talents of its practitioners may not be as dependable as their intentions. . . . The work of art is not a gem, as some schools of criticism would insist, but truly a lens. We look through it for the purified and honestly offered spirit of the artist.[2]

The question here is not with Stegner's talents, which are obvious, but with something beyond the "gift of words." Stegner has always sought to give us a look at life; his most ambitious works distinguish themselves from the rest in terms of their temporal and spatial scope, for life reveals its truths by accretion, and Stegner's novels reflect that process. For him, intentions are of crucial importance: the artist (as in some foreign traditions, African, for example) sees himself as a speaker of and to his society, and so more responsible and responsive to it. His fiction should be judged on those merits.

In a truly seminal essay on the subject of American literature and Western experience, "Born a Square," Stegner describes the situation of the serious Western writer with the image of a double-ended *cul de sac.* "The thesis of this piece," he begins, "is that the western writer is in a box with booby traps at both ends. . . . since any writer must write from what he knows and believes, the writer from the West finds himself so unfashionable as to be practically voiceless."[3] This offers a valuable insight into Stegner's anti-mythical stance as a novelist. His sane, realistic approach seeks to illustrate that some of the largest myths that burden the image of the West in our nation's consciousness—especially the fantasy of "man alone"—prevent us from perceiving important cultural truths about ourselves. He knows from long experience that the Western writer suffers from a backlash against such mythical configurations: the Matter of the Wild West, taken straight, offers few negotiable effects besides escapism, a point Richard Slotkin raises in his *Regeneration Through Violence:*

> What a mass audience expects from popular literature is a reflection of the images and symbols that are the outer emblems of its collective mythology, rather than a painful analysis or probing of the depths beneath the

surface. Popular mythology serves as a gloss for the painful or troubling aspects of a people's history, providing an illusory solution of real difficulties. . . .[4]

The West is the home of popular mythology, and Stegner has sought to function there as a serious artist, finding his materials from among the faded mythic props and settings, and trying to present them with the clear vision of traditional realism so that they seem "true," and able to convey Stegner's themes without being confused with the old stereotypes.

I think *Angle of Repose* best represents this approach. Not only is it Stegner's best novel to date, it also shows itself to be a descendent of and an improvement upon *The Big Rock Candy Mountain* (1943), and a culmination in his struggle to present Western realities. It illustrates that he has grappled with and solved some major technical problems that weakened earlier efforts, and has succeeded in giving us a vision of experience distinctively American.

II

The Big Rock Candy Mountain investigates the issue of the cultural and intellectual limitations of life in the interior West. A richer novel than the four that preceded it, which seem monocular in comparison, its scope allows Stegner to examine the influences of the West from several points of view; its characters include mature personalities beckoned to by the spacious country and young people who are actually formed by it. The book is filled with magic scenes (many conceived and published previously as short stories[5]), for Stegner is never better than when narrating youth's experiences of exploration and initiation, or sports contests, or trips by car or wagon.

The novel's most ambitious and difficult task is dramatizing and satisfactorily combining the paradoxical qualities of the West as Stegner sees it, "as good a place to be a boy and as unsatisfactory a place to be a man as one could well imagine."[6] The best scenes—invariably action sequences—illustrate the former, but they do not set the novel's tone. Primarily, Stegner wants to show the falseness of the candy mountain idea (the "idea of the West") and the deprivation that results from following it. The story is about victims; it stresses an unsatisfactory boyhood. Despite the shifting, limited point of view, with its implication that all four members of the Mason family will characterize themselves and be treated with similar detachment, the narratives are influenced both in voice and choice of events by the fact that the author identifies himself in some very important ways with Bruce and his mother Elsa. The father, Bo Mason, may be the novel's central character, as most critics have suggested, but Bruce is clearly most important in Stegner's mind. The narrative begins with Elsa (Bruce is very much his mother's son, inheriting less of value from his father than he, or perhaps Stegner, would have us believe) and ends with Bruce. The family's polarity is more than neutral fact: Bruce and Elsa are given fully three times as much narrative as Bo and his son and kindred spirit, Chet, and are regarded throughout as arch-victims of Bo's rootlessness.

Put very simply, Stegner's method in this novel is at odds with his personal feelings about the subject. A story seeking to present life on the last frontier by focusing in turn upon the different members of the family demands an evenness of authorial detachment. Since each character receives extensive narrative treatment, we would expect to learn how each suffers and profits from the situation. Stegner's quotation in the previous paragraph strongly implies that any mature intellect will find the marginal West "unsatisfactory," and the principle should apply to Bo Mason, an intelligent man. A careful analysis of such a character would reveal much about our historical love-hate relationship with the wilderness West, and about the anguish of one whose very existence embodies that paradox. But Stegner's purpose will not allow such detachment. *The Big Rock Candy Mountain* is dominated by an eagerness to show blame again and again; it is a son's novel, an attack upon paternal blindness. Its weaknesses, as I see them, result from the absence of a consistent sympathy toward all the Masons; there should be either a third-person-limited telling which really sees as each consciousness leads, or a first-person rendering, Bruce's. The broad scope of the novel demands the former, and its preoccupation with Bruce's search-for-identity theme the latter. More control in fusing the two might have resulted in a narrative stance similar to Wolfe's in *Look Homeward, Angel* (some later sections of Stegner's novel have precisely that tone); perhaps the very possibility prompted him to try another technique. But in the end, his greatest problems came from the intimacy of his material. He has said in several essays that he resented his father for the hardships and cultural deprivation (especially for the mother) that attended their wandering life; he has sought in later writing, notably *Wolf Willow* (1962), to indicate how much of the novel recreates his own experience both in general theme and specific incident. It may be, as Lois Hudson wrote, that the Western author must tie his fiction to the demonstrably "true" to avoid its dismissal as mere myth-on-myth,[7] but to do so while employing Stegner's chosen technique in *The Big Rock Candy Mountain* creates another difficulty. Detachment must not only be maintained, but also feigned.

Since the early portions of the novel use Elsa's consciousness as their limits, one would expect to feel first her boredom with her father's house, and then, after her escape from it, a great deal of sympathy from Bo, and lots of love's light-headedness. The malaise is well presented, but Elsa's emotions control less and less of the narrative as her love for Bo increases. Their relationship lacks joy and spontaneity; the events in this section not only hint that Bo is something less than deserving, they actually emphasize his shady business association, his dubious moral standards, and his propensity for cruelty and violence. What comes to seem obvious to the reader, though, is lost on Elsa, for she is innocent. At times, Stegner's concern with marshalling evidence against Bo becomes excessive, and Elsa's characterization suffers: for her to miss the implications of what she sees implies not merely innocence, but a monumental naiveté. A lighter touch would have left a subtler but more believable feeling of doubt about Bo. A good example of Stegner's skill is the scene of Bo's proposal—the couple sits in the middle of a vast, flat, snow-covered North Dakota field whose stark emptiness is implication enough that her agreement to marry him forebodes a bleakness of its own.

Because the account of their courtship seems less devoted to portraying the sources of their mutual attraction than it is to proving that Bo does not deserve her, the dramatic force inherent in many scenes never asserts itself. For example, the summary of Bo's early life loses some of its impact because, although we know that he relates it to Elsa on the front steps of her uncle's home in North Dakota, we do not get to watch him. When he boasts that his baseball skills would have taken him to the major leagues but for an injury, or tells of the time he memorized his McGuffey and then misbehaved until his teacher belittled him and demanded that he recite (hours later, "she reluctantly turned him and the rest of the class loose. He had reached page ninety-two with only a few minor errors"),[8] we miss both the raw edge of his bravado and the pleasure of seeing Elsa's reaction to it. Generally, the narrative does not allow Bo and Elsa to get very close together; it not only ignores the dimension in Elsa's personality that is attracted to Bo's sexuality, but actually tries to discourage any such implication. Jumping from the wagon at the end of a double date, Elsa sees Bo's best friend pull his hand from under his lady friend's dress; she is shocked, but too innocent to draw the obvious conclusion that she is mixed up with people of questionable morals. Because Elsa does not understand the dangers of her attraction, and because the narrative emphasizes those very dangers, the whole question of "love," and why she finds Bo irresistible, are neglected, with great loss to the energy of the narrative. The touching and silly expectations of first love do not get communicated, and consequently their disappointing relationship of future years never achieves the pathos it should. The curve on the graph begins low, already declining. Since the narrative denies Bo the same emotional depths the other characters possess, it limits its own force commensurately.

A similar narrowing principle arranges the events in Bruce's sections. We see almost nothing of him at school, at play with his mates, or growing up with his brother. Rather, the narrative occupies itself with demonstrating the abundant pain that energetic, impatient Bo brings to his life, and on the other hand, the compensations he derives from a close relationship with Elsa. This may be "true"; it may even be most important in his development; but it is certainly not all. Too many other important elements remain outside the narrative: we learn that he receives a high school award as a member of the "midget" basketball team, and that he is a natural athlete, but we see nothing of those interests or efforts; the earlier emphasis upon Bruce's small, weak stature actually makes them seem unlikely. When his mother dies, he laments that he spent too much time chasing girls, neglecting her, but never has he appeared with a date, or even with thoughts of girls on his mind. At one point, Chet teases him about his failure to relate with the opposite sex. Girls and sports are reserved for Chet's story, and both bring trouble. In fact, interests are divided so categorically between the brothers that they seem halves of a single, well-rounded personality.

The final third of the novel, when Bruce's consciousness comes to the fore and provides the dominant point of view, actually does little more than restate the case against Bo, consolidating all the arguments. There is evidence within the novel that Stegner perceived and tried to soften the effect, but there is no better evidence of its strength than Ray B. West's reading, wherein he quotes Bruce's harsh assessment of the father as "the words of the author through the consciousness of . . . Bruce":[9]

> At the end he degenerated into a broken old man, sponging a bare living and sustaining himself on a last, gilded, impossible dream; and when he could no longer bear the indignities which the world heaped upon him, and when the dream broke like a bubble, he sought some way, out of an obscure and passionate compulsion to exonerate himself, to lay the blame onto another.

Interpreting *The Big Rock Candy Mountain* requires judging West's response (which the entire novel, with both the "how" and "what" of its narrative, seems to support) against Stegner's hints of Bruce's bias. Near the end, he juxtaposes Bruce's inflexibility with Elsa's martyrlike patience (she tells him from her deathbed, "You never make allowances. . ." (p. 541). Stegner implies here that he wishes the novel to leave the reader not with a final judgment on Bo, but with a feeling that a just opinion lies somewhere between Bruce's and Elsa's positions. Bo, after all, did not live by "sponging," nor can his suicide and murder of his ex-mistress be reasonably interpreted as an attempt to lay blame on another for his own decline. We are not allowed to watch Bo in the last moments of his despair, and must rely upon Bruce's uncharitable reconstruction of events. The reader who sifts the evidence is still uncertain where the real source of authority in this novel rests.

Throughout the narrative, Bo's point of view is neglected; only a sixth of the novel focuses upon his consciousness, and those sequences underscore his abundant, almost manic energy (see especially the short story "Two Rivers," included in section IV; the first rum-run, section V; and the whiskey hijack episode in section VI) with clean skillful narrative. But notably lacking is any sympathy or desire to illuminate Bo's mind, his fears (in the largest sense), his conscience, or the influence of his family upon his thinking. We see him only as a man of action, of "furious compulsion" (he seems in many ways the twin of Vardis Fisher's Dock Hunter in *Toilers of the Hills*—they even have strong superstitious streaks, Dock with horoscopes, Bo with solitaire); the narrative, in other words, illustrates the blindness of the son toward the anguish of the father, emphasizing instead his size, power, and apparent freedom from his family's influence. Because Bruce's refusal to sympathize is indistinguishable from the narrative's attitude throughout, one can understand West's position.

Of the scenes Bo shares with Elsa, one in particular summarizes the difficulties of determining what voice controls the telling of the novel. After the planned trip to the Arctic gold fields collapses (significantly, when the boys fall ill), the family moves to Richmond, a small lumbering town in western Washington, where they live in a tent while Bo and Elsa try to establish a small diner. Bo's "westering" urge soon has him chafing and impatient, and the climax is this scene, where Bo attempts to fill a coffee-maker with boiling water:

> the urn was high; he had to strain to hoist the pail. The lip caught under the flange of the urn top, and he hung there teetering on the precarious stool. "Come here quick!" he said . . .
>
> You were over to him in three steps, looking to see what he wanted you to do. "The stool!" Bo yelled. "The stool, the stool, the stool!" He could have lowered the pail and started over, but that was not his way. Convulsed with fury and strain, he shouted at you and kept the streaming pail jammed as high as he could reach . . . Hot water slopped over him, and with a yell he dropped it and *leaped back to save himself.* The whole bucket of scalding water came down across your shoulder and arm. [italics mine] (p. 116).

The episode is rendered during an Elsa section (Bruce did not witness it), and the question of whose barely-controlled contempt tone of the passage conveys becomes even more clouded later when Elsa explains the scars to her sister: "The coffee urn tipped over." Then she adds, "Do you want to blame that on him, too?" She occasionally defends Bo against her family, but nowhere else does she lie to them. With all the emphasis placed upon his courage and physical strength, it seems incongruous to single out this scene as somehow characteristic of their relationship, yet the scars receive many references. The wound is made symbolic.

In another Elsa section, it is reported to similar effect:

> He was born with an itch in his bones, Elsa knew. . . . There was somewhere, if you knew where to find it, some place where money could be made like drawing water from a well, some Big Rock Candy Mountain where life was effortless . . . where something could be had for nothing (p. 94).

If this condescension represents Elsa's attitude toward her husband, something is amiss, for that personality differs radically from the one

Stegner creates in the rest of the novel, and this warping for the purpose of furthering the all-pervasive anti-herioc theme weakens Stegner's attempt to achieve pathos for her. Once again, near the end of her life, he has her ask Bruce (whom she for years has sought to soften toward Bo), "Did you know that your dad is keeping another woman?" (p. 574). A most serious violation of character. If Bo is as bad as this; if, as the narrative implies, she has always known it and is so stricken that she cannot avoid telling the very worst to their only surviving child, then we should view her long insistence on cleaving to this man not with pity and admiration, but with sad amazement. Actually, these examples do not dominate Elsa's characterization; they illustrate an unfortunate principle in the novel—attacks on the father outweigh basic demands of good fiction such as plausibility and consistency.

Obviously, the themes most important to Stegner at the time he wrote make *The Big Rock Candy Mountain* the son's book, and Bruce should have told it. Then, at least, the subjectivity of his account would have explained, for example, the habit of ending sections and chapters with devastatingly crisp testaments of Bo's obtuseness (for instance, IV, 5; V, 2; V, 8; the initial break in VI, 4; VII, 5; and VIII, 3), the intensity of the attack on heroic interpretations of westering, the preoccupation with showing virtually every one of Bo's kind impulses to be clumsy, tastelessly extravagant, and/or embarrassing to the family (the soiled Christmas gifts, the Shakespeare volume whose spine he cracks, etc.). One thinks again of West's interpretation: the narrator seems to have been filling in for the son until he can mature and assert himself, as Bruce does in the final third of the novel. Here, Stegner finds the center of his interest in Bruce's struggle to make sense of his heritage; such a theme, combined with the antipatriarchal bias to match Samuel Butler's, could best have been handled subjectively.

Once the reader understands this, the ending of the novel becomes less ambiguous. Stegner, fearing that he has overstated, tries to soften the son's denunciations. In the final scene, when Bruce attends Bo's funeral, he thinks to himself, "There is the makings of a man in that [Mason] family, and more of it than I ever thought will have to come out of the tissues of my father" (p. 633). The novel's last note is mollification, with both Bruce and the reader looking back to the loving scenes the family had:

> Perhaps that was what it meant, all of it. It was good to have been along and to have shared it. There were things he had learned that could not be taken from him (p. 634).

The reference is to those youthful scenes that Canzoneri observed are the sparkling moments of the novel, where "even the 'hated' father becomes so fully real and alive in his own person that the reader sees beyond the perceptions of the son and achieves understanding and compassion."[10] But the important question concerns just who that "son" is; many of those scenes are not narrated from Bruce's view—to say that they provide the real portrait of Bo is to ignore the effect of a far larger number of vividly-told events in Bruce's, Elsa's, and Bo's sections) that grant the father energy and misguided ambition, but no complexity or soul. The "hated"-Bo theme is so pervasive that it does not seem unreasonable to accept West's interpretation while disregarding Bruce's final statements as mere funeral sentiments. Yet Stegner surely meant Bruce's conclusion to be taken seriously as evidence of his maturity, intelligence, and ability to carry on as the last Mason. There is, in Canzoneri's words, understanding and compassion in the final pages, but Bruce's softening is too little come too late. The novel misses being a really great work because it remains the product of conflicting impulses; it is a narrative of parts not unified by technique.

III

Angle of Repose contains all the significant themes of *The Big Rock Candy Mountain*. Like that novel, it represents an ambitious bursting forth after a period of more confined stories: *A Shooting Star* (1961) and *All the Little Live Things* (1967) are studies of contemporary California, which seems to intrigue Stegner more than it inspires him. Between the 1940s and the 1970s, Stegner experienced California, saw more of time's sweeping changes in the West, learned a good many things about the craft of fiction, and (this may or may not be relevant) raised a son. As a result, *Angle of Repose*, a new attempt to deal with his largest themes (Western history and us, the search for identity, the incorrigibility of Hope) on a large scale, represents a culmination. Holding this view, I disagree in part with Canzoneri's preference: "[*The Big Rock Candy Mountain*] is in fact a once-in-a-lifetime book, and . . . it has not been and cannot be surpassed." I would agree that the earlier novel contains more youthful vigor, more immediate, vivid drama, and perhaps, as Canzoneri argues, it is the one "in which Stegner's brand of realism is most readily seen."[11] This may be analogous to arguing over the merits of a young Zinfandel and an aged Cabernet, but I believe that in terms of maturity and complexity and mutual reinforcement of idea and structure, *Angle of Repose* stands superior. It gains both unity and resonance (to say nothing of the bright and sassy personality of Lyman Ward) from its narrative style.

The best beginning would be to consider what the novel is not; a summary of that is a recent essay review entitled "Hung-Up on Virtue and Talent,"[12] a good illustration of the pitfalls of Stegner criticism. The writer's interpretation of the novel rests upon his identification of Stegner and crusty Lyman Ward, retired professor from Berkeley, Bancroft Prize winner, and victim of a progressive bone disease which has taken half a leg, fused his spine, and left him (symbolically) immobile. Lyman Ward believes we can learn from history, but convinced that he has no future of

his own, and loathing the hippy culture (an extreme form of historical
blindness) in particular, and contemporary America in general, he decides to lose himself in the task of reconstructing the life and times of his
genteel, pioneer grandmother, Susan Burling Ward. He gets preachy on
occasion, especially with his secretary, Shelley Rasmussen, and ex- and
crypto-hippy under constant temptation to re-enlist. To be sure, subject
profiles of Ward and Stegner would show some similar entries under "Interests," but this critic (whom I single out only because he is most articulate on the subject) assumes that since he has seen discussion of similar
themes in Stegner's essays he can reasonably state that "Stegner's purpose
in telling his story is highly polemical"; in other words, that Lyman's
quarrels with America's intellectual "deviations" should be taken as the
central issue, that Stegner has written a six-hundred-page novel to teach
us, to bait hippies (a word Lyman never encloses in quotation marks) and
sociologists.

It isn't so. First of all, Stegner denied such a possibility; in reference
to a recent doctoral dissertation on theories of history in his fiction, he
noted that the student's basic assumption is incorrect: "he has me up on a
soapbox."[13] To hold that Stegner employs his narrators as masks through
which he can speak out is to deny that he possesses the imagination to
create an intimate picture of anyone's mind but his own. He has of late
been identified not only with Lyman, but also Joe Allston, the grumpy,
argumentative narrator of *All the Little Live Things* who, like his creator,
lives in the hills west of San Francisco Bay. If one doubts Stegner's word
that he knows the difference between fiction and disquisition, there is
abundant evidence in the texts to disprove any identification. In the case
of Lyman Ward, the superficial likenesses are misleading: both men are
Bay Area Californians, retired professors, and writers of Western history.
There the similarities end. Until the final page, Lyman Ward's head does
not, literally or figuratively, turn. Wallace Stegner's does.

The differences in technique between *Angle of Repose* and *The Big
Rock Candy Mountain* result from the detachment Stegner plans as the
first principle of Lyman's narrative. Though he was reared by his grandparents, Oliver and Susan Ward, in the very house where he has returned
to write the history of their marriage, he did not share the passionate
years of their lives which had such an unsettling effect upon his own
father. He notes, in fact, that he has no interest in any events after 1890—
more than two decades before his birth—when the Wards separated following a rapid and mysterious succession of events that caused his father
tc cut ties with Susan for more than a decade. The novel is thus a mystery,
for Lyman attempts to uncover the lost details; the central irony of the
novel is that the story contains more mystery games than Lyman admits.

He claims that his research is no more than a diversion of a man who
has given up hope: "It is only Lyman Ward, Coe Professor of History,
Emeritus, living a day in his grandparents' life to avoid paying too much

attention to his own."[14] Yet he goes about the job with suspicious intensity. The last thing one expects to find in the writing of an author so given to realism as Stegner is an unreliable narrator, yet that classification, to a modest degree, describes Lyman and points out a change which began with Joe Allston, who knew himself less than he thought, and who in his aging years was surprised to find that he had much to learn. Likewise Lyman Ward, who misleads us, but no more, perhaps, than he does himself. Behind him Stegner cleverly manipulates: we begin the novel with the expectation that a historian of such stature (and self-professed objectivity) as Lyman's will give us the truth, and in fine style. During the opening "Grass Valley" section, he frequently intrudes with explanations of where he got evidence, statements of his historical theories, and exclamations of impatience with Susan's lack of appreciation for her husband. He sides openly with Oliver, who was in an almost archetypal sense "Western," and bowed predictably before her Eastern sophistication and learning. Lyman summarizes his own preference when he calls his grandfather a paragon of honesty and strength: "I refer my actions to his standards yet" (p. 29).

This bias becomes more apparent as the narrative progresses, having special influence where Lyman resorts to fictional techniques and seeks to influence our judgments by what he chooses to dramatize. Most obvious are the sex scenes: Susan, he implies, gets most aroused following some promising breakthrough, such as Oliver's development of a formula for cement, or Clarence King's requesting that he join the U.S. Geological Survey. Each apparent success bring them nothing, but Lyman's prejudice is clear: the success of the marriage will depend upon how well Oliver meets his wife's expectations for advancement in his engineering profession. Since Lyman knows that Oliver never achieved either fame or fortune, he tells the story with the smugness of a man who has made up his mind.

Yet as confident as he seems, it soon becomes apparent that the "biography" represents not the conclusions of an objective mind that has weighed all evidence, but rather the speculations and pre-judgments of a man groping his way along. We are witnessing the construction of a rough draft; his only sure courses are geographical and chronological. He knows that Oliver's attempts to gain a reputation in mining and civil engineering took the Wards to California, Colorado, Mexico, Idaho and back to California. He can tell the dates and name the people. But his façade begins to show cracks:

> I have never formulated precisely what it is I have been doing . . . What interests me in all these papers is not Susan Burling Ward the novelist and illustrator, and not Oliver Ward the engineer, and not the West they spent their lives in. What really interests me is how two such unlike particles clung together, and under what strains, rolling downhill into their future until they reached the angle of repose where I knew them (p. 187).

This formulation, coming a third of the way through his narrative, clearly offers us valuable information, but its candor can also be misleading. The reality of the Wards' demythologized odyssey through the West is clearly important to the novel, and to Lyman; and he has not satisfactorily explained why he is investigating the marriage when he has already interpreted its essence. All of this testifies to Stegner's skill in uniting a variety of interests in a narrative that allows several searches to progress simultaneously—we are aware of Susan studying herself and her husband, fighting her chronic discontent; of Lyman above them, ordering their experience and attempting to judge them; and finally, ourselves above it all. We accept Lyman's account because although he can be dogmatic, we are reassured by the abundant quotation from his grandmother's correspondence that her Victorian prudishness and desire for tangible success are not Lyman's inventions. He is remote enough from the events that we trust him despite vague misgivings; still, we watch him as well as the dead. Stegner chose right. Through Lyman he can introduce the "objective" rendering of the Wards' life and gradually include the subjective theme of how the telling influences the teller. It is, of course, one of his (and Lyman's) favorite problems, the relationship of past to present.

Stegner, playing with what Nabokov fondly refers to as the "astute reader," has, as already noted, aroused some suspicion about Lyman's motives in researching the Ward marriage, and he develops the theme quietly. We should look first to Lyman's sermons on the past. Initially, his explanations of history's "meanings" are directed at Shelley; he also directs monologues at the reader about his son the sociology professor, who will no longer listen to them himself. Lyman believes that a knowledge of history gives perspective, making radicalism naive. On those grounds, he rejects a multitude of contemporary movements from the aggressive social sciences to hippy communes. As his sermonizing continues, a suspicious pattern emerges—first, though his knowledge is extensive, he habitually overstates his case; second, he uses history like a club, directed always at others; and third, he is finally forced to admit that as his research and writing progress, he discovers (he may have known all along) that the Ward project is something more than a diversion, that he is looking for a specific answer to the problems of his own failed marriage, and not an answer that will repair it, but rather one that will justify his own conduct as honorable.

About a third of the way through the novel, Lyman's son comes as an emissary for his mother: Ellen Ward had run off with the surgeon who removed Lyman's diseased leg, and now she desires reconciliation. With characteristic bluster, Lyman rejects the idea. The attentive reader will later see the analogy between Lyman's and his grandfather's positions, and recall Lyman's admiration ("I refer my actions to his standards even yet.") Late in Lyman's account, we learn that Susan Ward, after more than a decade of wandering in the West, always aware and often ashamed of her husband's lack of culture and success, was unfaithful to him "in thought or act or both" (p. 503) (we can never know for sure) with his best friend. Here, the parallel Lyman wishes to make between his own marriage and his grandparents' is clear, and the narrative's early bias against Susan is explained. Lyman wants to believe that the Wards' only angle of repose was horizontal, the grave—that though they continued their marriage for nearly fifty years, Oliver never forgave her. Along with Lyman, the reader must judge the merits of Oliver's actions; independent of him, the reader should question Lyman's basic interpretation of the Ward marriage. Irony is the keyword to understanding Stegner's relationship with his narrator, and Lyman's notion that Oliver and Susan lived a kind of "cold war" marriage for half a century should be regarded with suspicion.

Lyman would have us believe they were reconciled because he must believe it himself. In doing so, he ignores the implications of several facts in his own narrative: one, that Oliver, after the 1890 separation, built Susan the beautiful house she had long dreamed of and made the very symbol of a different angle of repose than horizontal (Zodiac Cottage is so impressive that Lyman intends to donate it to the National Trust); and two, even before construction began, he planted a rose garden to replace the one in Idaho he had grimly uprooted to punish her for what he interpreted as evident adultery. Later, he worked a decade to perfect a rose he named Agnes, after a long-dead child, victim of negligence or perhaps that same guilt. Lyman thinks it very significant that they never spoke of that rose in his presence, as though that proved the flower a symbol of wounds still festering. He also fails to mention that by the time he was old enough to remember much about his grandparents' relationship, they were nearly eighty; his conclusions of angles he justifies with the memory that they did not seem very warm toward each other.

Yet our doubts would not matter much to Lyman, who judges evidence as best he can. Because we watch him while he searches the past, we see his limitations, and he becomes, as Stegner would say, not an unquestionable authority, but another one of us:

> In our wandering through the real fictional worlds it is probably ourselves we seek, and since that encounter is impossible we want the next best thing—the completely intimate contact which may show us another like ourselves.[15]

Lyman illustrates both the value and the hazards of such a course. He finally sees that Susan was not simply the victimizer in her marriage, but that there was a mutual lack of communication; mulish Oliver no more recognized his wife's discontent than Lyman saw Ellen's. By telling Susan's story in such detail, he has in effect lived Ellen's frustrations; his sympathy for Susan leaves him just one courageous, compassionate step from understanding his own life. If, in the end, he does not see everything—Oliver may have been a better man than his grandson suspects; he and Susan may have reached a separate peace—the old professor sees enough, for he considers facing a problem he himself had turned away from. He rests on his bed in the night, "wondering if I am man enough to be a bigger man than my grandfather," (p. 511) finding continuity a comfort and a challenge.

Stegner has given him a stiff neck, a leg and a half, social theories both inflexible and incomplete, and a son named Rodman who tries to bully him into a rest home. Lyman, it seems to me, is Stegner's response to critics with tunnel vision, and perhaps represents some authorial self-parody as well; he shares many of Stegner's reservations about contemporary life, but illustrates the dangers of prescriptive vision. Anyone who identifies him with his creator becomes guilty of that sin. Near the end of the novel, Stegner's ironic stance proves hilariously clear: Lyman comments predictably upon the Freudian interpretation "obvious" in Ellen's affair with the man who "dismasted" him, and later experiences a wild parody of Freudian dreams—bare-chested, buxom Shelley undresses him, his stump rises, but the climax is an explosive urination. This is not merely surrealism, however; it relates some of Lyman's preoccupations and a preview of the encounter with his wife he fears but in the end resolves to face. Behind it all, I sense Stegner, smiling.

From Stegner's point of view, it does not matter that Lyman cannot unravel the full truth; history is by definition inexact, and he refuses to undercut his narrator by providing external authority to detail how and where Lyman might have guessed wrong. Much of the reading enjoyment, in fact, comes from speculating. Yet Lyman is a formidable intellect, and can sustain himself as a convincing voice despite his prejudices and the irony Stegner makes at his expense. He carries on his main function, to picture the West as it probably was, with all its excesses and limitations, to view in Susan Ward the response of the cultured East (limited too, but significantly, she possesses resourcefulness and energy to rival her husband's), all without pandering to myths and stereotypes. The complexity and resonance of Lyman's "straight" narrative are impressive, and yet another subject. That Stegner can present both the contemporary and historical Wests in the same narrative with such complete control implies significant artistic growth. He has learned the value of detachment from Western history, a lesson he claims has been too long ignored by novelists of the region.

Notes

1. "Wallace Stegner: Trial by Existence," *The Southern Review*, IX, New Series (October, 1973), 796.

2. "Fiction: A Lens on Life," *Saturday Review*, 21 (April 22, 1950), 9.

3. In *The Sound of Mountain Water* (Garden City, N.Y.: Doubleday, 1969), pp. 170–171.

4. (Middletown, Connecticut, 1973), p. 550.

5. See *The Women on the Wall* (Boston: Houghton Mifflin, 1950), which includes five such stories.

6. *Wolf Willow* (New York: Viking, 1962), p. 306.

7. *"The Big Rock Candy Mountain:* No Roots—and No Frontier," *South Dakota Review*, IX (Spring, 1971), 3–6.

8. Wallace Stegner, *The Big Rock Candy Mountain* (New York: Simon & Schuster, Pocket Book ed., 1970), p. 27.

9. "Four Rocky Mountain Novels," *Rocky Mountain Review*, X (Autumn, 1945), 27.

10. Canzoneri, 803.

11. Canzoneri, 803.

12. Edward Twining, "Hung-Up on Virtue and Talent," *University of Denver Quarterly*, 6 (Winter, 1972), 106–113.

13. Stegner, in conversation, May, 1973.

14. Wallace Stegner, *Angle of Repose* (Greenwich, Conn.: Fawcett Crest ed., 1972), p. 67.

15. Stegner, quoted in Canzoneri, 827.

The Historical Ideal in
Wallace Stegner's Fiction

Barnett Singer*

In a period when historians have never been less sure of their art it is hard to speak of historical ideals or minds. But Wallace Stegner possesses the historian's requisite command of the concrete, and a historical vision unmarred by the tendency to mythologize. Few fiction writers show us, as Stegner does, that history matters; few, that chronology and literal facts about the past can be crucial to the novel. Why does Stegner possess this outlook? This is difficult to answer, but certainly there is in most of his novels an attempt to recover something—the milieus and people of his childhood, and, most importantly perhaps, a hated yet unforgettable father. By taking one's father's world seriously, and ingesting his past, one can, I believe, understand any past better. In fiction this permits an author like Stegner to impose historical limits upon his work.

Stegner's first major novel before *The Big Rock Candy Mountain* was, in my opinion, *On a Darkling Plain,* and the book is shot through with actual history. The action takes place in 1918, with World War I and the flu epidemic and major events involved. Even more pivotal in this novel than in *Big Rock Candy Mountain* or his own life, the epidemic is a symbol for what America was then trying to avoid—the ruined world created by the trench war. Stegner, writing on the eve of the Second World War, is thus probing the historical roots of American isolationism that persisted until Pearl Harbor. A major philosophical theme in this author's work is always the unavoidability of evil—history itself being a history of evils, a string of catastrophes that only vigilance prevents. The hero of *Darkling Plain* is a victim of mustard gas who, having vacated a bankrupt Europe for the quiet and peace of the prairies, finds, unavoidably, that he cannot stay out of life. He falls in love, and when the flu comes it unexpectedly takes away his special girl; and Vickers, the hero, subsequently converts back to involvement. The story, of course, reminds one of Camus' *The Plague*[1], also of Moravia's *La Ciociara* (inaccurately translated as *Two Women*). Such stories, in brief, are universal; how they are executed is the real test, and here Stegner does very well, Thickening the plot, he brings on the real danger in a slow, sure manner. The plague

*Reprinted from *South Dakota Review*, 1 (1977), 28–44.

travels like a train across the Midwest, enters Montana, hits Great Falls, and then Havre. Meanwhile in tandem, news of the final American offensives in the Argonne forests reaches this Canadian border village (Stegner's childhood area) where the action transpires. Finally it comes home, just as history would to all Americans after the halcyon period of the twenties was ended.

Problems of logistics take over with the flu. Where to find doctors, nurses, hospital space, supplies, gravediggers? Adeptly, Stegner switches from landscape writing to such specifics with no apparent difficulty, using an excellent eye for small detail. At the dead girl's funeral, for instance, we see "Ina's white pine coffin [with] frost on the heads of the nails."[2] Conferring importance upon such minutiae—things most take for granted—will be one of Stegner's enduring attributes, one that both good fiction writers and historians equally demonstrate.

What mars *Darkling Plain*, however, is its paltry scope. Characters are few though interesting, and the book is short—as sparse as the landscape. Perhaps its virtues and flaws are bound together.

The Big Rock Candy Mountain, Stegner's *David Copperfield*, was obviously written with an eye to removing this defect of scope. The book is nearly as endless as the West itself, but other problems creep in, as they usually do. Howard Mumford Jones calls *The Big Rock Candy Mountain* "a vast living untidy book," and Kerry Ahearn, in a recent article, views it as "a narrative of parts not unified by technique."[3] On the other hand there is something to be said for a good miss. Stegner's autobiographical novel may be flawed but it is a published document well worth reading, and the historical world it describes is a rich one. We have a West still holding its own against the coming of modernity, and ethnics in the process of becoming Americans—principally, Scandinavians of the plains caught between fjords and 100 per centness. Niggers are things you throw at in carnival booths; Chinks are pigtailed cooks one teases. Life is still violent and raw as the century cranks up, but the visual and aural stimuli now universal are just beginning to reach even the remotest areas. In *Big Rock Candy Mountain* Stegner has caught American rural history at a crucial point of equilibrium between its past and future: the boy Bruce (obviously Stegner) lives in a primitive town on the Saskatchewan-Montana border in the winter of 1918, yet hears the gravelly Harry Lauder and George M. Cohan on the gramophone and watches *Tarzan of the Apes* in installments at the movie house. Better than these artifacts of nostalgia is the feel you derive for minds unlike our own—minds which will not be reproduced. Stegner well depicts Bruce's youthful curiosity before paintings and his mother's gentle explanations of them. From the n'er-do-well father the boy hears Paul Bunyan and Hot Biscuit Slim stories, and improvised songs. Not to push the point too far, this sort of novel shows us all historically just how much of a certain self America has turned out—for good and ill.

Simultaneously, *Big Rock Candy Mountain* gains and loses by its slowness, with the baseball game near its beginning almost a metaphor for the whole book. Then as now ball games can be relaxing, but also dull. Stegner invites us to take our time and poke around in the furniture of the past, and some of that poking does feel good to the reader. When Elsa goes back to her house in Minnesota, we go with her:

> That house—the dark, quiet little parlor, the library table stacked with Norwegian newspapers, the glass-fronted bookcases full of sets, Ibsen, Bjrnson, Lie, Kjelland, the folksongs of Asbjrnson and Moe, the brass-and-leather Snorre, the patriotic *landsmaal* songs of Ivar Aasen—she knew the feel and look of everything there, . . .[4]

Here, there are some obvious historical lessons. As Louis Wright has shown how Anglo-Saxon culture was transported and transplanted out West,[5] perhaps it is time for other historians to study the cultured rural ethnics as well—the cultural larding in against isolation. Stegner also makes us understand that the immigrants did it for themselves, not for some grand thing called American pluralism and "aren't these just lovely little shops!" He shows us quite nakedly that the buck was uppermost in their minds—ethnic or non-ethnic; hence, the big rock candy mountain, or easy street. In fact he does not have to draw these lessons, for good history or fiction, by making them apparent in the drama, allows the reader to do so.

On another level Stegner's work fits into the Western formula. Bo Mason is the undisciplined type who yearns to wander, while Elsa is domesticating stability—a familiar, perhaps too familiar conflict. But in Bo we also have a typical American casualty to the spirit of do-it-yourself individualism, presaging Oliver Ward of *Angle of Repose*. Bo is a frustrated ball-player (with trick knee), then saloon owner, homesteader, goldminer, liquor runner. The second son Bruce pays for his frustrations.

Filling out the autobiographical resonances of *Big Rock Candy Mountain* and confirming them is Stegner's memoir cum history, *Wolf Willow* of 1962: all here again are the flu, the father, the Chinese cook induced to freeze his tongue on a doorknob, and the bleak country of the Cypress Hills region.[6] Ideally, *Wolf Willow* is read in conjunction with *Big Rock Candy Mountain;* what is interesting again is the contrast between 1918 and the second half of the twentieth century, the sheer accumulation of things our country has seen. It strikes me, for instance, that few new Bobby Hulls will spring fresh off outdoor farm rinks to stardom; in Stegner's Whitemud there is now a covered rink. No longer will a boy of twelve thrill at the sight of a bathtub or "W.C." as Stegner did; these things are now common. Each technological gain, as Daniel Boorstin shows, entails a narrowing of experience,[7] and Stegner now realizes he himself was lucky to be always catching up culturally—his fine phrase for it.[8]

The straight, expository writing of a book like *Wolf Willow* some-times moves a reader more than the over-written *Big Rock Candy Mountain*. Stegner is one of those unfortunates with a mind on the frontier of fiction and history, a person who loves mood and style but who also values objective historical fact. In history, as Bernard DeVoto found, such ambivalent types get the business from professionals, and as novelists, can be taxed with plodding literalism by critics.[9] But the worst problem is their own divided self. Stegner feels, for instance, that DeVoto wasted many years writing fiction when his style was more suited to the historical mode. As for Stegner himself, he has always been a novelist, but has also dabbled in history, most of it on Utah and very good. Finally, in *Angle of Repose* fiction and history are split down the middle. Once again this may be partly a matter of memory or of childhood—a person who can't divest himself of childhood trifles, as Stegner obviously can't, often remembers much else; and this kind of memory seems to be associated with a true sense of history.

As a child, Stegner had already had a divided consciousness. School and library were women's worlds to which he was attracted, but in the streets and with father the world was clearly masculine. Moreover, he was Canadian in winter, reading Toronto textbooks, singing God Save the King, playing ice hockey; and in summer was American—baseball, Fourth of July, New York magazines.[10] Then he lived in various parts of the West as a Scandinavian with no sure sense of roots (more of this later), and was exposed to a Mormon-dominated Utah. That this author writes both fiction and history, that he skillfully mixed modes, and that he writes as persuasively on the Mormons as he does on Whitemud or California perhaps reflects an elastic background.

Cultural awareness is on view in his one regional novel set outside the West, *Second Growth*. The scene is a summer New England resort town in the 1940's, with an amalgam including farmers before the freeways, Breadloafian Eastern intellectuals relaxing, and *Duddy Kravitz* Jews before the great surge uptown. There are several sub-plots, none too exciting, and a rural fellow going up to the city in the traditional manner. Just before T. V. Stegner fixes for us as well as most historians could an unspoiled spot in the East, not appreciably different, as one character says, from what it was in 1800.[11] He describes the village as follows:

> Back in the hills, too far off the roads for profitable farming, too far off for farm women to keep their sanity, too far for the school team or the snowplow to reach in bad weather, abandoned houses and barns the color of tarnished silver rotted slowly in the quiet, and every summer the goldenglow sprang up tall and yellow around their untrodden doors, and little by little the spruce marched in from the woods and engulfed the meadows, took them back (p. 67).

Andy, the boy off for the Ivy League and *déclassement*, can look over this landscape and see his forefathers who died in the Revolution or at Lundy's

Lane. History also figures in the thought of one of the Jewish characters, Abe Kaplan, whose exchanges with Ruth Liebowitz are a vehicle for Stegner's early thoughts on history versus the novel. According to Abe "storytelling is for children's bedtimes and silly women," (p. 43), and he reads John Reed on the Russian Revolution, the Beards, as well as *Middletown;* whereas Ruth vehemently defends the novel for its imaginative power.

One feels that Stegner had almost to sneak his history into his fiction, as historians like DeVoto snuck the mood of fiction into their history; and that one of his weaknesses as a novelist is that he compulsively marshals specifics like a historian, where, sometimes, he would do better to prune certain moments to pitch point. Particularly is this so in *Big Rock Candy Mountain,* virtually unfinishable without some skimming. Paradoxically, the historically-minded DeVoto embraced the moment over obligatory minutiae whenever he could. As he wrote to Garrett Mattingly, "When you get a scene, play it. I'd even sacrifice all the dispensable detail in order to get room for drama."[12] Of course when all goes ideally, both the accomplished fictionalist *and* historian use dramatic moments to resuscitate the past, as Saul Bellow did so well in *Mr. Sammler's Planet* or Samuel Eliot Morison does in his best work. The use of dramatic moments can be a heuristic element in saving the past, and Stegner, even though a novelist, sees a primary need of writing, and of Western writing in particular, as precisely this reclamation of the past. In a well-known essay he laments the fact that the West has no William Faulkner, and even wishes to place a candidature of himself, thoroughly aware of the difficulties. To Stegner, historical imagination must be kept alive to keep civilization in the American West (and elsewhere) from becoming "one gigantic anthill."[13]

His historical idealism, then, is a determined intellectual antidote to a bulldozed present. Nowhere is the problem more pressing than in California, the state in which he has mainly lived since 1946. His biographical-historical novel *Joe Hill* (originally entitled *The Preacher and the Slave*) took place in turn-of-the-century San Francisco, and its multiethnic drive is reminiscent of Stegner's prairie work—there are the same quaint Chinamen, Jews, and Cockneys, the same Scandinavian accents well mimicked by the author; but the novel could have easily been set in other port areas. In three novels of the 1960's and 70's, however, he finally confronts the new California or America of the suburbs. The first of the three novels, *A Shooting Star* (1961), depicts a heroine lost in a world of crisscrossing freeways and endless developments, and in that novel Stegner captures very well the hollowness of a suburban California dressed in fancy names:

> A street named for a shrub? They were all named for shrubs. From blurred street light to blurred street light the maze led her in circles and figure eights at whose re-entrant curves she found delusive names: Acacia,

Laurel, Laburnum, Palo Verde. They were all fictitious—they were all the same street.[14]

The story concerns a woman named Sabrina—even the human name exotic—who returns to her Bay Area home and, much like Stegner in *Wolf Willow*, finds her past obliterated. Anyone who has seen aerial photographs of San Jose circa 1950, filled with fruit trees, and the same place in 1965 as a welter of franchises can appreciate the theme. But the plot, despite adultery, lags a good deal, and Stegner's old problem of overwriting impairs the novel.

A turning point in his career came with *All the Little Live Things* (1967) and *Angle of Repose* (1972). These are tough fictions not submerged in style, and, coincidentally, they demonstrate more historical vision than any novels he had ever written. The Stegner who had always promised more than he delivered finally delivered a good deal.

The late sixties mix, of course, was a new one, and any writer worth his salt had to try to come to terms. Marijuana and a hopeless American war, Black Power and new consciousness, air pollution and the Mafia, adversary culture spread even among boobs, the latter once Babbits now "beautiful", all categories scrambled . . . it eluded precise analysis. What Stegner's main character in *Live Things* confronts head on is one late-sixties quality in particular, that of innocence. The innocent is a hippie named Jim Peck who squats on Joe Allston's land in the suburban Bay area, and who then proceeds to draw the youth and even some grown-ups of the neighborhood into his ken. Now I'm sure that Stegner does not oppose simple living—his admirable pro-wilderness essay in last year's Sierra Club calendar shows it. Where is the threat? The threat is Peck's apathy, his rejection of all rules, his desire for limitlessness, his simplicity—his innocence;[15] innocence more dangerous historically, suggests Stegner, than malicious intent. Joe (or Stegner?) uses all his wits to try and reconcile Peck to the civilization that clothes him, but as anyone knows who has argued with a frisbee-thrower living off the sun's kind rays the job is hopeless. Stegner's wit—this is the pity of the recent ambience—will mostly impress those who share his values.[16] For example.

> One at a time, in some coherent order and relationship, with discrimination and with some sense of the possible, I might take and approve most of the ingredients that went into the great underdone pizza of a Jim Peck's faith, but I didn't believe I could take them in combination, the mustard on the blueberry pie, the asparagus topped with chocolate ice cream.[17]

One would hope such a sense of humor might escape politicization, but probably it will not, for Stegner is taking on some of the central new pieties. His character mentions books where "love is about as romantic as a five-minute car wash," and disdains these new "theosophy-and-water faiths," a "University of the Free Mind," and so on (pp. 51, 155, 161). Such lines are bound to raise hackles. When you hear certain young people cheer at the humiliation of stiff Douglas Dumbrilles—meaning puritan Wasps—you do wonder at the fate of humor. Certainly the Dumbrilles are necessary foils for the Marx brothers, and of course that opposition is what produces comedy, so said Bergson; but a plain laugh at the contrast is different from one with clenched teeth.

Stegner, however, does produce his funniest novel here precisely because of such oppositions. The squatting hippie swings into his tree hut like an ape, while the bourgeois waters his flowers. (Actually Joe is a more sophisticated gardener than that implies.) At a hot-weather martini party, perfect grist for pot proselytizers' mills, Joe and other guests get tight while two Russians grimly take notes. The scene reminds one of Cheever's best, or of Flaubert's Emma Bovary at the agricultural fair. Yet Stegner goes beyond a Cheever because his main concern is not depiction but the reconciliation of philosophy against the facts. And that philosophy is that life matters, that things are serious (even humor), and that if we lose our sense of history we will lose much more in the process. Stegner's ideal of history is the novel's moral center. Morality and preachment can also kill a novel unless worked out in characters and plot, but let me show, with an extended quotation, how well he puts his arguments into opposing characters, believable on each side. The scene involves a woman dying of cancer named Marian, arguing for Jim Peck, or at least arguing tolerance; versus Joe Allston, who at the height of the dispute points to historical awareness and the lack of it as their key point of difference. A modern Paine versus Burke might not come out more interesting:

> "I feel sorry for young people [said Marian]. They seem to find it harder and harder to believe the world values them or has a place for them."
> "That's what comes of sneering at mere achievement. The world has a place for anybody who can do anything."
> "Joe," she said, "I think you *want* to keep your prejudice against that groping boy."
> "Groping!" I said. "Good God, he's the Mahatma, he's got the confidence of a road agent."
> "You think so? If he really felt that way would he have to keep on acting so sure of himself? I think he's as uncertain as he can be—look how he hunts and hunts through all those yeasty philosophies for something to believe in. I do feel sorry for him. People his age have every right to be appalled at the world they find themselves in, the bomb and all the rest of it."
> "Could Peck make a better world?" I said. "As for the bomb, I'm sick of the thing, hanging up there on its thread. It's no different from what's always hung there. And if anybody ever pushes the button, it'll be some nut like Peck, some wild-eyed enthusiast with no sense of history. It's his *temperament* I don't like—that True-Believer stance, and his faith in the emancipated individual. The whole history of mankind is social, not individual. We've learned little by little to turn human energy into social order. Outside the Establishment these kids despise so much, an in-

dividual doesn't exist, he hasn't got any language, character, art, ideas, anything, that didn't come to him from society" (p. 164).

Not to demean Marian's argument—for the boat *is* about full and the young *are* legitimately worried about placement—Joe wins this one because he takes the only realistic viewpoint available today: that one can't opt out. From at least Hegel's time to Norman O. Brown's, thinking men have wanted to jump out of history; not possible says Joe, with Stegner's obvious approval. In a letter to me the author put it nicely, comparing life to a coral reef that "didn't start yesterday." Further arguments would come from the very latest developments in cultural history. The counter-culture has now synthesized with both American business and the holy cult of pleasure, an interesting trinity. Long-hairs demonstrate ski turns to rock music at shopping centers financed by corporations while hard hats in chinos look on. No one escapes into ahistorical virginity.

Easy to say this on paper, of course, but as with Lyman Ward of *Angle of Repose*, Joe Allston has to struggle it out within himself. That makes the novel. For one, his own son had drowned (suicide?) after a fruitless life of searching, and the father who plumps for a sense of history had obviously failed to transmit it to his son. The boy had flitted from cause to cause including pacifism in World War II, and had never established roots. Even Joe himself has his problems in this department. As a child in Northfield, Minnesota, he had felt briefly Danish and much later "sniffed around" in Denmark for a sense of derivation, but ultimately derived little from his background (p. 195). This is a problem, I believe, peculiar to Nordic Americans who once found it relatively easier than others to assimilate, and who now find it difficult to trot out a buried heritage on demand. Stegner's own struggle with rootlessness, according to critics like Lois Phillips Hudson, is a perpetual problem in his work.[18]

The problem is compounded by the fact that he has mainly considered himself a Western writer. Western writers almost by definition have had to be historians, but the greater problem, according to Stegner, is putting together one's past and present.[19] And it is not easy to establish a sense of place or roots in the West. There is not even one writing capital—neither San Francisco nor Portland nor Salt Lake qualify.[20] The West, indeed, has always been many mini-Wests—in some parts of Eastern Washington fruit trees grow, and a scant twenty miles away they won't. So according to John Milton, "the far-flung materials need to be fused through the Coleridgean sense of the creative imagination":[21] he might equally have said "historical imagination." And the historical imagination not only becomes more elusive as the contemporary becomes universalized, but even seems gratuitous to its finest practitioners, legitimately worried about fading remnants. I think, for example, of A. B. Guthrie Jr., who recently concluded a speech in this manner: "My novels have been cast in a time known as the winning of the West. If I live to write another, it will be about the saving of it."[22]

This, however, is going far. Stegner's idea of putting together, or at least comparing, past and present is a viable one; and it has finally worked effectively in his most ambitious and multivarious novel to date, *Angle of Repose* (1971).

As Cyril Connolly once wrote in his exaggerated fashion, no writer should ever aim to write anything less than a masterpiece;[23] and if Stegner in *Angle of Repose* did not quite succeed in this, his high aim gave the book much worth. With Mary Hallock Foote's letters, now mostly published, he had ample material to exploit, and this is his most consciously professional novel of history. Its narrating character, Lyman Ward, is a crippled historian who had once won a Bancroft prize but who now in his declining years wants only to probe the life of his grandparents. The letters are there and the words, but what do they really say? Using the novelist's license, Lyman reads between the lines without missing the lines themselves. But his secretary, a bouncy young woman named Shelley, tends to laugh at what Lyman thinks tender in these lives of an almost prehistoric era; while for his son, Rodman, all such history is bunk. Rodman, a young sociologist, is perhaps too easy a target and Stegner may be overstating his case here, but as a historian who has seen the adverse effect of sociologizing (at the worst, eviscerating) the past, I share his prejudice. As the author writes caustically, "Rodman, like most sociologists and most of his generation, was born without the sense of history. To him it is only an aborted social science."[24] On the same page—the first page—Stegner counterposes in his narrator a Burkean respect for the historical organism: "I am much of what my parents and especially my grandparents were—inherited stature, coloring, brains, bones (that part unfortunate), plus transmitted prejudices, culture, scruples, likings, moralities, . . ." Near the end of the book he says in a similar vein: "God, those sociologists! They're always trying to reclaim a tropical jungle with a sprinkling can full of weed killer. Civilizations grow and change and decline—they aren't remade" (pp. 11, 463–64). Certainly these passages are strongly wordy, and too many such can constitute glibness, but the author avoids the trap.

His saving virtue is an industrious grasp of concrete things. Stegner's history of Susan Ward, talented Eastern woman on the frontier, and husband Oliver, talented engineer but slated to fail, is filled with tiny precisions about their times that do no violence to the actual atmosphere of early California or Idaho. There are many fine and varied descriptions—of Susan's outfits ("In that baldest of their bald frontiers at the very bottom of their fortunes, she dressed as if for a garden party") (p. 85); of Oliver's inventions, like an automatic garbage collector, so representative of nineteenth-century Jeffersons or Bordens; of flour-sack diapers (what *did* they do without diaper service out West?); and so on. Stegner also has an eye for outmoded belief systems—an eye that avoids the shoals of both irony and Lévi-Strauss primitive-worship. For example,

Susan Ward writes letters after childbirth with her eyes closed, in order not to damage them. None of this really goes beyond reporting the actual—which Stegner, the historian, obviously considers important *per se*—but as a novelist he must also strike off the typical.[25] For this purpose he mobilizes his imagination. A soundless world, without refrigerator or freeway buzz—how did it sound? (From one of Susan's letters: "I wish I could make you feel a place like Kuna. It is a place where silence closes about you after the bustle of the train, where a soft, dry wind from great distances hums through the telephone wires . . .") (p. 336). Marriage—how did one between a thwarted romantic and a realist last so long? Sex—how did it feel? The first night? For isolated neophytes? To whom a touch was electric? Stegner, answering, intrudes some wit but answer with wisdom:

> If I were a modern writing about a modern young woman I would have to do her wedding night in grisly detail. The custom of the country and the times would demand a description, preferably "comic," of foreplay, lubrication, penetration, and climax, and in deference to the accepted opinions about Victorian love, I would have to abort the climax and end the wedding night in tears and desolate comfortings. But I don't know. I have a good deal of confidence in both Susan Burling and the man she married. I imagine they worked it out without the need of any scientific lubricity and with less need to make their privacies public (p. 58).

More than this historical imagination, Stegner has plain historical savvy, which even some credentialed historians lack. With a viewpoint similar to Sir Lewis Namier's on eighteenth century England, he emphasizes the interconnections between frontier notables that made the settlers of the West far less individualistic than is often supposed. This give us food for revision of thought on Western history generally. As his Lyman says, "I am impressed with how much of my grandparents' life depended on continuities, contacts, connections, friendships, and blood relationships. Contrary to the myth, the West was not made entirely by pioneers who had thrown everything away but an axe and a gun (p. 35). Moral leaders were always there to fight anarchic tendencies, and, despite myths, Stegner suggests "there was never a time or place [the early West] where gentility, especially female gentility, was more respected" (p. 117).

The author also senses the importance that novels once had as a guide to nineteenth century conduct. Their displacement by various media and the diffusion of new moral standards are important historical transformations—transformations the author understands very well. His Susan Ward acts as heroines of novels then acted, and these novels help preserve her from adultery, for many then dealt with unfulfillable love.[26]

Susan Ward, gay, charming, creative, is a person cramped by her time and place—by the frontier, by her husband, and by mores of the period. She sketches and writes in this backwater; she goes for a walk with another man and pays for it—her daughter drowns. From then on her taciturn husband is almost totally silent. She stays; the main point is that she stays, *within* her time and place. Stegner, the novelist, might well have transposed her to more fertile ground; Stegner, the historian, could not do so. He wants the history to show through typical people bound by period and character.

Just as certain historical themes are worked out in the character of Susan, so others are illustrated in the career of her husband, Oliver. Oliver Ward is first and foremost a casualty of the age of growth in America, the age that created our leisure; and he corresponds to some of the real-life failures that Daniel Boorstin presents in his recent *The Americans: The Democratic Experience.* Just as Elias Howe came before his time and Isaac Merritt Singer received credit for the sewing machine (partly thanks to the Civil War and the need for mass-produced clothing), so Ward's great engineering schemes come to naught. It is at once a problem of moment and one of character. Lacking assertiveness and capitalistic know-how, Oliver allows the salesmen to absorb him—something that occurs time and time again in the history of inventions. Stegner's character is made to employ the term "talkee-talkee" for exactly what he lacks; others who possessed it

> would later take his formula, which he characteristically had not patented or kept to himself, and tear down the mountains of limestone and the cliffs of clay, grind them and burn them to clinker, add gypsum, and grind and roll clinker together into the finest powder for making of bridges, piers, dams, highways, and all the works of Roman America that my grandfather's generation thought a part of Progress (p. 168).

This is the kind of Stegnerian sentence that combines history and the novel in a most effective manner. If John Milton (of England) said the wise man refines gold from all kinds of books, *Angle of Repose* is a book containing enough such nuggets to make any man wise. One likes the factualness of Stegner's description quite as much as its sweep, and the quality of a writer-historian who misses neither the small nor the large, neither character nor structural background.

But if Stegner is a novelist with a historical sense, he *is* a novelist—he knows his base, as one must; and if anything mars the novel *Angle of Repose* it is in fact too *much* history. By this I mean not merely detail, but the long excerpts from Susan's letters that are meant to convey historical atmosphere. For the most part Stegner succeeds in doing that, but he should have deleted more pages. This is an age of impatience and novelists must accommodate to that fact, if not acquiesce. Rather than so much on each magazine article Susan sold or each knick-knack she added to her cabin, one would have welcomed more taut passages that catch large and small in one brush stroke. For example, Susan Ward standing over a mine:

It terrified her to think that the whole riddled mountain crawled with men like that one. Under her feet as she walked in sunshine, under her stool and umbrella as she sat sketching, under the piazza as she rocked the baby in his cradle, creatures like that one were swinging picks, drilling holes, shoveling, pushing ore cars, sinking in cages to ever deeper levels, groping along black tunnels with the energy of ants (p. 120).

With a combination of impressionism and realism, and contrasting perspectives, this passage recalls the best of *Germinal* or *Hard Times*.[27] Stegner is really at his best when he turns the obvious in history—the things we shouldn't forget but do—into exciting art. One last example:

Death and life were everyday matters to Grandmother. The breeding of horses, mules, cattle, the parturition of dogs, the smug and polygamous fornications of chickens, raised no eyebrows. When animals died, the family had to deal with their bodies; when people died, the family's women laid them out. In the 1880s you suffered animal pain to a degree no modern would submit to. You bore your children, more likely than not, without anesthetic (p. 401).

To repeat, *Angle of Repose* is dense with such nuggets, but it is also just *dense*; and the ordinary reader may tire even of the splendid passages.

Which would be a shame. This is an age when it is very hard to get read, yet Stegner is wise enough to deserve our attention. His ideals, of which the historical is only one, are vacillating, and he is not ultimately sure of them. He has trouble reconciling the ideal with the facts but that does not negate his idealism. Genuinely worried about discontinuity despite saucy pages on the generation gap; and taking seriously what J. H. Plumb calls the death of the past, he never defends history by relapsing into mere antiquarianism. Stegner has allowed a genuine anxiety about the value of history to give his fiction its unique philosophical stamp and quality.

Notes

1. See Merrill and Lorene Lewis, *Wallace Stegner* (Boise: Boise State College Western Writers Series, 1972), p. 12.

2. Stegner, *On a Darkling Plain* (New York: Harcourt, Brace, 1939, 1940), p. 200.

3. Jones cited in Lewis, *Wallace Stegner*, p. 15; Kerry Ahearn, "The Big Rock Candy Mountain and Angle of Repose," *Western American Literature*, 10 (Spring, 1975), 19.

4. Stegner, *The Big Rock Candy Mountain* (New York: World Publishing Company, 1945; originally published 1943), p. 155.

5. Louis Wright, *Culture on the Moving Frontier* (New York: Harper Torchbook, 1961).

6. Kerry Ahearn calls *Big Rock Candy Mountain* a "son's book," and *Wolf Willow* is the last of Stegner's books that remains wholly within that perspective. Ahearn, "Big Rock Candy Mountain," 19.

7. Boorstin first adumbrated this idea in *The Image: A Guide to Pseudo-events in American Life* (New York, 1961), *passim*.

8. Stegner, *Wolf Willow: A History, a Story, and a Memory of the Last Plains Frontier* (New York: Viking, 1962), pp. 24–25. On the latter page he adds that "anyone starting from deprivation is spared getting bored."

9. This has happened to Stegner, according to Robert Canzoneri. Canzoneri, "Wallace Stegner: Trial by Existence," *The Southern Review*, 9 (October, 1973), 796–797.

10. These details are found in *Wolf Willow*, pp. 81–83.

11. Stegner, *Second Growth* (Boston: Houghton Mifflin, 1947), p. 57.

12. Quoted by Stegner in "On the Writing of History," *The Sound of Mountain Water* (Garden City, N. Y., 1969), p. 221.

13. Stegner, "History, Myth, and the Western Writer," in *The Sound of Mountain Water*, p. 198.

14. Stegner, *A Shooting Star* (New York: Viking Press, 1961), p. 91.

15. Professor John Sisk of Gonzaga has spoken to these problems better than anyone else in articles that have appeared in *Commentary* and *American Scholar*.

16. Richard Hofstadter calls these shared values a "comity," in the concluding pages of *The Progressive Historians: Turner, Beard, Parrington* (New York: Vintage edition, 1970).

17. Stegner, *All the Little Live Things* (New York: Viking, 1967), pp. 109–110.

18. Lois Phillips Hudson, "The Big Rock Candy Mountain: No Roots—and No Frontier," *South Dakota Review*, 9 (Spring, 1971), 6, 9.

19. "Conversation with Wallace Stegner" (John Milton interview), *South Dakota Review*, 9 (Spring, 1971), 53.

20. See "Conversations," p. 20.

21. John R. Milton, "The American West: A Challenge to the Literary Imagination," *Western American Literature*, 1 (Winter, 1967), 284.

22. A. B. Guthrie Jr., "Why Write About the West?" *Western American Literature*, 7 (Fall, 1972), 169.

23. Cyril Connolly, *The Unquiet Grave: A Word Cycle* (New York: Harper Colophon edition, 1973), p. 1.

24. Stegner, *Angle of Repose* (Greenwich, Conn.: Fawcett Crest, 1972), p. 11.

25. I coined this term "striking off the typical" then read later in Stegner ". . . history reports the actual, fiction the typical." Stegner, "On the Writing of History," *Sound of Mountain Water*, p. 205.

26. He calls them "novels full of hopeless and enduring loves too lofty for treacherous thoughts or acts." "On the Writing of History", p. 400. Julien Sorel of the *Red and the Black*, as well as many other romantic heroes, acted according to literature. Goethe's *Werther* inspired countless suicides.

27. I also think of the middle-class lady with bored headaches contrasted to starving workers in Elizabeth Gaskell's *Mary Barton*, on Manchester in the 1840's.

The Big Rock Candy Mountain:
No Roots—and No Frontier

Lois Phillips Hudson*

Perhaps more than any other living American writer, Wallace Stegner embodies in his work and in his own life the cardinal fact of Western America in the Twentieth Century—namely, that our rootlessness has never had the compensation of frontier opportunity. The frontier was mostly myth, even some years before Frederick Jackson Turner proclaimed it so in 1890, and for a man of Stegner's broad vision and deep understanding, building an edifice of fiction upon fiction created problems which, it seems to me, shaped both his writing and his view of life itself. For rootlessness is bearable for most human beings only on the condition that it leads to material, social, and psychological stability. (Stegner would put cultural stability at the head of that list.) And though Stegner's own material rootlessness has long since ended in a long and happy association with Stanford University, he has, by his own repeated admission, never ceased to feel himself a cultural anachronism.

The artistic analogy with the lack of material opportunity in a non-frontier, then, is that the serious Western writer may feel, as Stegner seems to feel, that an ersatz frontier has not provided him with a richness that can compensate for the deprivation of cultural roots. Indeed, Stegner has reiterated aspects of this idea in his fiction and essays for thirty years. In his essay "Born a Square," included in *The Sound of Mountain Water* (1969), Stegner begins, "The thesis of this piece is that the western writer is in a box with booby traps at both ends," and he goes on to ask: "Why . . . should western books so often strike us as dealing with a past which has no present? Why haven't Westerners ever managed to get beyond the celebration of the heroic and mythic frontier?"[1]

It seems to me that Stegner answers his own question in the asking of it: That is, we cannot escape the myth precisely *because* the frontier always was much more myth than fact, as Stegner himself has observed elsewhere, and the history of a myth will always be just that—the history of a myth. And without a real history on which to build our own myths, we feel constantly obliged to discover and rediscover and prove the literal:

*Reprinted from *South Dakota Review*, 9 (Spring, 1971), 3–13.

> We have all written books that deal with the settlement and the mythic past, the confrontation between empty land and imported populations, which is the salient historical fact about the West, as about America at large. We have all found it difficult or impossible to make anything of the contemporary West except as articles for *Holiday*, and when we have finished our most personal books, we have taken refuge in history, fictionalized or straight (p. 178).

Thus, writing *The Big Rock Candy Mountain* was not enough. In his later essays, Stegner seems to go out of his way to tell us that the details in the novel are "real," "true." He has an extreme need, it seems to me, to tell us how precisely Bruce Mason is Wallace Stegner. They were both sickly, thin, "puny," "crybabies," lacking in the particular "masculine" qualities necessary for acceptance in frontier Whitemud, "mamma's boys" who had read all of the volumes of Ridpath's *History of the World* by the time they were eight—and they both even had their collarbones broken when their fathers "knocked [them] end over end across the woodbox." And Bo Mason is precisely Stegner's father, agonizingly scornful of his younger son (Stegner and Bruce are, of course, both by about two years the younger in a family of two boys), "big and dark," and always singing and cleverly improvising songs. Stegner is likely to tell us, years after the novel was published, that even very minor characters did, in fact, exist. In the novel, Elsa tells Bruce about Edna Harkness, who would get drunk in Whitemud and pull off her clothes to prove that "she wasn't ashamed of her shape." More than a decade later, he tells us about the real Edna Harkness, after he has "smelled" his way back to "Whitemud."[2]

The landscape of the novel is likewise a roadmap of Stegner's years in Whitemud, from the house on the "Whitemud" (Frenchman) River to the homestead on the Montana-Canadian border, with the Bearpaw Mountains to the south—those mountains the boy longed for, and finally was taken to in the family Ford. (This is a section of *TBRCM*, pp. 204, ff., often reprinted.) But though Stegner describes and feels the enormous and enormously varied western landscape as well as, or better than, any living Western writer (in *Wolf Willow* he tells us that instead of "culture" he experienced the boyhood of "a sensual little savage"), has the trek from Manitoba to the California Coast Range, by way of the Wasatch and the Sierra Nevada, given us a landscape that approaches the mythical size of Yoknapatawpha County, or of the relatively (in terms of actual square miles) tiny wilderness in which Roger Malvin lies buried? This is the sort of question Eastern critics like to ask, and that Western writers seem always to be trying to answer in terms of the literal truth of the hugeness of the West. (This summer an Eastern friend of mine, who has a Ph.D., has traveled to Europe many times, visited me in Seattle. She had the impression that she would travel *north* to see the redwoods. And Eastern critics drink martinis at 30,000 feet and doze across the West.)

And when a writer grows up in landscape unimaginably huge and rugged, compared to that of his literary ancestors, and in a cultural myth, what is left to him except to meet the myth and try to wrestle it, like Jacob, into truth? Literal truth. Stegner says of himself in *Wolf Willow*.

> I had grown up in this dung-heeled sagebrush town on the disappearing edge of nowhere, utterly without painting, without sculpture, without architecture, almost without music or theater, without conversation or languages or travel or stimulating instruction, without libraries or museums or bookstores, almost without books. I was charged with getting in a single lifetime, from scratch, what some people inherit as naturally as they breathe air (p. 24).

So he started, in *The Big Rock Candy Mountain*, to build, not a myth on a myth, but truth "from scratch." He felt compelled to literal accuracy, because otherwise he could be nothing but an anachronism—rootless, doomed to die before ever even becoming part of what critics like to call "a viable tradition." Homer could build on what Schliemann proved to be literal truth. And though Faulkner had, by comparison with Homer, a short time to create Yoknapatawpha County, he had, by Western American time, a long 104 years between the birth of great-grandfather Col. William C. Faulkner and his fictional reincarnation as Colonel Sartoris. And there was, behind Faulkner, what we restless Westerners might view as a crushing legacy of literalness—aristocracies, genealogies.

Western writers seem to be charged with the double burden of dispelling myth and then building fiction on the fact they must first insist upon. It is a heavy burden. Stegner says, in speaking of the disparity between the space in which he grew up and its infinitesimal history:

> In general, the assumption of all of us, child or adult, was that this was a new country and that a new country had no history. History was something that applied to other places. . . . Time reached back only a few years. . . . So the world when I began to know it had neither location nor time, geography nor history. . . . History? Seldom anywhere, have historical changes occurred so fast. From grizzlies, buffalo, and Indians still only half possessed of the horse and gun, the historical parabola to Dust Bowl and near-depopulation covered only about sixty years. Here was the Plains frontier in a capsule, condensed into the life of a reasonably long-lived man (pp. 28, ff.).

William Faulkner could say that he "sought to create out of the materials of the human spirit, something which did not exist before," but he never was faced with Stegner's rootlessness. How does a writer create something which did not exist before if he is not sure of his own past existence? In "The Question Mark in the Circle" (included in *Wolf Willow*), Stegner says, referring to such events as the ice-jam destruction of the Canadian Pacific Railroad bridge, described at length in the novel:

> I have used those memories for years as if they really happened, have made stories and novels of them. Now they seem uncorroborated and

delusive. . . . I am afflicted with the sense of how many whom I have known are dead, and how little evidence I have that I myself have lived what I remember (p. 15).

The great-grandson of Col. William C. Faulkner could hardly have been afflicted by such lack of evidence. The Colonel's descendants were all around, towns were named by them, or for them.

I belabor the obvious because Stegner has felt forced to do so, and because, it seems to me, any serious Western writer still must do so. We must establish fact, which is a hard job, since the television myths, among others, are still so pervasive, for we cannot erect fiction on fiction. At least we know of no precedent in literature for such an edifice. Holinshed may have written a great deal of fiction, but Shakespeare could build on him without fear of the kind of repudiation that Whitemud was born in: ". . . between the Frenchman and Milk [rivers] the boundary line was pushed through the carrion stink of a way of life recklessly destroying itself. . . . an ecology still furiously vital on the very eve of its extinction" (pp. 95, 96).

Holinshed's history was based on stories received by his readers as fact, but more importantly, it was set in a landscape understandable, if not known, to tens of thousands, for centuries. Hardly so with Whitemud, or any other Western place, where history was constantly eclipsed by geography. And this disparity between the spatial hugeness of the West and its relatively minuscule history—at least as time and space are perceived in human terms—has probably never been more deeply felt nor closely observed than it has by Wallace Stegner. So he goes back, insists again and again on fact, on autobiographical fact, for he himself is the only verifiable fact. Look for a minute at what the less sensitive, or less literate, Westerner makes of the geographical facts of our continent, which seem to astound alike both Europeans and Eastern Americans. The farther west one drives, the larger grow the plaster Paul Bunyans, each having proclaimed itself at its erection as "the tallest Paul Bunyan." They start in Michigan and Wisconsin, hardly "West" to Stegner, but still very far west to Eastern keepers of culture, who generally go to Europe on their vacations. (The East, it is true, first gave us Paul Bunyan, but so long ago that most Westerners find the idea surprising. Paul Bunyan has been dead in the East for some time now.)And beginning in Colorado, or even farther east, there are the Where-the-West-Begins plaster cowboys, till finally the parched driver, having crossed the Great Salt Desert of dry Utah (in little more than an hour, instead of the dreadful week of the Donner party), beholds like a monstrous mirage the beckoning electric arm of the towering winking cowpuncher at the Wendover state line—welcome to the first bar in Nevada. And finally the assiduous collector of "roadside attractions" reaches The World's Largest Animated Paul Bunyan in the Northern California redwoods. On the way there, he can, of course, drive his Detroit car (Detroit is very far East, in the West) through the trunks of any number of "living Redwoods."

But tall as he is, the cowboy at the Utah state line is ridiculously small against the bit of a foothill that rises up westward behind him. And the Paul Bunyan, with his animated axe, red shirt, and blue stagged pants, is nothing more than an affront, in his motel yard, to the three-hundred-foot redwoods living their ancient lives a hundred yards beyond the motel fence. The winking cowboy could put all of Homer's landscape in his skinny hip pocket. And Dante and Milton could be buried, with literal room to spare, in a single open-pit Utah copper mine. (Or a single Minnesota iron mine.)

When the landscape is so much larger than the myth, how does the writer see himself? He sees himself, as Stegner says, a being which "the world still reduces . . . to a point and then measures itself from me" (p. 19). And he gives us, in *The Big Rock Candy Mountain*, Bruce Mason's search as he drives west from law school in Minneapolis to still another new "home"—one he has never seen, a cottage his father is building on Lake Tahoe: "Where is home? Maybe it's Minnesota, because my mother came from here. . . . and second and third cousins, and great-aunts and great-uncles, in a dozen towns where Norwegian is still spoken as much as English. Does that make Minnesota home?"[3]

But already, as Bruce muses on Minnesota, he is driving West, through North Dakota, where his parents met in the mythical town of Hardanger. And here it seems appropriate to refer to Stegner's earlier Hardanger, and to his most recent evocation of that place, under another name. In *Wolf Willow* Stegner describes his yearning to place himself in time and space:

> [I] wanted a past to which I could be tribally and emotionally committed. . . . I had to fall back . . . upon Norway (my maternal grandfather and grandmother had emigrated from it). . . . All through my childhood I signed my most personal and private books and documents with the Norwegian name that my grandfather had given up on coming to America. It seems to me now an absurdity that I should have felt it necessary to go as far as the Hardanger Fjord for a sense of belonging (p. 112).

In *All the Little Live Things*, published in 1967, twenty-four years after *The Big Rock Candy Mountain*, Joe Allston, an unusually literate and sensitive retired success, seeking peace in the farthest mountains of California, speaks of his own search:

> At past sixty . . . I could find no place that was mine. The crisscrossing trails of my mother's life had confused all the scents. In the end, we made, one after the other, the two moves that are possible to Americans and lost dogs. We smelled our way back to the old country [as Stegner smelled "wolf willow" and found the "Whitemud" of three decades ago?] and

sniffed for a while around Copenhagen and around the little island of
Taasinge . . . where my mother was born. . . . I didn't smell one thing
that was familiar or that meant anything personal. . . . So we did the
other thing that Americans and lost dogs can do, we quit trying to
backtrack and went forward. We turned our backs on everything
remembered and came out to make a new beginning in California. It
wasn't a radical act, in a way. It was a habitual one, it conformed to
twenty generations of American experience.[4]

Joe Allston "went forward," which meant going from the East Coast
to the West Coast. That was what Bruce Mason, in *The Big Rock Candy
Mountain*, was doing, driving through North Dakota, where he experiences a rare sensation of connection with a recognizable past. He has a
moment of seeing himself as his mother, "Elsa Norgaard of Hardanger."
But he drives on through an Americana that is as oppressive as ever
Humbert Humbert's was, and he renounces North Dakota as "home"
because it is not far enough West. Driving on alone in the night he tell
himself:

I'll take it. I love it, whatever good that does. Even if I don't know where
home is, I know when I *feel* at home. . . . Anything beyond the Missouri
was close to home, at least. He was a westerner, whatever that was . . .
As long as the road ran west he didn't want to stop, because that was
where he was going, west beyond the Dakotas toward home (p. 458).

Hardanger Fjord "seemed an absurdity" to Stegner, after sending
Elsa and Bruce to the fictional Hardanger; yet he sent Joseph Allston to
Taasinge in 1967. (Minus a few fictional years.)

And since there are no roots in Taasinge, either, Joe Allston tries
desperately to find them in his seemingly secure retirement in the Coast
Range a few miles from Palo Alto—very near, indeed, to Stegner's own
home. Allston plants and plants; he *wills* flowers, trees, shrubs to root
around him. Yet he encounters nothing but anarchy, mutilation and
death—the ineluctable consequences of rootlessness and anachronism.
Always, like Webster, Stegner has seen "the skull beneath the skin;/And
breastless creatures under ground."[5] Indeed, some of the strongest images
of death are identical, confronting (in their order of publication) first
Stegner-Bruce Mason, then the reminiscent Stegner, then Stegner-Joe
Allston. Both Bruce and Stegner lose a colt with a broken leg. Allston must
preside over the killing of a horse with *all four* legs broken. Both Bruce
Mason and Allston must watch a loved woman die of breast cancer, and
one feels, somehow, that at least in the case of Elsa, there is a connection
between her search for freedom and the final "anarchy."

In the first chapter of *The Big Rock Candy Mountain*, Elsa Norgaard
is traveling West to Hardanger: "The train was rocking through wide
open country before she was able to put off the misery of leaving and
reach out for the freedom and release that were hers now." But Elsa finds
little freedom in a disordered life with Bo Mason, and she dies "breastless"

before she is even "under ground." Bruce see the beginning and the end of "this way of life":

> . . . she was contemplating the battleground of her own body, warring cells going crazy, multiplying, proliferating, spreading and crowding out the healthy cells, leaving her less and less of herself. A body completely replaces itself in seven years, but that was done to pattern, according to a plan. This was something else, an insane crowding of formless hostility, a barbarian invasion, blotting out the order and the form and the identity (p. 476).

The last sentence of this description of cancer could also describe the hippie group that is squatting on Allston's property in *All the Little Live Things,* providing one of the major social manifestations of the anarchy and mutilation all around as Marian Catlin dies:

> . . . in the organs and blood stream of the girl who liked the hard and painful things because they could so persuade her she was fully alive, and who believed the universe began in order and proceeded toward the perfection of consciousness, the stealthy cells, rebellious against the order that had created them, went on splitting to form their fatal isotopes (p. 214).

The Catlins had come to California for Marian's health. Stegner, the literal Western writer, tells us just how golden are the promises of the Golden Gate, where the seekers of freedom and life have flocked since 1849. (My own great-great-grandmother died of tuberculosis in San Jose in that year of the great migration, having crossed, by wagon, most of the continent in search of health.)

The anarchy surrounding Marian's death is overwhelming. The hippies have completely corrupted the teen-aged sons and daughters of Allston's neighbors. It is while Allston is driving Marian to the hospital that the horse breaks its legs in a plank bridge they must cross. And as for the material promise of the frontier, a "developer" is the only one who collects:

> That was the afternoon when Tom Weld drove his caterpillar across the tottering bridge and began tearing great wounds in the hill. We saw him as we walked slowly home from our afternoon visit, and full of the bitterness of being able to do not one thing for Marian, we took refuge in fury at that barebacked Neanderthal and his brutish machine. I associated his mutilation of the hill with the mutilations that Marian had suffered and was still to suffer . . . we could no more resist the laws of property . . . and Weldian notion that mutilation was progress, than we could stop the malignant cells from metastasizing through Marian's blood stream (p. 262).

And as the Allstons return from Marian's funeral, on an October day, they see that a cherry tree Joe has been nursing is blooming out of season because it is dying. Here it still is—the anarchy of the West which makes anachronisms of Westerners, restricts us to the literal, loses us in that sunset we have sought since the migrations of our Gothic ancestors. But the dream of the Bo Masons and Joseph Allstons does die hard, like the snake we all remember, which some brave boy has killed. It lies wriggling after its skull is crushed and its slim perfection is mangled—wriggling still. And the boy assures us that it is really dead, but that it won't die till the sun sets.

The Western father and his son met only once on common ground. Bruce Mason's only affectionate memory of his father occurs when he recalls:

> . . . the great snake his father had killed by the roadside, and the gopher that had come slimy and stretched from the snake's mouth, and the feeling he had had then was like the feeling he had now: it was a good thing to have been along and seen, a thing to be remembered and told about, a thing that he and his father shared (p. 563).

They shared, in other words, death. Otherwise, the frontier was a place of confused isolation. Bruce muses on his father:

> In an earlier time, under other circumstances, he might have become something the nation would have elected to honor, but he would have been no different. He would always have been an undeveloped human being, an immature social animal, and the further the nation goes the less room there is for that kind of man (pp. 561–562).

Bo Mason was one kind of anachronism, Stegner was another. Perhaps it is not unfair to say that Stegner's thoughts of himself as an anachronism reach the point of genuine obsession:

> The accident of being brought up on a belated, almost symbolic frontier has put me through processes of deculturation, isolation, and intellectual schizophrenia that until recently have been a most common American experience *(Wolf Willow,* p. 22).

> We have had our own grain, and our knots as well, but prairie and town did the shaping, and sometimes I have wondered if they did not cut us to a pattern no longer viable (p. 24).[6]

And when Bo Mason understood, at last, that he was an anachronism, there was nothing left but suicide. Bruce see his father

> . . . always chasing something down a long road, always moving on from something to something else. At the very end, before that fatal morning, he must have looked down his road and seen nothing, no Big Rock Candy Mountain, no lemonade springs, no cigarette trees, no little streams of alcohol, no handout bushes. Nothing. The end, the empty end, nothing to move toward because nothing was there (p. 552).

That, of course, is what the Mission District winos and the suicides who sometimes come all the way across the continent to fling themselves from the Golden Gate Bridge have found out. Only in death did Bo Mason find order and continuity. Bruce found, going through his father's papers, that at the end of a chaotic life the "old man" had left everything neatly arranged—the last of his bills paid up, including his burial insurance, and the last of his materialistic vision of the Big Rock Candy Mountain, consisting of

> One pair of worn shoes, one worn suit, a dozen spotted neckties, a third interest in a worthless mine, [and] a cemetery lot with perpetual care (p. 556).

Notes

1. *The Sound of Mountain Water* (Garden City, N.Y.: Doubleday, 1969), p. 16.

2. *Wolf Willow* (New York: Viking Compass edition, 1966), p. 18. (It has seemed unnecessary to cross-footnote all the corresponding details between Stegner's reminiscences in these two books and the novel.)

3. *The Big Rock Candy Mountain* (New York: Hill and Wang, American Century Series edition, 1968), p. 458.

4. *All the Little Live Things* (New York: Signet edition, 1968), p. 165.

5. T. S. Eliot, "Whispers of Immortality."

6. *Wolf Willow*, p. 24.

Western Fiction and History:
A Reconsideration

Richard W. Etulain*

Serious study of western American literature is of recent origin.† Not until the 1960s did scholars organize a group devoted to the examination of the literature of the American West. Such well-known authorities as Franklin Walker, Bernard DeVoto, and Henry Nash Smith had published significant works on western writing, but few scholars followed the trails they blazed.

But in the 1960s and 1970s a new interest in western literature has arisen. The Western Literature Association was organized in 1965 and began sponsoring the journal *Western American Literature*. Five years later the Southwestern Literature Association was organized and launched its journal, *Southwestern American Literature*. Meanwhile, a national group, the Popular Culture Association, commenced in 1967 and founded the *Journal of Popular Culture*. These three associations and their magazines have provided a powerful impetus for students and scholars interested in doing research on western authors and their works. Although scholarly study of western literature still lags behind serious historical research on the West, literary studies have increased appreciably in number—and in merit—since the 1960s. For the first time one can speak of western American literature as a subject that is attracting a large number of competent scholars.[1]

Some of these interpreters have begun to discuss such large questions as, What is the nature of the literary West? Is there a single outlook that unifies western literature, or are there several dominant themes? The first answers to these and other significant questions indicate no unanimity of approach or findings. In fact, the plethora of research methods and the variety of opinions about western literature demonstrate that scholars have not come to similar conclusions about the subject. Nonetheless, without overemphasizing agreement, one can distinguish a few points of view that dominate research about western writing.

*Reprinted from *The American West: New Perspectives, New Dimensions*, edited by Jerome O. Steffen (1979) University of Oklahoma Press, 152–174.

†I am indebted to the Idaho State Research Committee and the American Philosophical Society for grants that made possible the research for this chapter.

The oldest thesis has its roots in early American history and reflects a conflict that arose between seaboard and backcountry areas of the first colonies. Frontiersmen were convinced that their eastern brethen dismissed them as illiterate barbarians innocent of any cultural attainments. Whether that conviction was accurate is still being debated, but many westerners considered it to be correct.

The idea of the frontier or the West as a colonial culture has continued into the present era. During the first thirty years of this century the southwestern novelist Eugene Manlove Rhodes argued heatedly against considering the West as culturally inferior. Near the end of Rhodes's life the western historian-novelist-essayist and general disturber of the peace Bernard DeVoto took up the battle for the West, sometimes from Harvard Yard and sometimes from the editorial offices of *Saturday Review* and *Harper's*. DeVoto spoke of the West as a "plundered province" and implied in several of his works that the East too often dominated the culture of the West and tended to emasculate the freshness and uniqueness of its literature. Robert Edson Lee argued the same point in his stimulating book *From West to East: Studies in the Literature of the American West* (1966). Others have championed this view—for example, Vardis Fisher, the best of Idaho's authors, and several leading interpreters of western American literature.[2]

A second approach to western literature follows closely the ideas and research methods in Henry Nash Smith's pathbreaking book *Virgin Land: The American West as Symbol and Myth* (1950). Smith emphasized the importance of understanding the myths about the West that many Americans came to believe in the nineteenth century. He argued that students must scrutinize these patterns of thought as they clustered around three themes: "A Passage to India," "The Sons of Leatherstocking," and "The Garden of the World." In the years since its publication *Virgin Land* has had more impact than any other study upon students of the literary West, especially those who received their training in departments of American studies or popular culture. Scholars have been particularly drawn to his discussions of Cooper's fiction, the heros and heroines of the dime novel, and imaginative writings about western agriculture.[3]

A third thesis has become increasingly popular since 1960. Proponents of this view contend that the literature of the American West is primarily a land-oriented and nonrational literature, that it is akin to the philosophies of many Native Americans, that it is Jungian rather than Freudian, and that its books are (to use the terminology of critic Richard Chase) more often mythic *romances* than realistic *novels*. If one centers his attention on the work of such western writers as Frank Waters, Walter Van Tilburg Clark, and John Steinbeck and the western poet Gary Snyder, he finds a good deal to support this point of view. If one reads much recent commentary on western American literature, he will realize how pervasive this thesis is. Among others, the editors of the two most important scholarly journals dealing with the American literary West, *South Dakota Review* and *Western American Literature,* are advocates for this view.[4]

A fourth group of interpreters stresses the importance of viewing the West as an arid and spacious environment. Wallace Stegner, for example, argues that in the interior West aridity and openness are the major forces shaping writers and their work. As he points out, the westerner has difficulty finding himself "in any formed or coherent society. . . . His confrontations are therefore likely to be with landscape, which seems to define the West and its meaning better than any of its forming cultures, or with himself in the context of that landscape."[5] Several other scholars have noted that on occasion western writers have been so enthralled with their awesome environment that they have fallen into overly romantic descriptions of setting or have limited their plots to conflicts between men and nature.[6]

These four theses are important for a broad understanding of western literature. They augment our comprehension of a new and intriguing subject. But I should like to point to another significant emphasis in western fiction, one that has not received sufficient attention. This is the noticeable tendency among many western novelists to search for a useful or usable past. In common parlance, western writers have a hangup on history. At the center of their work is a concern for understanding the western past and for communicating the connections or continuities between past and present. It would be incorrect to argue that this is *the* most important theme of western literature; it is equally mistaken to omit its importance in a discussion of the major themes of western writing. To judge from the attention paid to history by several western novelists, historians should reexamine their assumptions about the relation of western fiction and history.[7]

In this chapter I shall discuss three ways in which western writers have used history. Vardis Fisher illustrates those who have thoroughly researched their historical subjects in order to write stirring narratives. A. B. Guthrie, Jr., who is also interested in the use of history in fiction, moves beyond Fisher in his desire to interpret as well as narrate his historical materials. Finally, Wallace Stegner takes the giant step. I treat his *Angle of Repose* at length because he has produced a western novel that is more than *about* history; he has written a first-rate fictional interpretation *of* the historical development of the West. I am convinced that an examination of the significant relationship between western history and the western novel will open new vistas of research for historians and literary scholars.[8]

Some students of the life and works of Vardis Fisher are convinced that he was born with a cocklebur in his diaper. They describe his life as one spent either trying to rid himself of the irritant or attempting to understand why he was not chosen one of the elect. It is true that few western writers have been as emotionally involved as he in searching out his own past and that of other persons. From his first novels, published in the late 1920s and early 1930s, until his last novel, *Mountain Man* (1965), Fisher was on a lifelong quest to narrate man's movement through history. During his productive career Fisher dedicated himself to the fruitful union of history and literature in an attempt to recount the past.[9]

For Fisher, first of all, the story was a personal one. His first seven novels (including the Vridar Hunter tetralogy), published between 1928 and 1937, were regional novels dealing with frontier life in the Antelope Hills area of Idaho. They were autobiographical works that dealt with Fisher's tortured feelings about his early life in the region. The son of pioneer Mormon parents, Fisher battled throughout his early years with his ambiguous responses to his backgrounds. He was not sympathetic to the teachings of the Mormons, and he thought them often bigoted and self-righteous. Yet he praised the leadership of Brigham Young and the loyalty and perseverance he inspired among his followers. Similar tensions are evident in Fisher's feelings about his father. He frequently pictured his father as epitomizing the worst kind of religious fundamentalism. On some occasions his father figures are unfeeling men, introverted and blindly idealistic. But Fisher also admired his father's individualism and his hard work; these were qualities that Fisher tried to emulate in his own life.

In his tension-filled, love-hate reactions to his formative years Fisher displayed his inordinate interest in reporting his past. Some have suggested that his earliest novels were primarily excursions toward self-understanding. What is apparent is that he found some satisfactory answers for comprehending his life, and thus he was able to move back to Idaho—"to come home again"—and to carve out his ranch and build a home in Hagerman Valley. Other questions, however, still vexed him: What about the nature of man? Had people changed through the centuries? What were the forces that had the largest impact on history?

To deal with these questions, Fisher set out on one of the most ambitious projects in American literary history. His ten-volume Testament of Man series (1943–1960) is a monument to Fisher's tenacity, to his unwillingness to let go of the past until it had yielded up at least partial answers to some of its mysteries. The series, which chronicled man from his prehistoric origins to the modern era, was, in one sense, a continuation of his earliest work, although now the issues raised were less personal and more universal. Anyone who has plowed through the series—or even part of it—must admire the prodigious amount of research involved in the project. Fisher the historian-novelist shines through in every volume.[10]

Most of Fisher's western historical fiction also illustrates his thirst for narrating the past. In his most controversial book, *Children of God* (1939), Fisher sought to record how by 1900 the Mormons had evolved into a powerful institution. He had little sympathy for the doctrines and religious practices of the Church, but he exhibited a great deal of interest in the humanity of several of the early Mormon leaders. His own unsatisfying experience with the Latter-day Saints colored his interpretations, but it is noteworthy that, while devout Mormons at first harshly criticized the novel, some have recently recommended it with reservations.

Fisher's search for the historical West led him to the Donner party (*The Mothers*, 1943), the beaver wars of the Northwest (*Pemmican*, 1956), Lewis and Clark (*Tale of Valor*, 1958), and finally the western fur trappers (*Mountain Man*, 1965). His final novel illustrates several of the techniques that he used repeatedly in historical fiction. *Mountain Man* is based on wide research in original sources dealing with the trappers. Fisher seldom wrote about a subject that he had not researched as if he were writing a doctoral dissertation (he received a doctorate in English literature with high honors from the University of Chicago in 1925). At the same time the novel betrays the strong feelings Fisher had about contemporary issues rooted in the freedom, the spontaneity, and the perseverance that the lives of the mountain men illustrated. He also celebrated, through his hero Sam Minard, the strong feelings for nature that he shared with mountain men. In short, Fisher's final novel was a combination of his desire for historical veracity and his goal of demonstrating how the past is related to the present.

A. B. Guthrie, Jr., the Montana novelist, shares Fisher's strong interest in the historical novel. In accounting for his late arrival as a writer of historical fiction (Guthrie was forty-six when *The Big Sky* was published), he says that early in life he fell in love with the West and wanted to explain in fiction the artifacts he found and the men he encountered in diaries and journals. But he kept putting off rounding up his ideas. Then in 1944, on the strength of a Nieman Fellowship to Harvard, he was able to spend a vigorous year reading, researching, and reflecting upon the era of the mountain man. Three years later *The Big Sky* illustrated Guthrie's extensive work in historical documents.[11]

Guthrie's subsequent novels seem less and less based on factual research. As one moves from *The Big Sky* to *The Way West* (1949), to *These Thousand Hills* (1955), to *Arfive* (1970), and on to *The Last Valley* (1975), the last of his five-volume fictional history of the West, one moves gradually across the frontier of fact into the region of Guthrie's remembrances of the West. Each of the first four novels deals with a crucial era in the historical development of the West: the years of the mountain men, the coming of the overlanders, the rise of the cattle ranchers, and the beginnings of town building. The final book in the series treats several themes of the era 1920 to 1945.

In writing *The Big Sky*, Guthrie used many of the standard historical sources dealing with the 1830s and 1840s. He ransacked the works of travelers like Nathaniel J. Wyeth and Washington Irving, as well as the writings of later historians, such as Hubert Howe Bancroft and Hiram H. Chittenden. The writer he seems to have followed most was George Frederick Ruxton, an Englishman who traveled extensively throughout the frontier West. Guthrie may have borrowed much of his trapper talk and perhaps some of his characters from Ruxton's semifact, semifictional work, *Life in the Far West*.[12]

But *The Big Sky* is much more than the scissors-and-paste product of Guthrie's reading and research in western history. He shapes incidents, scenery, and characterizations to fit his thematic concerns. Guthrie once remarked, after finishing his first two novels, that his major thesis was that man kills or destroys the things he loves most. *The Big Sky* illustrates this theme in several ways. Boone Caudill, the major character in the novel, kills his best friend and destroys his marriage to an Indian girl because he mistakenly thinks they have been sleeping together. Besides specific incidents that epitomize Guthrie's thesis, the entire novel deals with the seeds of destruction the trappers bring to the mountains. They love the out-of-doors and sense a new freedom and exhilaration in their occupation. At the same time they strip the Rocky Mountains of its beaver, kill more meat than they are able to use, and exhibit wanton wastefulness in their yearly rendezvous. Boone realizes the destructiveness of his life, as well as that of his companions, when near the end of the novel he tells a friend that they have "spiled" the mountains and that he does not want to return.[13]

In *Arfive*, the penultimate novel of Guthrie's series, he deals with what historian C. Vann Woodward has called the twilight zone of man's experience—that shadowy era in which history and memory overlap. The novel describes a Montana town in the period of Guthrie's boyhood, the years around the opening of World War I. The emphasis is on a small community and its citizens' efforts to adjust their frontier backgrounds to changes thrust upon them. The two major characters have to realize that the past is gone, that new ideas and problems have arisen, and that they too must change if they are to adapt to a fluctuating environment. *Arfive* is a persuasive picture of an important era in our past—when the West ceased to be a frontier and gradually began to take on the appearance of a settled region.[14]

The Last Valley, which Guthrie claims is the last of his fictive treatments of the West, illustrates his absorbing interest in history, his preoccupation with the ideas of change and progress, and some of the similarities in method of historians and novelists. Guthrie uses the central figures of *Arfive*—Benton Collingswood and Mort Ewing—in *The Last Valley*. They are employed as Dick Summers, the mountain man and overland guide, was in *The Big Sky* and *The Way West;* they function as bridges from the past to the present and as commentators on the dangers and benefits of change and progress. And they serve another important purpose. Novelists and historians face analogous tasks of selection and omission when they try to produce a book that portrays a twenty-five-year period without drowning the reader in a deluge of facts.[15] Guthrie attempts to solve this problem by selecting specific events in the 1920s, 1930s, and 1940s and allowing his major characters to react to these occurrences. Their diverse reactions—which Guthrie deals with repeatedly—are similar to what historians call historiography, that is, varying interpretations of a single happening. The technique of probing several reactions to one event or idea allows historians and novelists to broaden the perspectives of their works and to demonstrate the complexity of the past.

Guthrie's most recent novel is also a first-rate treatment of the fluidity of time, of the shadowy boundaries between past, present, and future. Collingswood, Ewing, and Ben Tate, a journalist and Collingswood's son-in-law, are reflective persons, and on several occasions, as they ponder their present circumstances, remembrances of past experiences flood in and condition their thoughts and actions. By uniting past and present—sometimes jamming them together—Guthrie shows how much human history is a flow, an ongoing current rather than a series of separate, isolated eras. The painting on the dust jacket of *The Last Valley* further illustrates Guthrie's method and message. In the background verdant mountains loom above the rest of the setting, but a town, with its streets, buildings, and smoking chimneys, occupies the center of the painting. In the immediate foreground a single horseman rides away from the town. He is not in headlong flight, but he is leaving. The mountains, the town, and the horseman are not distinctly separated; they are merged. Like the novel, the painting hints at some of the tensions between nature and civilization, between past and present. Alongside the evidences of tension and conflict and emphases on juxtaposition and continuity. In fact, the major themes portrayed in the painting and treated in *The Last Valley* are the key ideas dealt with in all of Guthrie's western historical novels. In a speech he summed up his ambiguous response to the inevitable movement of history and to change: "I accept the fact that progress leaves us no retreat. We can only insist *no undue haste*. We can only try to guide it. We can't stay it. Neither should we."[16]

The interest in history, so evident in the work of Fisher and Guthrie, is even more prominent in the recent work of Wallace Stegner, whom many commentators have come to consider our best contemporary western writer. Norman Cousins, in a review in *Saturday Review/World* of Stegner's superb biography of Bernard DeVoto, has even higher praise for Stegner, calling him the leading man of American letters. Throughout his distinguished career as historian, biographer, and novelist, Stegner has been profoundly interested in western history. Nowhere is this concern better demonstrated than in his novel *Angle of Repose* (1971), which won the Pulitzer Prize for fiction in 1972.[17]

On one level the novel is the story of an eastern woman, Susan Burling, who marries another easterner, Oliver Ward, goes west, and tries to acclimate herself to western ways. On another level the book is about Susan's grandson, Lyman Ward, a retired history professor, who is an amputee and alienated from his world of 1970. By shifting back and forth between the late nineteenth century and events and ideas of the 1960s, Stegner deals with a full century of western history. It is a huge task and one that Stegner accomplishes through two major themes of western history: (1) What is the relationship between East and West? Should the emphases be placed on continuities or on differences? and (2) What comparisons and contrasts can be made between the frontier West and the New West of the 1960s? Because it deals with the major questions involved in a discussion of the nature of western history, Stegner's work is a paradigm for the western novel as history.[18]

The first theme of eastern influence upon the West is developed primarily through the character of Susan Burling Ward. She lives most of her life in the West as she follows her husband to the mining camps of California and Colorado, to the new community of Boise, and finally to Grass Valley, California. Unlike her husband, she never becomes a westerner. Throughout her life she holds on to her eastern, genteel symbols. Her clothing, her maid, and governess (probably the one household in Boise in the 1880s to have both), her eastern literary friends, and her allusions to the East and the classics—all these illustrate her connections with the East.

Through adroit use of symbolic action Stegner represents how much Susan is a stranger to western ways. On one occasion, while standing on an elevated porch and speaking to a Mexican worker, she drops her handkerchief. The laborer quickly retrieves it and hands it up to her. She reaches down for the handkerchief but quickly withdraws her hand when she realizes what she is doing. She cannot—in fact will not—take the handkerchief from his hand; finally she calls her maid to get it back. Another night, while she and Oliver are returning to Leadville—Colorado's riproaring mining town—they are forced to bed down in a flophouse. Oliver hesitates, for he realizes that his wife is horrified by the prospect of sleeping in a curtained-off section of a room no more than snoring and belching distance from rough miners and dirty vagabonds. Susan is queasy about the situation, and she lies awake most of the night—first in fear and then, true to her character, in dreaming about how she will picture this "rough" West for eastern magazines. Obviously much of the truth will be brushed away and large doses of romanticism applied before the "dreamed up" West will be publishable in *Century* and *Scribner's*.

A third scene—from which Stegner wrings multiple meanings—is the most revealing incident about Susan's attachment to a nonwestern perspective. Before this scene Oliver and Susan have argued about the suitability of an eastern man who has come west. Susan, overcome by her respect for his reading and his obvious exposure to eastern culture, declares him a cultivated gentleman. She is amazed and upset when Oliver says that the man is worthless in the West—in fact a hazard because he knows so little about mining and engineering. Susan does not see that his lack of experience in these professions should be held against him. One night soon after this discussion Susan and Oliver sit down to dinner, and she mentally criticizes Oliver for not washing before eating—there appears to be smudge on his thumb. Later a third person tells of the day's happenings (the account does not come from Oliver, for, as Susan says, he does not like talkee, talkee). Oliver, the eastern engineer, and others were in the mines when someone shouted a warning. The easterner froze in his tracks, and had it not been for Oliver's quick thinking and fast reactions the gentleman might have lost his life. The smudge on Oliver's thumb is an ugly bruise suffered by aiding a man whom he does not respect. At the end of the scene the reader realizes—and so does Susan—how much her perspective prevents her from understanding the West and what it demands from its residents.

Susan's life in Boise—her longest stay in one place in the West before the family moves to Grass Valley—epitomizes the tensions that eat at her even after she has lived in the West for more than a decade. Stegner catches her dilemmas in one ironic sentence of description: "There sat Susan Burling Ward, tired-eyed after a day's drawing, dragged-out after a day's heat, and tightening her drowning-woman's grip on culture, literature, civilization, by trying to read *War and Peace*" (p. 421). Like the local colorist she is, Susan loves the scenery, the wild and picturesque part of the Boise Valley; but once she faces the problems of living "in" the Boise area, she finds its remoteness and crassness repugnant and is stifled by the boosterism of its residents. Life in Boise seems acceptable only when she withdraws from it—when she and Oliver move up a river canyon and when she tries to establish a western miniature of Brook Farm.

Yet she becomes attached to the West, despite her reluctance to do so. Near the end of the Wards' stay in Boise, disappointments, failures, and tragedies seem to engulf them. Oliver's irrigation schemes will not hold water, their youngest child drowns (ironically, in an irrigation ditch), Oliver takes to the bottle, and a young engineering friend complicates Susan's problems by declaring his love for her. Susan almost gives up on the West; she leaves Oliver, ships her oldest son to an eastern boarding school, and thinks of remaining in the East. But she cannot remain in the East; something draws her west again—back to Oliver, back to disappointments, back to the dreadful West. She realizes, in spite of herself, that she has become attached to things in the West—even if she is not yet a westerner.

It would be a mistake to picture Oliver as the archetypal westerner—as the exact opposite of Susan. But he does take on characteristics ascribed to many westerners. His dreams are expansive—and expensive—but he is a diligent worker. Because he realizes the need for help in achieving his dreams, he is less class-conscious than Susan and evaluates a person more by his abilities than by his cultural achievements. Though he is overly protective of his wife, he does not allow an excessive gentility to blind him to the realities of a region that demands a ruggedness unknown to Susan's eastern friends.

He is not a local colorist caught up in the picturesque, picnic West. For him the region is a place where his dreams can be put to work; it is a place to be conquered. He finds Susan's classical allusions to miners and their arduous work "about used up" (p. 139), and he bluntly tells her that the cultured gentleman who claims to be an engineer is worthless in the West. At times Susan realizes that Oliver is different: "It was his physical readiness, his unflustered way of doing what was needed in a crisis, that she most respected in him; it made him different from the men she had known" (p. 234).

Oliver's dreams are pregnant with promise, although most of them eventually miscarry. He invents devices to save time and money. He discovers the necessary ingredients to make cement. He lays out a usable scheme to irrigate an entire western valley. But he cannot bring his dreams to fruition, and a major reason for his lack of success is a problem that plagued many western dreamers: he is dependent upon eastern capital, and too often sources of eastern capital are as untrustworthy as Lady Fortuna. All of Oliver's dreams prove workable—but only after he has left the scene. Like many westerners, his schemes and partial successes are destroyed by his inability to control sources of financing.

Stegner, sometimes through his narrator and sometimes as omniscient author, also comments on the relationship between East and West. Early in the novel Lyman Ward says: "I am impressed with how much of my grandparents' life depended on continuities, contacts, connections, friendships, and blood relationships. Contrary to the myth, the West was not made entirely by pioneers who had thrown everything away but an ax and a gun" (p. 41). On other occasions Stegner contrasts Susan's romantic perceptions with what the West was really like.[19] By depicting these two kinds of Wests, Stegner makes clear how much eastern visions defined what the West was to Americans. Most of these foreign interpreters overstressed the uniqueness of western life and underplayed the continuities between East and West. The point Stegner argues is the central thesis of Henry Nash Smith's brilliant book *Virgin Land* and among the major contentions in the writings of the western historian Earl Pomeroy.[20]

The second theme in Stegner's novel is his depiction of the West as it moves from frontier to settled community and finally on to the Bay Area counterculture of the 1960s. By keeping two eras of western life before the reader and by commenting on the transitions between the two periods, Stegner continually narrates and interprets the historical development of the West. Susan's life, as it moves from raw Leadville to semisettled Boise and finally to the security of Grass Valley, illustrates the flow of western history that Stegner is narrating. Throughout the novel the life and mores of the Wards are placed alongside the Berkeley fever of Lyman's young neighbor, Shelley Rasmussen, and his son, Rodman. And Lyman is the link. As he says, "I really would like to talk to somebody about my grandparents, their past, their part in the West's becoming, their struggle toward ambiguous ends." He likes the idea of seeing how "a fourth-generation Trevithick should help me organize the lives of the first-generation Wards" (p. 50). What Lyman notes is the irony of Shelley, who is a descendant of a Cornish miner, helping him interpret the meaning of the lives of a family who "ruled" her ancestors. And more to the point: It is a Trevithick (Shelley's mother) who, more than any of his kin, keeps Lyman moving physically. Stegner implies that the social and cultural history of the West has leveled some mountains, elevated some valleys, and bridged several chasms.

Stegner also suggests that if contemporary westerners paid more attention to their past they could learn from their history. Shelley is excited about the commune that her husband is planning, and she is disappointed that Lyman does not share her enthusiasm. Her problem, Lyman says, is that she could learn from Susan's experiences in trying to set up a psuedo Brook Farm in the Boise Canyon and from other historical precedents. What Lyman preaches (and one hears Stegner in the background at this point) is that if one knows the past one can better manage the present and plot the future.

It is from Lyman Ward, who acts as narrator, as commentator, as synthesizer, that one receives the most explicit comments about history, especially on the frontier becoming the New West. From the opening pages of the novel Stegner establishes a fluidity of time for his narrator. This fluidity is important, for Lyman switches from present to past and to present again as he searches for an understanding of his life. As he tries to seize hold of his present circumstances, he perceives the paradoxical truth that as soon as he defines the present it has become the past. And he realizes, too, that his life is cumulative: he is *in* and *of* the past just as he is tied to a complicated present. Both periods impinge upon him; he can escape neither. In his attempt to comprehend fully the relationship between the Old and the New Wests, Lyman utilizes two geological terms. The first is "angle of repose," the incline at which rocks cease to roll. He wishes to study his grandparents to discover how they achieved an angle of repose in their lives. The second term, the Doppler Effect, defines the way in which he wishes to undertake his study. It is not enough, he thinks, to stand in 1970, look back to the late nineteenth century, and write about his ancestors. Instead, he must place himself alongside his grandparents and, in a sense, live their lives with them. Like the good historian, he wishes to be past-minded, to climb into their shoes, and to relive their lives with understanding and objectivity.

But several pressures keep Lyman from producing the kind of history he wishes to write. In the first place, so few of his contemporaries think his subject or his method is correct. Lyman wants his son and the Berkeley generation to understand how much they are tied to the past. The problem is, he says, that they are "without a sense of history. . . . [To them] it is only an aborted social science." His son, Rodman, sums up the view that his father fears: "The past isn't going to teach us anything about what we've got ahead of us. Maybe it did once, or seemed to. It doesn't any more." But Lyman wants to study the past. It is, he argues, "the only direction we can learn from." He continues: "I believe in Time, as they did, and in the life chronological rather than in the life existential. We live in time and through it, we build our huts in its rivers, or used to, and we cannot afford all these abandonings" (pp. 15–16, 17, 18). The Berkeley generation has not yet learned this lesson; the youth of the 1960s, he says, are "by Paul Goodman out of Margaret Mead."[21]

Nor does Lyman want a distorted meaning of the past once it is scrutinized. Too many readers are like Rodman, who wants the drama and the color of something like the life of Lola Montez. But to Lyman this kind of writing is worthless: "Every fourth-rate antiquarian in the West has panned Lola's poor little gravel. My grandparents are in a deep vein that has never been dug. They were *people*" (p. 22).

Most of the time Lyman the historian practices what he preaches. He establishes what the region was like when Susan went west. The reader sees her trip in the context of early transcontinental rail travel and within the tense atmosphere that Americans experienced a few weeks after Custer's defeat in the summer of 1876. Here Lyman utilizes the Doppler Effect when he draws close to his subject, near enough for the reader to discern the sounds of her inner struggles. In addition, he wants to make sure that his readers see the continuities in the time periods he describes. When he summarizes the authoritarianism of mine owners and the illtreatment of miners in the 1870s, he reminds his listeners that much will change in the next century. The Western Federation of Miners, the Industrial Workers of the World, and the United Mine Workers are yet to come. One cannot hurry history; one must study it and write about it as it was, not as he wishes it had been. Nor must he remold it entirely by the outlook of his contemporaries. Lyman implies that presentist historians make these mistakes and thus distort history.

Lyman also realizes that the historian (or even a entire society) can easily fall in love with the past and use it as a refuge from an oppressive present. In fact, in spite of his vows not to fall victim to an alluring past, Lyman does so. On one occasion when the counterculture seems to be knocking at his door, he muses: "I am not going to get sucked into this. I'll call the cops in a minute if I have to. And this is all, absolutely all. I am going to think about it. I am going back to Grandmother's nineteenth century, where the problems and the people are less messy" (p. 170). Or, in another situation, he catches an epiphany-like glimpse of himself: "This is not a story of frontier hardships, though my grandparents went through a few; nor of pioneer hardihood, though they both had it. It is only Lyman Ward, Coe Professor of History, Emeritus, living a day in his grandparents' life to avoid paying too much attention to his own" (p. 409).

It would be a mistake to consider Lyman merely the mouthpiece of Wallace Stegner. Students of literature avoid the error of always identifying the ideas of a character with those of its author, but historians need additional warning about the pitfalls of such comparisons. Yet much of what Lyman talks about, Stegner has spoken for on other occasions. Stegner shares some of Lyman's distaste for the student radicalism of the 1960s. Stegner remarked in 1972 that the student movement "started at Berkeley and we inherited it at Stanford. The kids didn't come to learn, they came angry and with answers—not questions." He added, "I don't know why when you get mad at Mr. Smith, you break Mr. Jones's windows."

Much of this misplaced anger, Stegner argued, would have been avoided if we were better students of our past:

> In times of crisis people turn to history. Certainly, as some of the protesters . . . argue, we may be prisoners of the past, but we also are imprisoned in the human species. We have to keep our ties with the past to learn and grow. Cut loose from the past and we become nothing. It doesn't make any difference if there are flaws in the marble or not; that's the marble history must be carved from.[22]

In an interview with John R. Milton, Stegner was even more explicit about some of the ideas contained in his novel: "This is what I would really like to see some western writer manage to do, to put together his past and his present." This statement led to *Angle of Repose*, which Stegner described as

> a novel which involves some pretty refined *eastern* characters who are going to have some of the refinement ground out of them. . . . It's a Willa Catherish kind of theme. She keeps pointing out that the frontier breaks the really refined. . . . The frontier was a brutalizing experience, but it also could be, for people who weren't actually broken by it, an experience which changed them in other ways. It could be a coarsening experience but also a strengthening one. So I've got some genteel-tradition folks who are going to have to develop a few callouses.[23]

Not only does Stegner ask the most important questions about the making of the modern West; he seems to give the best answers. A full discussion of his answers would be the subject of another chapter, but allow me to summarize briefly what I think he says about the nature of western experiences. Scratch a westerner deeply enough, and one will find an easterner who has carried along much of his cultural baggage and has had to readjust his thinking and living to fit a new environment. In other words, the westerner is not something entirely new; he is a product of his past as well as his present.

Second, if one wishes to understand the modern West, he ought, Stegner hints, to study and comprehend the meaning of such nineteenth-century activities as the gold rush, labor disputes in the mines, and political malcontents like the Populists. In short, what Lyman seems to learn is that the American West is the product of two angles of repose: it is East *and* West; and it is the frontier *and* the Berkeley generation. The answers that Stegner provides are the products of a probing mind trying to decipher the nature of the American West. He shows that the open marriage of history and literature will lead us to the best fictional treatments of the West. And thus, if I were asked to name the most significant western novel of the last decade, I would nominate *Angle of Repose*. I know of no other novel of the last ten years that says as many meaningful things about the American West as Stegner's book. It is a model for subsequent novels written about the West.

At this point one must ask, If such novelists as Fisher, Guthrie, and especially Stegner have made notable use of history in their western novels, why is it that this tendency has not received much notice? I am convinced that the answer to this worthwhile question is rooted in the current trends of scholarship in history and literature and in the inclinations of western historians.

In the past few years historians have been urged to employ more of the research techniques of the social sciences. They are told that the use of statistics, demography, and social psychology, for example, will enhance the specificity of their studies. Many students of history have heeded this urging, and historical monographs and essays in historical journals evidence an increasing use of social-science methods. This trend has not been detrimental to historians, for these new techniques have broadened their perspectives. At the same time there is a decreasing interest among historians in utilizing literature in their studies; the scrutiny of novels, poems, and plays as a source for historical knowledge seems less and less acceptable to a generation of historians taught to search for exactness in history.

In the field of American literary studies current research continues to move in the direction of myth criticism and the study of linguistics and popular culture. Here too contemporary emphases have widened our viewpoints and added to our understanding of American literature. On the other hand, few critics emphasize literary history or the historical consciousness of novelists. Thus neither historians nor literary critics have recently shown much interest in trying to focus on subjects that cross the disciplines of history and literature.[24]

There are other reasons why the relationship between western history and western literature has not been studied. By and large, western historians have paid scant attention to the literature of the West. The major western-history textbooks contain no extensive discussions of western writing, and there is no published history of western American literature. Western historians, unlike historians of the South, seem unaware either of the historical value of their literature or the historical consciousness evident in the region's fiction.[25] Part of this oversight is due, no doubt, to the widespread but mistaken notion among historians that any novel written about the West is "just another western." It is true that some western writers have chosen to follow the patterned westerns of Zane Grey and his descendants, but to pigeonhole most western authors as writers of westerns—as some historians have done—is to make no distinctions between Zane Grey and A. B. Guthrie, Luke Short and Wallace Stegner, or Frederick Faust (Max Brand) and Vardis Fisher. As we have seen, Guthrie, Fisher, and Stegner have not written Zane Grey westerns.[26]

Other commentators are equally contemptuous of western historical fiction. As one writer has pointed out, the historical novel is treated as if it were " 'a kind of mule-like animal begotten by the ass of fiction on the brood-mare of fact, and hence a sterile monster.' "[27] Here again there is some basis for this negative attitude. For example, James Michener's bestselling novel *Centennial* (1974) illustrates some of the pitfalls of too much popularization in western historical fiction. Michener gives some sense of the vertical (old to new) and horizontal (East and South to West) history of the West, he deals with some ethnic patterns that helped form the mosaic of western society, and he knows how to write appealing narrative history. But the weaknesses of his popular approach limit the historical value of his widely read novel. He conveniently kills off too many of his characters, and he invokes too many chance circumstances to keep his thousand-page novel on the move. He sensationalizes too much of his material. He places too much emphasis on faddish topics: Indians, cowboys, and mountain men. And, on the other hand, he does little with populism, radical farmer groups, or local, state, and federal governmental squabbles, and he generally scants the twentieth century. Michener has "used" (perhaps "abused") western history; he majors on lively and flashy narrative and minors on useful interpretation of the historical materials he utilizes. But to point to Michener or to writers of westerns as the only source of western fiction is to distort the evidence, and some historians have been guilty of this distortion.

Now, allow me to snub down my maverick points. The works of several important novelists, as we have seen, evidence a strong interest in history. But current trends in historical and literary scholarship and contemporary predilections among many western historians have kept students from noting this historical consciousness in western fiction. One hopes that western novelists continue to mine the rich lode of western history as well as they have in the past. If they do, literary critics and historians will soon realize that many authors make use of regional history in their western fiction and that this theme merits more attention.

Notes

1. Recent trends in the study of western American literature are summarized in Richard W. Etulain, "The American Literary West and Its Interpreters: The Rise of a New Historiography," *Pacific Historical Review* 45 (August, 1976).

2. For two sources that discuss this point of view, see W. H. Hutchinson, *A Bar Cross Man: The Life and Personal Writings of Eugene Manlove Rhodes* (Norman: University of Oklahoma Press, 1956); and Wallace Stegner, *The Uneasy Chair: A Biography of Bernard DeVoto* (Garden City, N.Y.: Doubleday, 1974). The best treatments of the American West as a colonial culture are Gene Gressley, "Colonialism: A Western Complaint," *Pacific Northwest Quarterly* 54 (January, 1963): 1–8; and the more comprehensive Gerald D. Nash, *The American West in the Twentieth Century: A Short History of an Urban Oasis* (Englewood Cliffs, N.J.: Prentice Hall, 1973).

3. Books and articles that depend heavily on the insights and methods of Smith are discussed in Etulain, "The American Literary West and Its Interpreters."

4. John R. Milton, editor of *South Dakota Review*, expresses this view in "The Western Novel: Sources and Forms," *Chicago Review* 16 (Summer, 1963): 74–100; and in *Interpretive Approaches to Western American Literature* (Pocatello, Idaho: University of Idaho Press, 1972), pp. 7–21. See also Max Westbrook, *Walter Van Tilburg Clark* (New York: Twayne, 1969). The latest substantiation of the same view is by Thomas Lyon (editor of *Western American Literature)* in *Frank Waters* (New York: Twayne, 1973).

5. Wallace Stegner, *The Sound of Mountain Water* (Garden City, N.Y.: Doubleday, 1969), p. 11.

6. John R. Milton, "The American West: A Challenge to the Literary Imagination," *Western American Literature* 1 (Winter 1967): 267–84; Wilson O. Clough, "Regionalism," in *Rocky Mountain Reader*, ed. Ray B. West, Jr. (New York: Norton, 1946), pp. 414–17. Clough enlarges his discussion of this subject in *The Necessary Earth: Nature and Solitude in American Literature* (Austin: University of Texas Press, 1964).

7. A few authors have dealt briefly with the relationshps between western history and literature. For example, see the scattered comments in James K. Folsom, *The American Western Novel* (New Haven: Yale University Press, 1966); and in Helen Hitt, "History in Pacific Northwest Novels Written Since 1920," *Oregon Historical Quarterly* 51 (September 1950): 180–206. The best article on the subject is Don Walker, "Can the Western Tell What Happens?" in *Interpretive Approaches to Western American Literature*, pp. 33–47.

8. Although I discuss only three western novelists here, many others could have been cited for their interest in and use of history in their fiction. For example, in the Middle West, Willa Cather, Ole Rölvaag, and Frederick Manfred; in the Southwest, Conrad Richter, Paul Horgan, and Larry McMurtry; in the Far West, Jack London, John Steinbeck, and H. L. Davis.

9. For Fisher's use of history I am drawing upon Wayne Chatterton, *Vardis Fisher: The Frontier and Regional Works* (Boise: Boise State College Western Writers Series, 1972); and Ronald Taber, "Vardis Fisher: New Directions for the Historical Novel," *Western American Literature* 1 (Winter, 1967): 285–96.

10. Fisher's role as historian-novelist is treated in detail in Joseph M. Flora, *Vardis Fisher* (New York: Twayne, 1965); and George F. Day, "The Uses of History in the Novels of Vardis Fisher" (Ph.D. diss., University of Colorado, 1968).

11. Guthrie discusses his interests in history in his autobiography, *The Blue Hen's Chick* (New York: McGraw-Hills, 1965); and in "The Historical Novel: Tramp or Teacher," *Montana: The Magazine of Western History* 4 (Autumn, 1954): 1–8.

12. Richard H. Cracroft, *"The Big Sky:* A. B. Guthrie's Use of Historical Sources," *Western American Literature* 6 (Fall, 1971): 163–76. A companion article is David C. Stineback, "On History and Its Consequences: A. B. Guthrie's *These Thousand Hills," Western American Literature:* 6 (Fall, 1971): 177–89.

13. These comments on *The Big Sky* are taken from my tape, "The Mountain Man in Literature," Western American Writers Series (Deland, Florida, 1974).

14. See Richard W. Etulain, "The New Western Novel," *Idaho Yesterdays* 15 (Winter, 1972): 12–17, for more on *Arfive.*

15. I am drawing here on the useful comments of Russell Nye, "History and Literature: Branches of the Same Tree," *Essays on History and Literature,* ed. Robert H. Bremner (Columbus: Ohio State University Press, 1966), pp. 123–59.

16. "Author Guthrie—'Going Toward the Sunset,' " *Exponent* [Montana State University], April 2, 1971. Guthrie added to these ideas in his luncheon address at the Montana Historical Conference at Helena in October, 1975.

17. Wallace Stegner, *Angle of Repose* (Garden City, N.Y.: Doubleday, 1971). Some of the ideas in the previous paragraphs and in the section on Wallace Stegner appeared in different form in my "New Western Novel" and "Frontier and Region in Western Literature," *Southwestern American Literature* 1 (September, 1971): 121–28.

18. I have not dealt here with several other significant themes in *Angle of Repose.* For example, no one yet has studied carefully Stegner's use of the letters and autobiography of Mary Hallock Foote, [Editor's note: See the essay by Dr. Walsh included in this volume.] the western local-color writer who has the model for Susan Burling Ward. Foote's autobiography has been superbly edited by Rodman W. Paul, *A Victorian Gentlewoman in the Far West: The Reminiscenses of Mary Hallock Foote* (San Marino: The Huntington Library, 1972).

19. Stegner makes these comparisons throughout his novel, but especially notable are those that deal with setting; see pp. 81–82, 84–85, 97–103, 134–35, and 218–36. Near the end Susan is less tied to her perspectives; she begins to see the West in less romantic terms.

20. Earl Pomeroy discusses the ideas of innovation and continuity in western history in his pathbreaking article "Towards a Reorientation of Western History: Continuity and Environment," *Mississippi Valley Historical Review* 41 (March, 1955): 579–600. The same discussions are at the center of his *The Pacific Slope: A History of California, Oregon, Washington, Idaho, Utah, and Nevada* (New York: Knopf, 1965).

21. Stegner has said: "I am forced to believe in Time. I believe we are Time's prisoners, I believe Time is our safety and strength. I think we build our little huts against it as the latter-day Illyrians built their huts within and against the great palace of Diocletian at Split." *The Sound of Mountain Water,* p. 12.

22. Quoted in *Salt Lake Tribune,* June 11, 1972.

23. John R. Milton, " Conversation with Wallace Stegner," *South Dakota Review* 9 (Spring, 1971): 53, 54.

24. There are, of course, some exceptions. Notable among these are Harry B. Henderson III, *Versions of the Past: The Historical Imagination in American Fiction* (New York: Oxford University Press, 1974); Nelson Manfred Blake, *Novelists' America: Fiction as History, 1910–1940* (Syracuse: Syracuse University Press, 1969); and David Levin, *In Defense of Historical Literature* (New York: Hill & Wang, 1967). The outstanding example of a scholar who continues to work the rich relationship of history and literature is Russel Nye; see his extremely useful *The Unembarrassed Muse: The Popular Arts in America* (New York: Dial, 1970).

25. A model for western historians is F. Garvin Davenport, Jr., *The Myth of Southern History: Historical Consciousness in Twentieth-Century Southern Literature* (Nashville: Vanderbilt University Press, 1970). Robert V. Hine's *The American West: An Interpretive*

History (Boston: Little, Brown, 1973), is notable for its extensive use of literature as a source for history.

26. I have attempted to distinguish between the western and the western novel in "The Historical Development of the Western," *The Popular Western: Essays Toward a Definition*, eds. Richard W. Etulain and Michael T. Marsden (Bowling Green, Ohio: Bowling Green University Press, 1974), pp. 74–84.

27. In David E. Whisnant, *James Boyd* (New York: Twayne, 1972), p. 140.

The Compassionate Seer:
Wallace Stegner's Literary Artist

Sid Jenson*

> The word "artist" is not a word I like. It has been adopted by crackpots and abused by pretenders and debased by people with talent but no humility. In its capital A form it is the hallmark of that peculiarly repulsive sin of arrogance by which some practitioners of the arts retaliate for public neglect or compensate for personal inadequacy. I use it here only because there is no other word for the serious "maker" in words or stone or sound or colors.
>
> Wallace Stegner
> "Fiction: A Lens on Life"

Paul Horgan, speaking about the art and discipline of writing, says:

> We must go beyond the pencil boxes, as it were, and look beyond the page to consider the writer's vision of life, which all simple and habitual mechanics of writing exist to serve. Where many literary workers fall short of making significant works is just where spiritual values come into focus in a point of view.

Wallace Stegner, I am sure, would agree. I am also sure that Stegner would agree with Mr. Horgan when he says:

> The spiritual life of the modern world becomes increasingly fragmented. Modern writers, like everybody else, long for a nourishing explanation of life; but all too many turn to recent and fugitive systems of imposing orderly but incomplete designs upon life's teeming and elusive variety, and in doing so, seem to lose the deepest well of their inspiration and their artistic intuition.

Mr. Horgan concludes his comment about the source of man's creative powers with this comment:

> When aesthetic perception approaches its fullest realization, it is akin to man's religious vision, whatever form this may take. Faith is a supernatural grace. The true artist is he who knows without learning. His own intuition is closer to the supernatural than it is to any prevailing temper of the pluralistic and pragmatic modern culture.[1]

*Reprinted from *Brigham Young University Studies* (Winter, 1974), 248–62.

Wallace Stegner may not agree with every letter and line quoted above, but I am sure he would agree with the tenor and tone, with the basic point of view Paul Horgan has toward the creative artist.

Wallace Stegner has been described as a non-religious humanist,[2] but his theory of literary art is based on a belief in literature which is not unlike the religious faith that Jonathan Edwards had in the "divine and supernatural light," or the faith that Ralph Waldo Emerson had in "Reason," or that the devout Mormon has in the "Holy Ghost." Stegner's literary beliefs center on the idea that the aesthetic experience is a private, subjective, mystical experience that is "never quite communicable,"[3] and that the aesthetic experience is not subject to empirical verification. Art has its own peculiar sort of truth, the ancient and unverifiable "knowledge of things *as experience,*"[4] and this truth is just as important as, and is complementary to, measurable, scientific truth. The artist, for Stegner, is the "man aware," the man who can record the knowledge of things as experienced. But today we live in the age of the transistor and too often ignore or distrust the subjective, mystical experience; and says Stegner, this makes us like little children "trying to spell [the word] God with the wrong blocks."[5]

Another contemporary problem with the creative artist is that he has quit. In "Born a Square," Stegner says that, "from the Western writer's square, naive point of view, the trouble with Modern Man, as he reads about him in fiction, is that Modern Man has quit."[6] The modern literary generation specializes in "despair, hostility, hypersexuality, and disgust" (p. 171). Today's artist too often gives himself the status of "Man as Victim." The artist by his own definition is "a victim, a martyr, a loser, a self-loather, a life-hater" (p. 176).

Wallace Stegner, who comes from the West and has "incorrigible hope," (p. 185), wants none of this. He advises the western writer to keep his values, "to hang on to his basic hopefulness, instead of giving it up for a fashionable disgust" (p. 182). Stegner advises, "The West's own problems are likely to be more to the western writer's purpose than any that he can borrow, especially when in borrowing he must deny his own gods" (p. 184).

Stegner's literary theory and practice do not categorize nicely into any of the traditional groups, such as classicism, naturalism, or realism. If one must have such a handle, he might try soldering the word "archetypal" onto Stegner's works, but don't put too much pressure on the handle by overloading the pan or all your beans will be in the fire. Labeling Stegner's fictional work with a term which describes literary technique or type is not the best approach. What is needed in Stegner's case is a philosophical focus, an examination of Stegner's life and his moral-ethical-philosophical beliefs.

In this short paper one cannot trace the life of Stegner. For our purpose, we need only say that he had an abnormally migrant childhood which gave him an acute sense of physical and moral dislocation. Because of this moral rootlessness, Stegner's writing has taken on the purpose of bringing order to disorder, helping to make this earth a place where children will not have to experience all the disorder and early sorrow Stegner did. From the sorrows of the bleak life on a Saskatchewan farm, from the disorder of the sooty life in cities, Stegner has tried to find physical and moral order.

In *Wolf Willow* Stegner has said that he ranks fictional or poetic truth a little above that of historical truth.[7] He felt he could get more truth in a fictionalized account of the cattle industry on the Saskatchewan plains than he could with any historical summary. The personal impetus for Stegner's study and writing of history was his search to find himself and to know his roots. In *Wolf Willow* he says, "I may not know who I am, but I know where I am from."[8] Historical knowledge satisfied his question, "Where am I from?" but the more difficult question, "Who am I?" is better answered by poetic truth.

We read poetry (or literature), Stegner feels, primarily because we are searching for ourselves. "In all our wandering through . . . fictional worlds it is probably ourselves we seek."[9] But we never find ourselves. What we do find is how the author, "another waif in a bewildering world, has made out to survive and perhaps be at peace."[10]

Out of this belief comes Stegner's principal literary theme, the search for individual identity. In an early work, *Fire and Ice*, Paul Condon unsuccessfully struggles to find himself: "It's pretty clear to me that I didn't know myself," and "The biggest wrong I did was not to know myself better."[11] At the end of the novel, he leaves Salt Lake City, walking straight east, heading back toward where his countrymen came from, with the resolve to answer the question, "who am I?" "I'm going to do nothing but work and read and think till I've got an answer of my own that suits me. . . . Freshman Condon in search of the Grail."[12]

Lyman Ward, in Stegner's latest novel *Angle of Repose*, asks the same question, "Why then am I spending all this effort trying to understand my grandparents' lives?"[13] Lyman Ward is trying to write a history of his grandparents in order to understand them. He hopes that if he understands them, he will understand himself. Lyman Ward's search is not eastward like Paul Condon's, but westward, all over the West. In the end their search must be inward, but both start their search as Galahads of the public library.[14]

In the libraries these characters find literature, and literature for Stegner is a lens on life. In *The Writer in America*, he says "The work of art is not a gem, as some schools of criticism would insist, but truly a lens. We look through it for the purified and honestly offered spirit of the artist" (p. 13). Literature is a tool by which man can enlighten himself about the human predicament. Reading literature "is precisely like the act of putting a smear of culture on a slide for inspection under the microscope" (p. 11). Literature is not life; it is a way of seeing life; and for Stegner, it is the best way. As Ruth Liebowitz says in *Second Growth,* "But anybody with any sense can learn more from novels than he can from all the textbooks in your box. Novels give you an understanding of people."[15]

Stegner recognizes that literature does have its limitations. A microscope, no matter how well it illuminates a particular problem, has a very narrow range of vision. Its range is limited in proportion to its degree of magnification. The writer's vision is limited by his life, by his experience, his keenness of mind, and his ability of expression. But "the most inclusive vision is not necessarily his aim; it is the *clearest* vision he is after."[16] Limited though the microscope and literature may be, they both give a penetrating view of a small part of the world. "Certainly, no writer can see or know all or get all life into his fiction. His quality will be measured by the amount he does succeed in getting without blurring the edges of his simplifying frame."[17]

Stegner realizes that, like the microscope, art distorts life. Unlike the microscope fiction need not always be absolutely true to fact. Discussing some factually inaccurate farming details in *On a Darkling Plain*, Stegner warns that the writer must convince, and he must continuously maintain his dramatic illusion.

> For he *must* convince; he *must* drug his reader into complete acceptance of the premise of his story, and maintain his dramatic illusion by never slipping into inaccuracies of fact that may haul the reader up short.[18]

Stegner warns that specific facts had better be accurate or the dramatic illusion may be broken for the informed reader. Stegner notes the exact date Mark Twain used in *The Connecticut Yankee.* That fact is central to the plot; Mr. Clemens would not want to be called on the point by some astrologer or astronomer.

But the greater literary truth of *The Connecticut Yankee* does not rely on an accurate date at all. An author can fake, and "fake shamelessly" the factual materials of a story as long as the dramatic illusion is maintained, and just so long as the work is true to human experience.

> For here is the incontrovertible fact about fiction: that the details in scene after scene can be faked, spurious, or even absolutely false, and the validity of the novel's message be unimpeachable.

Stegner cites Keats' use of Cortez instead of Balboa to prove his point: "That passage, for all its spuriousness and in spite of its bald error, says so much, and so truly, about the essential human qualities of wonder and surprise that the details are overlooked."

In contrast to a historical novelist like Vardis Fisher, Stegner makes this suggestion to the writer: "Look up your details when they are important and must be exact, but fake them where hunting them down would be tedious and unnecessary labor." You should "spend most of your time, most of your thought, on the people, the psychological rightness, the ultimate implications of your story. . . . Those are things that cannot be faked, skimped, or rendered impressionistically. . . . Keep the attention focused on the people, where it belongs."[19]

The essential truths of literature are not simply historical facts or ideas. Ideas, says Stegner, have an important place in fiction, "but ideas are not the best *subject matter* for fiction."[20] Some writers, Stegner notes, begin with ideas and make them into flesh and blood as Nathaniel Hawthorne did. Other writers start with flesh and blood and let them work themselves out into ideas, as Mark Twain did.[21] Regardless of the method, the artist's goal is "dramatized belief."[22] No fiction should state its meaning flatly: "It does not state; it imitates or reflects, and is witnessed."[23]

For Stegner, human dramatization is the writer's key tool. Chisel a great character and you have great literature—Oedipus, Don Quixote, Hamlet, Ahab, Huckleberry Finn. The meaning of life lies in people. Literature must be drawn from "people, places, and things—especially people. If fiction isn't people it is nothing, and so any fiction writer is obligated to be to some degree a lover of his fellowmen, though he may, like the Mormon preacher, love some of them a damn sight better than others."[24]

Even when writing history (which he considers a branch of literature), Stegner tries to focus on people. The spirits and bodies of William Clayton, Patience Loader, and Margaret Dalglish all come alive in *The Gathering of Zion*. Margaret Dalglish was one of those stout-hearted pioneers of the Mormon migration who journeyed with the ill-fated Willie-Martin Handcart Companies. Stegner describes her actions as she entered and overlooked for the first time the Great Salt Lake Valley:

> Margaret Dalglish of the Martin Company, a gaunt image of Scottish fortitude, dragged her handful of belongings to the very rim of the valley, but when she looked down and saw the end of it she did something extraordinary. She tugged the cart to the edge of the road and gave it a push and watched it roll and crash and burst apart, scattering into Emigration Canyon the last things she owned on earth. Then she went on into Salt Lake to start a new life with nothing but her gaunt bones, her empty hands, her stout heart.[25]

Quoting Joseph Conrad, Stegner says in "One Way to Spell Man" that the task of the artist is, "by the power of the written work to make you hear, to make you feel—it is, before all, to make you see." (p. 44). "Creative writing begins in the senses," Stegner says. "Without senses the writer cannot create images, and images are his only means of making his reader hear and feel and see."[26] Lyman Ward, the narrator of *Angle of*

Repose, tries to help the listener of his tapes *see* the time and place. Susan and Oliver Ward are headed for Leadville, Colorado for the first time:

> Tiny figures at the foot of a long rising saddle, snowpeaks north and south, another high range across the west. The road crawled toward the place where the saddle emptied into the sky. The wind came across into her face with the taste of snow in it, and not all the glittering brightness of the snow could disguise the cold that lurked in the air. In the whole bright half-created landscape they were the only creatures except for a toy ore wagon that was just starting down the dugway from the summit (p. 231).

If you have had mountain experience, if you have imagination and if you read carefully, you *see* what is happening.

Following in the tradition of T. E. Hulme's idea of the "image," Stegner believes that images (concrete things drawn from experience to symbolize the human truths of experience) are what make the reader *see.* For example, in *Second Growth* Stegner uses the image of a porcupine trapped in a flashlight beam to represent a trapped man: "The eyes reminded the old man of the eyes of a porcupine trapped in a flashlight beam, eyes that stared glassily and yet seemed constantly to swim in every direction at once, looking for an escape."[27] But images have their limitations. For just as the reader who does not know how to fish misses the import of Eliot's Fisher King fishing after he crosses the Waste Land, the reader who has never seen a porcupine in a light will not *see* the effect.

Stegner recognizes this. "Literature is a game played between writer and reader, both of whom must be products of essentially similar cultures."[28] To be successful, the game of literature must be played by two sympathetic people. Just as the writer must be emotionally and intellectually linked with his materials, so must the reader.[29] "The proof of art," for Stegner, "is in the response, in the esthetic experience." And that experience is subjective, even somewhat mystical. We attempt to analyze the aesthetic experience, but ultimately we cannot explain the reader's experience any more than we can explain the creative principle or act of the writer.

The writer's or the reader's aesthetic experience is not subject to empirical measurement. Art is cumulative, unlike science which is progressive. Ibsen does not replace Shakespeare, nor does Shakespeare replace Aeschylus. But Harvey does replace Galen, and Einstein does replace Newton. "Artistic insights tend to remain discrete; they do not necessarily make the building block of future insights; the [literary] tradition accumulates less by accrual than by deviation and rebellion." For these reasons, "anyone who speaks for art must be prepared to assert the validity of non-scientific experience and the seriousness of non-verifiable insight."[30]

Since all fiction begins from the artist's experience, Stegner feels that a serious artist needs a broad, deep experience with life. This experience, short of crippling, must have hurt him.[31] "Hurt" is not the only word proper here. "Annoyed" or "outraged" might also be used. But Stegner's idea is correct. A writer must have deeply felt his experiences. A writer's emotions as well as his intellect must be moved before he can move his readers.

In addition to feeling his experience, the artist must be a special kind of person. Stegner quotes Joseph Conrad to explain:

> A novelist who would think himself of a superior essence to other men would miss . . . his calling. . . . I would ask that in his dealings with mankind he should be capable of giving a tender recognition to their [mankind's] obscure virtues. I would not have him impatient with their small failings and scornful of their errors. . . . I would wish him to look with a large forgiveness at men's ideas and prejudices. . . .[32]

Stegner's ideal artist is a person of sensibility, intelligence, but most of all, a person of artistic and personal control.[33] The artist is essentially a common man, but a man who has uncommonly developed humility, patience, and impartiality. He forgives easily; and because he is compassionate, rebukes softly. The artist realizes, as Lyman Ward does in *Angle of Repose,* that it is love and sympathy which makes him capable of reconstructing the lives of his grandparents (p. 439).

Lyman Ward is a good example of Wallace Stegner's idea of the creative artist. As he struggles with the problems of writing his grandparents' history, as he struggles with his dying, paralytic body, as he struggles to behave properly towards his unfaithful wife, we see that Lyman has come to realize, "that most lives are worth living even when they are lives of quiet desperation." Lyman has come to realize that "the point is to do the best one can in the circumstances, not the worst" (p. 184).

Lyman Ward, unhappy with his present, turns to to the past, searching for an angle of repose. As he studies his grandparents' lives he slowly recognizes what caused the slow decay of their marriage. He slowly compiles the "cumulative grudges" which caused the decline and fall of their marriage. His grandmother, Susan Burling Ward, lived for the future all her married life, and "what she resisted was being the wife of a failure and a woman with no home" (p. 277). She looked for her angle of repose in the future, but it was not there, just as it is not in Lyman Ward's past.

The term "angle of repose" is a geologic one which means the slope angle, abut 30°, at which dirt and pebbles stop rolling. But Susan and Lyman Ward are too alert to the possible figurative, human possibilities of the phrase to allow it to be a mere descriptive term for detrital rest. They both apply it to themselves. Lyman says Susan never achieved her angle of repose, "as Grandmother's biographer, I'd have to guess she was never really happy after, say, her thirty-seventh year, the last year when she lived an idyll in Boise Canyon" (p. 538). Susan Burling Ward was a proud, Victorian lady. Why wasn't she happy? Lyman thinks he knows.

> Because she considered that she'd been unfaithful to my grandfather, in thought or act or both. Because she blamed herself for the drowning of her daughter. . . . Because she was responsible for the suicide of her lover—if he *was* her lover. Because she'd lost the trust of her husband and son (p. 560).

Earlier Lyman had explained Susan Ward's failure to find repose in another way. She was:

> a woman who was a perfect lady, and a lady who was feeling, eager, talented, proud, snobbish, an exiled woman. And fallible. And responsible, willing to accept the blame for her actions. . . . She held herself to account, and she was terribly punished (p. 534).

But Lyman Ward could never figure out what the phrase "angle of repose" meant for his grandmother, except that he knew the phrase was too good for mere dirt. But he knew what it meant for him.

During a moment of depression, in a nightmare dream, he once said it meant "Horizontal. Permanently" (p. 562). Later he recanted this part of his dream and explained:

> some cowardly, hopeful geometer in my brain tells me it is the angle at which two lines prop each other up, the leaning-together from the vertical which produces the false arch. For the lack of a keystone, the false arch may be as much as one can expect in this life (p. 568).

Lyman begins to realize that those final years that Susan and Oliver Ward spent in Zodiac Cottage produced a "false arch" between them. In some quiet, non-spoken, non-touching, non-kissing way, Susan and Oliver Ward had made a kind of angle of repose, an accommodation of sorts. While this may not seem like much, maybe, thinks Lyman, maybe this was all these Victorian people needed. But a false arch is not enough for grandson Lyman. He still searches with his hopeful geometer for the keystone.

Lyman Ward, a product of the twentieth century, needs to speak, touch, to kiss. A silent accommodation will be no angle of repose for him. With the inherited pride of his grandmother and the stubbornness of his grandfather, he continues his search for repose. As a historian, Lyman Ward looks at the past and the present, seeing the sharp contrasts between his grandparents' life and the present flower children like Shelly Rasmussen, his secretary-assistant. Lyman does not like the hippie cult with its utopian dreams "because their soft headedness irritates me. Because their beautiful thinking ignores both history and human nature" (p. 421). Also, Lyman thinks that his wife, Ellen, has become a victim of the casual fornicating of this generation.

Lyman notes the failure of previous utopian communities which the hippie generation unknowingly has copied. Brook Farm, New Harmony, Amana, the Shakers, the Icarians, the Oneida Colony, the United Order of Zion, all failed, and why? Depravity. Not that Lyman especially cares about utopian schemes or about reforming hippies; he just does not want to personally repeat failure.

Shelly Rasmussen will not accept Lyman's historical argument: "You're judging by past history." "All history is past history," Lyman replies. "All right. . . . But it doesn't have to repeat itself," Shelly says. "Doesn't it?" Lyman replies, well knowing by this time that his own history is in the final stages of repeating his grandparents'. Shelly is not convinced; she does not believe history can teach her generation much. Shelly's crowd quotes Whitman and Thoreau to support their beliefs on nature, free love, meditation, communion, and communal living. Lyman the scholar rebuts, "I never liked Whitman, I can't help remembering that good old wild Thoreau wound up a tame surveyor of Concord house lots." Shelly does not understand the significance of this, "What's that supposed to mean, that about Thoreau?" Lyman explains:

> How would I know what it means? . . . I don't know what anything means. What it *suggests* to me is that the civilization he was contemptuous of—that civilization of men who lived lives of quiet desperation—was stronger than he was, and maybe righter. It out-voted him. It swallowed him, in fact, and used the nourishment he provided to alter a few cells in its corporate body. It grew richer by him, but it was bigger than he was. Civilizations grow by agreements and accommodations and accretions, not by repudiations. . . . Civilizations grow and change and decline— they aren't remade (p. 519).

Lyman Ward has expressed his own situation. He simply cannot reject his wife as young Thoreau and the hippie cult reject the establishment. "You can't retire to weakness," Lyman says, "you've got to learn to control strength" (p. 519). Lyman must control his strength, not retire to weakness. He must not let his grandmother's pride or his grandfather's stubbornness keep him from making an accommodation with his wife. Ellen has made a mistake; she may have been living a life of quiet desperation; she may have a chemical imbalance; she may have been influenced by the present loose sex standards; she may not have relished the idea of living with a paralyzed grotesque for the next forty years.

Lyman Ward who has yet to figure out for sure why his wife ran off with his doctor, knows only this, he must not repeat his family's history. To stop the cycle, he will have to accept the false arch with its modified angle of repose and quit searching, quit hoping for the keystone. With this, the tape of the novel ends, but ends somewhat ambiguously with Lyman wondering, "I lie wondering if I am man enough to be a bigger man than my grandfather" (p. 569).

But the ambiguity is not true ambiguity at all. After watching

Lyman Ward wrestle with his wheelchair and his marriage problem for almost six hundred pages, the reader knows whatever else Lyman Ward is, he is kind, considerate; he is a gentleman. He will accommodate, he will accept a modified angle of repose, realizing that maybe this is "as much as one can expect in this life" (p. 568).

This accommodation, says Anatole Broyard in a review of *Angle of Repose,* is regrettable:

> [When Lyman pardons] his bitchy wife, his brash son and his gang-banging secretary, not every reader is going to feel that he has risen above his distaste for our times. Whatever the author intended, we're more likely to see this last-minute reprieve as a perversion of character, a regrettable crumbling of a good, crusty character.[34]

Mr. Broyard is wrong. Lyman Ward still strongly dislikes much of the 20th century life; his cultural tastes have not changed. But his dislike does not mean he should condemn those things or people he dislikes. Lyman knows what he dislikes, but he also knows what he ought to like. He ought to like whatever is honorable and proper. He ought to behave kindly. He ought to love the sinner (including himself) and hate the sin.

Earlier in his review Mr. Broyard states that in sifting through his grandmother's materials, Lyman Ward was "looking not only for a story but for the *standard of conduct* whose loss he feels as keenly as he does that of his leg."[35] This is quite right. Lyman is determined to behave properly. His grandmother, Susan Ward, had told him once, "I was never never *never* to behave *beneath* myself. She had know people who did, and the results were calamitous" (p. 313). Lyman now understands because of his study that those people who behaved beneath themselves were his grandparents. But in spite of their calamity, Susan and Oliver Ward had set an example of civilized conduct. "They respected each other. They treated one another with a sort of grave infallible kindness" (p. 562). Lyman Ward follows his grandmother's advice and example. This is the least he and his wife, Ellen, can do for each other—be kind.

Lyman Ward learns that even though he tries never to behave beneath himself, personal disaster and heartbreak will probably still be his lot, but that his grandmother's Victorian principles (what Mr. Broyard calls "standards of conduct") will guide and sustain him toward a life of muted joy.

Lyman Ward is a good example of Wallace Stegner's creative artist. He is a common man who lives in the world, among people. He is a man who matures "the strength of his imagination among the things of this earth."[36] He matures from a literary craftsman to an artist when he developes Pauline charity, when he becomes a compassionate seer.

The primary aim of literary art, Stegner believes, is to celebrate the human spirit. Literature today, he also believes, has assumed much of the spiritual responsibilities traditionally belonging to religion. "Literature has become for many of us . . . the source of wisdom and the receptacle of values." Along with the wisdom and values, Stegner's theory of literature also includes an element of mysticism which traditionally belongs to religion. Neither the creative act nor the act of reading can ever be reduced to the laws of measurable science. The aesthetic experience is "an insight communicated by example from writer to reader"[37] and is never quite explainable. The writer and the reader are men fishing in obscure depths; they are dealers in mystery. When the writer reveals to the reader the truth he has found, he is a seer; and Stegner quotes Conrad again, these revelations "bind men to each other, . . . bind together all humanity—the dead and the living and the living to the unborn." The creation and understanding of a piece of literature are mystical experiences. This experience is a kind of private insight by which man gets a "clear-eyed"[38] view of the ambiguities of human life.

Notes

1. Paul Horgan, "The Way to Writing," *Intellectual Digest,* 5 (July 1970), 57.

2. James J. Conlon, "From Pioneers to Provincials: Mormonism as seen by Wallace Stegner," *Dialogue: A Journal of Mormon Thought,* 1 (Winter 1966), 111.

3. Wallace Stegner, "One Way to Spell Man," *The Saturday Review,* 41 (24 May 1958), 43.

4. "One Way," p. 10.

5. "One Way," p. 9.

6. Wallace Stegner, "Born a Square," in *The Sound of Mountain Water* (Garden City, N.Y.: Doubleday, 1969), p. 184.

7. Wallace Stegner, *Wolf Willow: A History, A Story, and A Memory of the Last Plains Frontier* (New York: Viking Press, 1962), p. 307.

8. *Wolf Willow,* p. 23.

9. Wallace Stegner, *The Writer in America* (Folcroft, Pa.: Folcroft Press, 1969), p. 12.

10. *Writer,* pp. 12–13.

11. Wallace Stegner, *Fire and Ice* (New York: Duell, Sloan and Pearce, 1941), p. 212.

12. *Fire and Ice,* p. 213.

13. Wallace Stegner, *Angle of Repose* (Garden City, N.Y.: Doubleday, 1971), p. 439.

14. Stegner, *Fire and Ice,* p. 213.

15. Wallace Stegner, *Second Growth* (Boston: Houghton Mifflin, 1947), p. 42.

16. *Writer,* p. 5.

17. *Writer,* p. 11.

18. Wallace Stegner, "Truth and Faking in Fiction," *Writer,* 53 (February 1940), 41.

19. "Truth," p. 43.

20. *Writer,* p. 7.

21. Wallace Stegner, "Creative Writer as an Image Maker," *Writer,* 76 (October 1963), 24.

22. Wallace Stegner, "To a Young Writer," *Atlantic,* 204 (November 1959), 89.

23. "One Way," p. 11.

24. *Writer*, p. 6.

25. Wallace Stegner, *The Gathering of Zion: The Story of the Mormon Trail* (New York: McGraw Hill, 1964), pp. 255–256.

26. Stegner, "Creative Writer as an Image Maker," p. 24.

27. *Second Growth*, p. 38.

28. "One Way," p. 43.

29. Wallace Stegner, "Regionalism in Art," in *Modern Writing*, ed. W. Thorp and M. F. Thorp (New York, n.d.), p. 293.

30. "One Way," p. 9–11.

31. *Writer*, p. 11.

32. *Writer*, p. 31.

33. Wallace Stegner, "Sensibility and Intelligence," *Saturday Review*, 41 (13 December 1958), 24.

34. Anatole Broyard, "Were the Old Times Really Better?" *Life*, 70 (26 March 1971), 14.

35. Broyard, p. 14.

36. *Writer*, p. 4.

37. "One Way," pp. 10–11.

38. "One Way," p. 43.

Narrative Voice in Wallace Stegner's *Angle of Repose*

Audrey C. Peterson*

In *Angle of Repose* Wallace Stegner uses a narrative technique that is both older than Fielding and newer than Nabokov. Ever since Henry James expressed a preference for consistency in point of view, or more accurately ever since theorists codified James's remarks into rules for fiction, it has been not only unfashionable but almost unthinkable for the teller of a tale to "intrude" upon the narrative to make comments. Earlier novelists, from Defoe to Hardy, have been scored for such inartistic practices and then forgiven on the ground of living before the dawning of enlightenment.[1] Yet in *Angle of Repose* the narrator is both an old-fashioned commentator and a contemporary manipulator of the action. Like Nabokov's "editor" in *Pale Fire* he molds his source material into his own creation, but while Nabokov's mode is satiric, Stegner paradoxically achieves an effect of solid realism. My purpose in this paper is to show how the narrative voice presides over and controls the novel, engaging in commentary which enriches rather than intrudes, and engaging in manipulative strategies without apparent loss of credibility.

Stegner accomplishes this tour de force by creating in Lyman Ward a fictional narrator who is himself so believable that the reader comes to accept whatever conventions he dictates. Ward, confined to a wheelchair by a painful and crippling bone disease, finds therapy in recreating the lives of his dead grandparents from letters and papers found in their house in Grass Valley, California, where Ward himself grew up. As his research progresses he records his findings on tape. He also records his own personal dilemma—his wife has left him and his son wants him to abandon his independence and enter a sanatorium. Within this narrative framework, Ward moves back and forth between past and present, stressing always his thesis that the present has a good deal to learn from the past: "Well, Grandmother, let me back out of this desk and turn around and look at you over there in your walnut frame . . . [Is there nothing in your life or art to teach a modern or a one-legged man something?"[2] Fragments of the grandparents' story emerge sporadically, rendered through a mixture of telling techniques. Quoting from letters and reminiscences, mak-

*Reprinted from *Western American Literature* (Summer, 1975), pp. 125–33.

ing wry comments on his own physical plight, carrying on imaginary conversations with his grandmother, Ward slips deftly into the beginnings of third person narration: "The West began for Susan Burling on the last day of 1868, more than a century ago. It had not figured in her plans. She was in love with Art, New York, and Augusta Drake" (p. 32). This appears to be the beginning of omniscient narration, but the narrator's voice is immediately present again, telling us that he "may as well quote" from Susan's reminiscences and following the quote with his comments upon it. Gradually longer passages of Susan's story are rendered by a third person narrator, but Ward's controlling voice is never entirely absent. Sometimes the narrative is punctuated by brief commentary, sometimes by long digressions, but it never continues for more than twenty pages or so without some intervention by the narrative voice.

What makes Stegner's method unique here is that it combines with apparent ease a number of conventional modes which might not be expected to mix well. In one such method, for example, Lyman Ward, a conventional first person narrator, would "tell" all of the novel, both past and present, in his own voice. In another, the author might set up an editorial frame to create verisimilitude, as in a novel like *Henry Esmond* where Thackeray appears on the title page as the "editor," or to take a more recent example, in Thomas Berger's *Little Big Man*, where the fictional "scholar" secures the taped story of Jack Crabb. In this method, Lyman Ward would disappear from the action and the central novel—the past story—would be rendered without his direct presence. In a third method, the author might use a simple alternation of story past and story present, rendering the past through an omniscient narrator and returning to first person only for separated sections of Lyman Ward's own story. Instead, Ward as narrator appears to break all rules of fiction by blithely moving from first to third person, interrupting his own omniscient narrator with pungent comments, and even discussing his own role in "creating" scenes in the novel, yet all the while holding the reader so firmly in his spell that his machinations are largely unobserved.

Just as form in poetry is inextricably linked to meaning, or ought to be, the narrative form in *Angle of Repose* is exactly suited to the need for a confrontation between the values of the past and those of today. The commentary in the novel is crucial to this purpose, as we can see at once if we try to imagine the novel without it. If Stegner had meant to write only a chronicle of the West, the materials were there. Susan Ward's story is based upon the life of Mary Hallock Foote. Stegner worked from unpublished letters and from Mrs. Foote's reminiscences (since published),[3] acknowledging in a prefatory note that he freely adapted his material for "fictional needs." The tale of the Eastern girl, artist and writer living in the unpolished West, is in itself rewarding and well worth a fictional retelling. What Stegner has given us, however, is not merely the frontier story but that story as perceived by a sophisticated twentieth century mind.[4] Ward's witty, irreverent voice breaks in at odd moments, inter-rupting letters "*What*, Grandmother?" he will exclaim when her letters to her friend Augusta sound gushingly romantic, addressing her directly ("Grandmother, take it easy, don't be a Victorian prude"), or, in a more serious tone, assessing his own desire to find that "angle of repose" at which all detritus comes to rest.

The way in which the commentary functions may be seen in some characteristic passages in the novel. Take, for example, two scenes during Oliver Ward's courtship of Susan. It is 1873 and he has come to her home in the East:

> Susan guided him upstairs to his room, the one they called Grandmother's room. There he set his carpetbag inside the door and shook himself out of the ulster, and she watched him lay on the dresser, which had never seen anything rougher than a Quaker bonnet or a book of poems in limp leather, a curved pipe, and a great, wooden-handled revolver.
>
> Was he showing off? I suppose so. God knows why else a man would bring a pistol to his courting. His character and his role were already Western, and he had only that way of asserting himself against the literary gentility with which her house was associated in his mind (p. 60).

The narrator here begins his analysis with a question—"Was he showing off?"—as he does frequently throughout the novel. He wonders aloud about the motives and feelings of the characters and the reader shares in his speculations. Sometimes the narrative voice becomes wryly ironic, as in the following passage, which occurs a few days later:

> On this day she lay down and hung her face over the cliff to see down the waterfall [with] Oliver Ward hanging onto her ankles to make sure she didn't spill over.
>
> Anxious? Not on your life. In these days when a girl goes to bed with anybody who will pat her in a friendly way on the rump, few will be able to imagine how Oliver Ward felt, holding those little ankles. He would not have let go if fire had swept the hilltop, if warrior ants had swarmed over him from head to foot, if Indians had sneaked from the bushes and hacked him loose from his hands (p. 62).

The narrator here is clearly on the side of Oliver and his romantic clinging to those little ankles. His tongue-in-cheek commentary does not intrude upon the fiction but rather enriches it by pulling out a scene from the past and scrutinizing it through contemporary eyes, forcing a constant re-assessment of values.

Concepts which may seem out of fashion today are thus constantly reexamined through the commentary. Moderns, says Ward, lack a sense of history. His sociologist son Rodman "is a great measurer" but "he never goes back more than ten years," while Ward identifies with his grand-parents: "I believe in Time, as they did, and in the life chronological rather than in life existential. We live in time and through it, we build our huts in its ruins, or used to, and we cannot afford all these abandonings" (p. 14). Like "time," the concept of "home" is given a fresh look. Susan weeps as she sees a bit of sentimental verse on the front of the Franklin stove, in the home in New Almaden which they are forced to leave:

> Sentimental? [says the narrator.] Of course. Riddled with the Anglo-American mawkishness about home, quicksandy with assumptions about monogamy and Women's Highest Role, buttery with echoes of the household poets. All that. But I find that I don't mind her emotions and her sentiments. Home is a notion that only nations of the homeless fully appreciate and only the uprooted comprehend. . . . So I don't snicker backward ninety years at poor Grandmother pacing her porch and biting her knuckle and hating the loss of what she had never quite got over thinking her exile. I find her moving (p. 159).

Again, when Susan has to abandon yet another home, the narrator comments: "I doubt that anyone of Rodman's generation could comprehend the home feelings of someone like Susan Ward." The moderns, he continues, "have suffered emphathectomy, their computers hum no ghostly feedback of Home, Sweet Home. How marvelously free they are! How unutterably deprived!" (pp. 277, 278).

To summarize, then, the passages quoted above should give some notion of the way in which the narrator's commentary becomes an indispensable part of the fabric of the novel. Without it, Susan Ward's story would still be a compelling tale, but we would lose the moral and intellectual play of Lyman Ward's mind upon the fiction. Delivered by an omniscient narrator, many of his pronouncements would have an air of didacticism, but coming from Ward, whose own character is fully established in the novel, they emerge as the reflections of an incisive, amusing, and refreshingly unorthodox mind.

His use of commentary freely mixed with third person narration is, however, only one aspect of Stegner's unusual technique in this novel. I should like to turn now to what I have called the narrator's role as manipulator." It is one thing to interrupt the narrative with comments; it is another for the narrator to announce, often at crucial moments in the novel, that scenes did not "really happen," he simply made them up. But Stegner's narrator does just that, and manages his strategy so subtly that readers seem to suffer no loss of belief. Reviewers, for example, beyond noting that it is a "novel-within-a-novel,"[5] or that the narrator is both "interpreter" and "participant,"[6] complain of no loss of illusion because of the narrative method but treat the novel in realistic terms.[7]

The narrator in *Angle of Repose* is a manipulator in the largest sense because he is dealing with actual source materials which he in turn molds into fiction. But instead of producing a finished product, an artifact called a novel which is then presented whole and complete, the narrator shares with the reader the process of creation. Stegner gains an effect of absolute immediacy through the device of the tape recorder—the novel has not already "happened" and is now being "told"; it is itself in the process of unfolding. The Lyman Ward who records the story is not recounting what happened last year or even last month; he is recording what he is thinking and feeling—and writing—at this moment. He does not "know" at the beginning what the end will be. Almost half way through the novel, he is not even sure what kind of book he is writing. When, for example, Rodman remarks that Ward is writing a book about Western history, he denies this:

> 'I've written enough history books to know this isn't one. I'm writing about something else. A marriage, I guess. . . .'
> Rodman is surprised. So am I, actually—I have never formulated precisely what it is I have been doing, but the minute I say it I know I have said it right (p. 211).

As historian-turned-novelist, Ward continues to explore the nature of the book he is writing. In a superb scene with his young secretary, Shelly—who, like Rodman, represents the contemporary scene—Ward deals with the rights and privileges of an omniscient narrator. "This afternoon [he begins] she asked me if I didn't think I was being a little inhibited about my grandparents' sex life. 'Because it's a novel,' she said. 'It isn't history—you're making half of it up, and if you're going to make up some of it, why not go the whole way?' " (p. 266). Ward replies that he may look to her like a novelist but he is "still a historian under the crust." Moreover, he deplores the contemporary obsession with explicit sex and respects the Victorian attitude toward privacy. Her grandmother had discipline, self-control, modesty:

> 'Modesty, there's a word 1970 can't even conceive. Is that a woman I want to show making awkward love on a camp cot? Do you want to hear her erotic cries? . . .'
> 'I didn't mean that, exactly. I was just thinking from the point of view of the modern reader. He might think you were ducking something essential.'
> 'That's too bad. Hasn't the modern reader got any imagination?'
> 'Well, *you* know. . . . How would it be if every modern novel did it like Paolo and Francesca—"That day they read no more"?'
> 'O.K., so I haven't fooled you with my dishonest methods,' I said. 'Just leave me there with old hypocritical Dante' (p. 269).

This passage illustrates the way in which the narrative technique reinforces meaning in the novel. By using a narrator who is himself exploring fictional techniques, defending his right not to "tell" more than he chooses, Stegner makes an amusing point about values in the contemporary novel.

Perhaps the most significant use of manipulation in the novel can be shown in three key scenes, all involving the central dramatic conflict: the attachment between Susan and her husband's young assistant with whom she could talk so congenially of books and art and life. The first of these scenes occurs when Frank returns to Boise canyon after a three-year absence. The narrator begins with speculation: "What would Susan Ward and Frank Sargent have said to each other in the two hours before Oliver and Ollie returned from town? . . . Their words, like their actions, would have been hedged by a hundred restraints. She was incorrigibly a lady, he was self-consciously honorable" (p. 449). Then, after two pages or so of speculation and commentary, the narrator abruptly states: "And now I can't avoid it any longer. I *have* to put words in their mouths" and proceeds to render, as third person narrator, a totally moving scene.

In the above instance the reader is told first that the scene is being created. In a second scene manipulation is carried a step further as the revelation comes afterward. Frank and Susan, alone on the veranda of the house on the mesa, struggle with temptation and renunciation, in what is surely one of the most memorable scenes in the novel. The narrator then says: "What went on on that piazza? I don't know. I don't even know that they were there. I just made up the scene to fit other facts that I do know. . . . I gravely doubt that they 'had sex,' in Shelly's charming phrase. . . . I only know that passion and guilt happened in some form" (p. 508).

The third such scene occurs at the dramatic climax of the novel—the accidental drowning of Susan's young daughter. In this case the scene is rendered not in narrative form as accomplished "fact" but through a series of questions by the narrator, who again "does not know" what happened. He asks:

> [Was Frank] there all the time—had he been sitting in that tall sage with his arm around Susan Ward, or with Susan Ward's two hands in his, pleading his urgent, ardent, reckless, hopeless cause? Were those two so absorbed in themselves that they forgot for a while to wonder where Agnes had got to? Did Susan, pushing away the misery of their parting, or whatever it was, stand up at some point, looking anxiously around in the growing dusk . . . and call out, and have no answer? (p. 536)

"I made up the scene." "I put words in their mouths." "I don't know what happened." "Was he there all the time?" This is indeed a remarkable series of statements for a novel that is praised for its solid realism. Moreover, most readers undoubtedly accept each of these scenes and others similarly created, as true and faithful renditions of what did "happen" in the story of Susan Ward. The very questioning of what is fiction, what is truth, seems to substantiate rather than betray the illusion of reality.

A final manipulation by the narrator occurs at the end of the novel when the return of Lyman Ward's wife is revealed as Ward's dreams of what might have happened. All of the manipulative strategies in the novel—the discussions of the novel form, the revelation that scenes were "made up," the dream device—are used in various ways by some contemporary novelists, often in non-realistic or absurdist modes. Perhaps the closest parallel to Stegner's method is that used by John Fowles' *The French Lieutenant's Woman,* in which the illusion of reality is challenged by the narrator. After presenting twelve chapters of a conventional "Victorian" novel, Fowles' narrator announces: "This story I am telling is all imagination. These characters I create never existed outside of my own mind."[8] Then follows a witty discussion of changing modes in fiction and of the tendency of characters to gain autonomy and move out of the author's control. He brings the novel to a first conventional ending which he then says did not happen but was only imagined, and ultimately gives two alternative versions of the "real" ending because he cannot decide which is better. Both Fowles and Stegner are concerned with questioning the assumption by moderns that contemporary attitudes toward life represent "progress"; both suggest, through the device of exploring earlier modes of fiction, that earlier attitudes may also be valid. What interests me especially, however, is that while Fowles' readers are almost invariably aware of his pyrotechnics,[9] Stegner's readers, as I have stated above, willingly suspend their disbelief.

In closing, I should like to suggest that a final dimension in the novel is the dramatic irony surrounding the character of Lyman Ward. It is essential not to confuse Ward with Stegner. As Robert Canzoneri observes in speaking of *All the Little Live Things,* we must not think Stegner "so naive as to speak in his own voice while operating Joe Allston's mouth like that of a puppet" (p. 823). Lyman Ward's views very often coincide with those of Stegner; in this sense he is what Wayne Booth calls a "reliable narrator," because his norms are in accord with those of the implied author. But the reader is clearly intended to see Ward as a dramatized character, subject to human frailty. He is embittered by personal loss; he valiantly clings to a productive life in the face of progressive physical paralysis. The reader is aware that the violent expression of his opinions is often dictated by physical or even more by emotional pain. He is admirable for maintaining his wry sense of humor despite such odds. The final measure of Stegner's achievement is that *Angle of Repose* is the creation of a narrator so convincing that he in turn creates and controls all the levels of fiction in the novel.

Notes

1. For the best defense of authorial "telling," see Wayne C. Booth, *The Rhetoric of Fiction* (University of Chicago Press), 1961.

2. Wallace Stegner, *Angle of Repose* (New York: Doubleday, 1971), p. 7. All citations are from this edition.

3. *A Victorian Gentlewoman in the Far West: The Reminiscences of Mary Hallock Foote,* ed. Rodman W. Paul (San Marino, California: Huntington Library, 1972).

4. Robert Canzoneri makes a similar point, but does not develop it in detail, in "Wallace Stegner: Trial by Existence," *Southern Review*, 9 (Autumn 1973), 825.

5. Janet Burroway,(*New Statesman* 17 September 1971), p. 369.

6. William Abrahams, "The Real Thing," *Atlantic*, 227 (April 1971), 96.

7. In a minority opinion, Glendy Culligan finds the novel lacking in "vitality," not however because of the narrative technique but because she finds Lyman Ward too "cerebral" (*Saturday Review*, 20 March 1971, p. 30).

8. John Fowles, *The French Lieutenant's Woman* (Boston: Little, Brown, 1969), p. 95.

9. Reviewers typically note that the "author intervenes in the narrative" (*New Statesman*, 13 June 1969, p. 850); that the narrator is a poseur who "holds his reader skillfully with story-tellers' tricks"(*TLS*, 12 June 1969, p. 629); or that the narrator "acts more like an impresario than a novelist" with a result that "delights" and "bewitches"(*Saturday Review*, 22 November 1969, p. 85).

Angle of Repose and the Writings of Mary Hallock Foote: A Source Study

Mary Ellen Williams Walsh*

In *Angle of Repose*, Lyman Ward sits at his desk in Grass Valley, California, surrounded by the papers of his grandmother, Susan Burling Ward, using the papers to write a kind of biography of Susan and her marriage to Oliver Ward. The papers include hundreds of letters Susan had written to her friend, Augusta, an unpublished reminiscence written late in Susan's life, copies of her published and unpublished essays, stories, novels, and illustrations, and numerous photographs of Susan and members of her family. As Wallace Stegner wrote *Angle of Repose*, he sat at a desk surrounded by the papers of Mary Hallock Foote, a nineteenth-century writer and illustrator, renowned in her day for her portrayal of the Western American experience in both her prose and her drawings. Foote's papers included hundreds of letters she had written to her friend, Helena DeKay Gilder; an unpublished reminiscence Foote wrote in the early 1920s; copies of Foote's published and unpublished essays, stories, novels, and illustrations; and numerous photographs of Foote and members of her family.

Two confusions have developed as a result of the complexity of this parallel situation. One centers on the extent to which Stegner borrowed from Mary Hallock Foote's papers in composing the novel. The other centers on how closely the Susan Burling Ward story reflects the life story of Mary Hallock Foote. The purpose of this paper is to clarify both situations, because as a result of the first, Stegner's indebtedness to Mary Hallock Foote's art has been underestimated, and as a result of the second, Mary Hallock Foote's character and personal life have been wrongly interpreted. The clarifying of these situations leads almost inevitably to a consideration of the ethical issues involved in Stegner's use of Foote's life and art. I will, therefore, first present the evidence of Stegner's borrowings from Foote's papers. Second, I will demonstrate the differences between the life of Susan Burling Ward and the life of Mary Hallock Foote. Finally, I will examine the ethical issues involved in the composition of the novel.

*This essay was written especially for this volume and appears here for the first time with the permission of the author.

I

The confusion concerning the extent to which Stegner borrowed from Mary Hallock Foote's writings in composing *Angle of Repose* is apparent in the published appraisals of the novel. Most critics and reviewers have apparently been unaware that Stegner worked closely and directly from Foote's papers, quoting and paraphrasing extensively, using her broad story line, her significant scenes, her authentic details. The publication of Foote's reminiscences a year after the publication of the novel made it possible for readers of both the novel and the reminiscences to discover the major source of the Susan Burling Ward story. In fact, in the "Bibliographical Note" that accompanies his edition of the reminiscences, Rodman Paul pointed out that "the basic settings [of *Angle of Repose*] and the cast of characters have been re-created out of Mary Hallock Foote's own descriptions, with few changes and only the thin disguise of a slight alteration of names. . . ."[1]

Much criticism of the novel, however, has played down the Susan Burling Ward story and has focused on what the critics consider to be Stegner's own great creation, the narrator, Lyman Ward. Perhaps the most significant discovery I have made in my research into the sources of the novel is that Stegner also "re-created" Lyman from a character in Mary Hallock Foote's unpublished story, "The Miniature."[2] The story is set in a California mining district in the stone-pillared house of the manager of a mine. In a cottage on the grounds live the caretakers, an old gardener and his wife. The hero is a cripple, confined to a wheelchair. His mind, however, is very active. He introduces himself to the heroine as "the family skeleton on wheels." He is surrounded by women—a nurse, an aunt, his mother—for whom he feels a "morbid sensitiveness." His nurse is "five feet eight, stalwart and soft-shod" and can "pick up Dick with no more effort than if he were a baby." He is powerfully affected by dreams of a young woman who had once lived in the house, dreams which he recounts fully to the heroine and about which he cautions her not to say " 'Freud' " or " 'psycho.' "[3] In other circumstances, the obvious correspondences between "The Miniature" and *Angle of Repose* could be explained away as coincidental. Given Stegner's use of Foote's writings for the Susan Burling Ward story, however, it seems accurate to conclude that the situation of the hero in "The Miniature" provided the idea and the basic outline for the character of Lyman.

Although the Susan Burling Ward story has received less critical attention than has the narrator of the story, both early reviewers and other more recent critics have singled out aspects of that story for special notice. In doing so, they have inadvertently praised Stegner for creating material that he actually found in Foote's writings. Glendy Culligan, in *Saturday Review*, pointed with admiration to the inclusion of "such 'historical personages' as Helen Hunt Jackson and Clarence King, the latter fresh from

converse with his old friend Henry Adams."[4] Stegner was able to make
such felicitous use of these historical personages because they visited Mary
Hallock Foote's "salon" in Leadville; she described these visits and those
of other well-known geologists and financiers in her reminiscences, including such details as the "beautiful white buckskins" worn by S. F. Emmons (Gentlewoman, pp. 179–86).[5] William Abrahams, in the Atlantic,
praised Stegner for the wide range of "his settings—California, New
York, the Dakotas, Idaho, Mexico. . . ."[6] Actually, the settings are the
places where Mary Hallock Foote lived; they are all richly described in
the reminiscences, the letters, and her published work. Abrahams also ex-
tolled Susan's letters as "a triumph of verisimilitude, perfectly matched to
Mr. Stegner's carefully rendered locales and social discriminations."[7]
Mary Hallock Foote wrote the majority of the letters, from the locales
which she herself exquisitely renders.[8] In recent critical essays, Kerry
Ahearn has written: "In a nice touch, Stegner has Oliver 'rescued' from
the inactive irrigation scheme with an invitation from John Wesley
Powell to join the Geological Survey,"[9] and he credits Stegner with
another "nice touch" for placing the separation of Oliver and Susan "in
Vardis Fisher country."[10] As Mary Hallock Foote records in her
reminiscences, Arthur Foote was hired by John Wesley Powell when Arthur's irrigation project was slowly dying (Gentlewoman, pp. 307–8). Arthur and Mary lived for years in "Vardis Fisher country."

An examination of Mary Hallock Foote's papers reveals that, in addition to these items praised by the critics, her writings are the source of the
title of the novel, the metaphor and the theme associated with the title,
the outline and most of the major events and scenes of the Susan Burling
Ward story. The examination further reveals that in working with Foote's
writings, Stegner did not always bother to "re-create" her material. He
sometimes simply incorporates passages from her writings directly into his
novel. For some of these passages, he provides the semi-documentation
that Lyman is quoting from Susan Burling Ward's papers, when Stegner
is in fact quoting from Mary Hallock Foote's papers. The semi-
documentation serves no real purpose, of course, in identifying his
sources. On the one hand, many readers of the novel will assume that
Stegner has created the reminiscences, letters, and other papers from
which he purports to be quoting, just as William Abrahams assumed in
his Atlantic review. On the other hand, the reader who knows that
Stegner based the novel on the life of Mary Hallock Foote is likely to
assume that the semi-documented passages and only those passages are
quotations from Foote's writings. Both assumptions are completely in
error. In addition to the semi-documented passages, Stegner incorporates
other directly quoted passages and numerous closely paraphrased
passages. He also incorporates numerous details which provide crispness
to the narrative texture and authenticity to the tone of the novel. Most of
the significant scenes incorporate the structure that Mary Hallock Foote

provided. Even the names of the major characters were pulled from the Hallock and Foote family trees. "Burling" was the maiden name of Mary Hallock Foote's mother. "Lyman" and "Ward" are both family names in Arthur DeWint Foote's family. "Rodman" is the name of the Footes' son-in-law. Most of the names of other characters are taken directly from Foote's writings.

To demonstrate the range and extent of Stegner's borrowings from Foote's writings for the Susan Burling Ward story requires extensive documentation. The analysis which follows is organized according to the appearance of the borrowed material part by part in *Angle of Repose*. I have chosen this organization because the chronology of the borrowings corresponds very closely to the chronology of the source material in Mary Hallock Foote's reminiscences, the major source. I have also cited the letters and other writings as they appear part by part. This organization demonstrates how fully each part derives from the writings of Mary Hallock Foote.

Part I Grass Valley

In introducing Susan Burling Ward, Stegner uses passages from Foote's reminiscences that provide both the title and a major theme of the novel. In her narration of the closing of the Footes' time in Boise Canyon, Foote describes the letters she received from miners and other professional men all over the world who had read her stories and wondered how she had learned so much about their work *(Gentlewoman,* pp. 305–6). As she ends this description, she speculates on the phrase "angle of repose," remarking that it is "too good to waste on rockslides or heaps of sand. Each one of us in the cañon was slipping and crawling and grinding along seeking what to us was that angle, but we were not any of us ready for repose" *(Gentlewoman,* p. 306). A few pages later, she writes: "All of which would tend towards that angle of repose which one finds and loses from time to time but is always seeking in one way or another" *(Gentlewoman,* p. 309). Using these passages from Foote, Stegner describes the letters Susan Burling Ward receives from miners and closes the paragraph with a speculation on the phrase "angle of repose." In a paraphrase of Foote, he writes of Susan: "But you were too alert to the figurative possibilities of words not to see the phrase as descriptive of human as well as detrital rest. As you said, it was too good for mere dirt; you tried to apply it to your own wandering and uneasy life" *(Angle,* p. 24).

The major events in Susan Burling Ward's early life that Stegner develops in Part I are borrowed from events in Foote's life and are narrated primarily following the chronological order in which Foote describes them in her reminiscences *(Gentlewoman,* pp. 73–117). One significant deviation from the chronology is the introduction of Augusta, the fictional version of Mary Hallock Foote's friend, Helena DeKay

Gilder. In Foote's reminiscences this passage follows her account of her meeting Arthur. In the novel, the passage from Susan's reminiscences that describes her meeting with Augusta at school in New York is a direct quotation, with only minor deletions, of Foote's description of her meeting with Helena (*Angle*, p. 33; *Gentlewoman*, pp. 97–9).

Stegner's account of the New Year's reception at which Susan and Oliver meet (*Angle*, pp. 34–43) replicates very closely Mary Hallock Foote's description of her meeting with Arthur (*Gentlewoman*, pp. 75–82). Mary and Arthur, like Susan and Oliver, met at the home of Moses Beach, where Mary was visiting at the invitation of Emma Beach. Foote's account provides the broad outlines for Stegner's scene: Henry Ward Beecher's holding forth to a group which Mary tries to escape (*Gentlewoman*, p. 77); a discussion of Beecher's use of the Beach's library (*Gentlewoman*, pp. 77–78); a description of the arrival of the young men callers (*Gentlewoman*, p. 79); an account of her meeting with Arthur in the library (*Gentlewoman*, pp. 80–81). In addition to the broad outline, Foote's account is the source of the following details in Stegner's narration:

- the large window in the Beach house (*Gentlewoman*, p. 75; cf. *Angle*, p. 35)
- the discussion of Katie Bloede, her background, her marriage to Thayer (*Gentlewoman*, p. 76; cf. *Angle*, pp. 35–36)
- Foote's comment on Katie Bloede, "her face was his inspiration" (*Gentlewoman*, p. 76), a sentence which Stegner paraphrases as follows: "As Grandmother said, 'Her face was his fortune' " (*Angle*, p. 36)
- the Elwood Walter sketch (*Gentlewoman*, p. 69; cf. *Angle*, p. 36)
- the George Haviland sketch (*Gentlewoman*, p. 67; cf. *Angle*, p. 36)
- Mrs. Beach's remonstrance, " 'Mary Hallock, sit still!' " and " 'Lizzie will see to it' " (*Gentlewoman*, p. 77), sentences which Stegner paraphrases as follows: " 'Susan Burling, sit down!' " and " 'Minnie will let them in' " (*Angle*, p. 37)
- the description of the young men at the party as "almost too boastful" (*Gentlewoman*, p. 79), a phrase which Stegner uses in the following sentence: "Grandmother thought them 'almost too boastful' . . ." (*Angle*, p. 36)
- Foote's description of Arthur as having "a restfulness of manner which seems to go with certain occupations or with the temperaments that seek them—sailors and horsemen and farmers" (*Gentlewoman*, p. 80), an idea which Stegner paraphrases in his description of Oliver as having "an air of quiet such as she had known in men like her father, men who worked with animals" (*Angle*, p. 38)

- Foote's report that Arthur "merely said how jolly it must be to have work that one liked and make it pay" (*Gentlewoman*, p. 80), a remark which Stegner paraphrases in the following dialogue: "But he only said, 'It must be wonderful to do what you like and get paid for it' " (*Angle*, p. 39)
- the information that Arthur Foote had gone to Florida to grow oranges and had had malaria after he had left Yale and the Sheffield Scientific School because of his eyesight (*Gentlewoman*, p. 80; cf. *Angle*, pp. 39–40)
- the discussion of Arthur's "Beecher blood," which is described as follows in Foote's account:

He corrected me with emphasis: 'I have no Beecher blood. . . .'
The connection was on the Foote side: Roxanna Foote, his father's sister, was the mother of Henry Ward and Thomas and Catherine Beecher and Mrs. Stowe, and 'Cousin Mary Perkins,' who was heard to say once that she began life as the 'daughter of Lyman Beecher' and grew up as the 'sister of Harriet Beecher Stowe,' and now she was finally settled and accounted for as 'the mother-in-law of Edward Hale' (*Gentlewoman*, p. 81),

a passage which Stegner paraphrases as follows:

He looked annoyed. 'I have no Beecher blood. . . .'
Like one patiently explaining incriminating circumstances, he said, 'My father's sister married Lyman Beecher. She's the mother of that whole brood—Henry Ward, Thomas, Catherine, Mrs. Stowe, and Cousin Mary Perkins, the best of the litter. . . . The other night she was telling me of the story of her life. She said she grew up the daughter of Lyman Beecher, and then became the sister of Harriet Beecher Stowe, and finally hit rock bottom as the mother-in-law of Edward Everett Hale' (*Angle*, pp. 40–41)

- Foote's closing reflective paragraph on her meeting with Arthur (*Gentlewoman*, p. 82), a passage which becomes Lyman's quotation from his grandmother's memoirs on her meeting with Oliver and which differs from Foote's original only in the following wording in the penultimate sentence, "I had my drawing pad with me" and the insertion of "with me" before the final phrase of that sentence (*Angle*, p. 42)

Stegner's account of the five-year interval which elapsed between the meeting of Susan and Oliver and their wedding (*Angle*, pp. 51–52) is drawn from Foote's description of a similar interval in hers and Arthur's life (*Gentlewoman*, p. 101–104). Foote's description includes the following details which Stegner incorporated into *Angle of Repose*:

- Arthur's work on the Southern Pacific's "Loop" at the Tehachapi Pass (*Gentlewoman*, p. 103; cf. *Angle*, p. 51)
- the detail that Arthur "had been in Sutro Tunnel, roasted, steamed

out at a temperature underground that made strong men faint"
(Gentlewoman, p. 103), a passage which Stegner paraphrases in
his statement that Oliver "boiled alive in the Sutro Tunnel" *(Angle,*
p. 51)

- the visits by George W. Cable and George Macdonald to Milton
  (Gentlewoman, pp. 100–1; cf. *Angle,* p. 52)
- her illustration of Longfellow's *The Hanging of the Crane*
  (Gentlewoman, p. 102; cf. *Angle,* p. 52)
- Foote's statement that she "bragged of [her life] to my strategist in
  the West. It was ungenerous and crude of me . . ."
  (Gentlewoman, p. 103), a remark which becomes Stegner's state-
  ment about Susan that "she admits she boasted, 'ungenerously' "
  (Angle, p. 52)
- John LaFarge's reading the Rubáiyát *(Gentlewoman,* p. 113; cf.
  Angle, p. 51).

Stegner describes Oliver's arrival for his wedding by means of the
significant details from Foote's paragraph describing Arthur's similar arrival. In *Angle of Repose,* Oliver wears a "great hooded cloak or ulster"
for which he apologizes, explaining that "it was his field coat, his town
coat was stolen in San Francisco" *(Angle,* p. 59). Susan conducts him to
"his room, the one they called Grandmother's room," where "she
watched him lay on the dresser, which had never seen anything rougher
than a Quaker bonnet or a book of poems in limp leather, a curved pipe,
and a great wooden-handled revolver" *(Angle,* p. 60). Mary Hallock
Foote reports Arthur's arrival at her home in the following passage from
the reminiscences: "He came—in a great hooded ulster belted around
him, his field overcoat; his new one had been stolen by a hat-rack thief
from the front hall of the house where he was a guest on the night before
his journey—and that was a blow if you like! He unpacked his leathery
luggage in the room we still called 'grandmother's room' and laid his pipe
and pistol on the bureau where her chaste neckerchiefs had been wont to
lie . . ." *(Gentlewoman,* p. 104).

Stegner's brief description of Susan and Oliver's wedding *(Angle,*
p. 67) corresponds to Foote's equally brief description of her wedding to
Arthur, including the mention that Helena was unable to attend
(Gentlewoman, p. 105). And finally the circumstances of Susan's leaving
for the West are to be found in Foote's description of her own departure:

- the hiring of a servant Lizzie Griffen, who with her small baby
  would serve as a model for Hester Prynne in Foote's illustration of
  the *Scarlet Letter (Gentlewoman,* p. 115–6; cf. *Angle,* p. 70)
- Arthur's being unable to send her money for the trip and her embarrassment at having to pay her own way *(Gentlewoman,* p. 115;
  cf. *Angle,* p. 71).

In addition to heavy reliance on Foote's narrative in her
reminiscences, Stegner incorporates letters written by Foote as the letters

of Susan. Susan's "Fishkill Landing" letter is excerpted from a much longer letter written by Mary Hallock to Helena DeKay from Fishkill Landing on September 23, [1873]. Stegner omits long explanatory and chatty paragraphs from Foote's letter which diffuse the sense of anguish that is present in the compressed form. Stegner also changes the wording of a crucial sentence. Foote wrote: "I love her as wives do (not) love their husbands as *friends* who have taken each other for life. . . ." Stegner omits the phrase "do (not)" and the emphasis on the word "friends": "I love her as wives love their husbands, as friends who have taken each other for life" (*Angle,* p. 57). Stegner adds the following sentences to the letter: "And oh! what a sick sunk feeling to see the *Mary Powell's* lights already out in the river, going every second farther away! I was distracted. I stood on this landing and wept, and then I walked, and it is only now, two hours later, that I have enough control of myself to huddle here on the bench and write you this by starlight and ask you to forgive me" (*Angle,* p. 57).[11] Susan's letter to Thomas (*Angle,* p. 58) is excerpted and directly quoted from Mary Hallock's letter to Richard Gilder, written from Milton on December 13, [1873]. Susan's letters from Guilford on her honeymoon (*Angle,* pp. 67, 68, 69) are excerpted with few minor changes from two of Foote's letters written from Guilford on her honeymoon, one undated and one written February 18, [1876]. Foote's February 18, [1876], letter from Guilford is also the source of the information in *Angle of Repose* that Oliver's ancestor General Ward had received a letter from George Washington and that Oliver's great-great-grandmother had received a love letter with the salutation "Honored Madame," from which she had torn the signature (*Angle,* p. 69). Susan's letter to Augusta apologizing for Oliver (*Angle,* p. 70) is excerpted and directly quoted from a letter Foote wrote to Helena from Milton in March, [1876].

Part II New Almaden

In Part II, Stegner uses not only Foote's reminiscences and letters but also her *Scribner's* article on New Almaden, "A California Mining Camp."[12] Stegner also describes a photograph of Susan in the Boise Canyon (*Angle,* p. 98) which is an actual photograph of Foote and appears on the cover of *A Victorian Gentlewoman in the Far West.*

In addition to once again following the broad outlines of the New Almaden experience as Foote recounts it in the reminiscences (*Gentlewoman,* pp. 121–39), Stegner uses the following specific details and scenes:
- Foote's arrival in San Francisco without her trunks and her borrowing clothes from her sister-in-law, Mary Hague (Gentlewoman, p. 122; cf. *Angle,* p. 81)
- Arthur's wedding presents of a grass mat and fan from Fiji and a water cooler from Guadalajara inscribed "Help thyself, little

Tomasa" (*Gentlewoman*, p. 123; cf. *Angle*, p. 87)
- the Footes' dinner at Mother Fall's (*Gentlewoman*, p. 124; cf. (*Angle*, p. 95)
- Foote's using her maid Lizzie for the model for Hester Prynne (*Gentlewoman*, p. 133; cf. *Angle*, p. 110)
- the visit of Hamilton Smith (*Gentlewoman*, p. 128; cf. *Angle*, p. 122)
- Mary Hague's visit, which Stegner describes as Mary Prager's visit to Susan by quoting with minor deletions the Mary Hague passage in the reminiscences (*Gentlewoman*, p. 134–5; cf. *Angle*, p. 123)
- Georgiana Bruce's making the rag doll for Buster (*Gentlewoman*, p. 134; cf. *Angle*, p. 125)
- the crib quilt made by a Cornish miner (*Gentlewoman*, p. 138; cf. *Angle*, p. 133)
- the Chinese flag which sheltered Foote's son (*Gentlewoman*, p. 159; cf. *Angle*, p. 133)
- a description of Foote's drawing expeditions accompanied by Marian C. and the baby (*Gentlewoman*, p. 136; cf. *Angle*, p. 134)
- a description of the *aguador* drawn by Foote (*Gentlewoman*, p. 128; cf. *Angle*, p. 146)
- the "no smoking" sign posted in Arthur's office (*Gentlewoman*, p. 128; cf. *Angle*, p. 148)
- the firing of an old miner for bringing stovepipe from San Jose and the tearing down of his house (*Gentlewoman*, p. 126; cf. *Angle*, pp. 150, 154–55).

In many of the instances in which Stegner quotes directly from Foote's reminiscences, he prefaces the quotation with an indication that he is quoting from Susan Burling Ward's reminiscences. In Part II, in the first of several instances, he quotes directly from Foote's reminiscences without providing even the fictional documentation that he has previously supplied.
- One of these direct quotations is Foote's sentence, "an engineer's capital is his experience" (*Gentlewoman*, p. 139; *Angle*, p. 151).
- The other directly incorporated quotation is a more extensive one from Foote's description of the visit of Georgiana Bruce. The passage appears in Foote's reminiscences as follows:

> Mrs. Kirby before her marriage was Georgiana Bruce, one of the Brook Farm transcendentalists, devoted to the improvement of society and the world. She had not been with us two days before she saw a missionary work before her in the training of that embryo man who went by the name of *Buster. He was destructive,* she said, *because his latent tenderness had not been appealed to; boys* especially *should play with dolls, to teach them to care for others* and paternal *responsibility—brickbats and tiles they would find for themselves* (*Gentlewoman*, pp. 133–4; italics mine).

The passage appears in *Angle of Repose* as follows:

> [S]he had been Georgiana Bruce, and she was one of the Brook Farm transcendentalists. All her life she had been saving the world. . . . She cast her bright enameled blue eye on Georgie, known as *Buster* because he busted everything within reach, and told dismayed Lizzie that *he was destructive because his latent tenderness had not been appealed to. Boys should play with dolls, to teach them care for others and* to stimulate their later parental *responsibility—brickbats and tiles they would find for themselves* (*Angle*, pp. 124–5; italics mine).

Mary Hallock Foote's letters are also a rich source for Stegner's New Almaden narrative, especially a letter written July 18, [1876], the letter that Stegner describes when he quotes from it as Susan's "serial" letter. The July 18 letter contains the following information:

- a description of the Footes' house and its situation (cf. *Angle*, p. 86)
- an account of the dog Stranger (cf. *Angle*, p. 88)
- an account of Mary and Arthur's having tea on the veranda on the first night of her arrival (cf. *Angle*, p. 90).

Stegner also directly quotes parts of this letter (*Angle*, pp. 95, 97). Parts of two letters, one undated and one dated July 19, [1876], written by Foote to Helena expressing her grief at the death of Helena's child are combined by Stegner to form Susan's similar letter to Augusta (*Angle*, pp. 100–1). Foote's letter written August 25, [1876], contains a brief account of a visit she made down into the mine; it is also directly quoted in part by Stegner as Susan's first letter describing her homesickness (*Angle*, p. 102). Susan's second letter on her "wistful memories" of home (*Angle*, p. 103) is excerpted from Foote's letter to Helena written October 21, [1876]. The greater part of Susan's letter describing their visit to San Francisco (*Angle*, pp. 117–9) is excerpted from Foote's lengthy letter to Helena written December 7, [1876]; the last paragraph of Susan's letter is quoted from Foote's letter to Helena written on January 16, [1877]. Susan's letter on contraceptives (*Angle*, pp. 119–120) is quoted from Foote's letter to Helena written on [January] 21, [1877].

Mary Hallock Foote's descriptive essay on New Almaden, "A California Mining Camp," is the source of names, details, and descriptions used by Stegner:

- the names of Tregoning, Tyrrell, Trengrove ("Camp," p. 481; cf. *Angle*, p. 84)
- the meat boxes nailed to posts by the Cornish miners and a description of the Cornish camp ("Camp," p. 481; cf. *Angle*, pp. 84–85)
- a description of the various levels of the camp: Hacienda, Cornish camp, Spanish camp ("Camp," passim; cf. *Angle*, p. 101 passim)
- the scene of the wood carrier tossing his scarf to the veranda ("Camp," p. 490; cf. *Angle*, pp. 107–10)

- the miner's salute, "Bueña salud, Señoras," before drinking ("Camp," p. 482; cf. *Angle*, p. 143).

Part III Santa Cruz

Stegner's sources for Part III are Mary Hallock Foote's reminiscences (*Gentlewoman*, pp. 140–53) and her letters. In addition, Stegner cites an article by Susan as providing the background for Lyman's imagining of what Santa Cruz was like when Susan and Oliver were there. The article to which Stegner refers is one written by Mary Hallock Foote, "A Sea-port on the Pacific."[13]

In addition to the broad outlines Stegner found there, Foote's reminiscences provide the following specific information:

- a telegram from Hague and Janin describing Arthur as "entirely competent" (*Gentlewoman*, p. 150), a phrase Stegner uses to describe Oliver (*Angle*, p. 172)
- Mrs. Kirby (Georgiana Bruce) on birth control (*Gentlewoman*, p. 142; cf. *Angle*, p. 182)
- Mrs. Kirby's remark, "and I took the little tanner" (*Gentlewoman*, p. 144) a sentence which Stegner incorporates as follows: "So I took the little tanner' (*Angle*, p. 183)
- the following account of Mrs. Kirby: "She never could forget that once she had wiped dishes with Margaret Fuller and sat on doorsteps on spring nights and talked philosophy with George William Curtis . . ." (*Gentlewoman*, p. 144), a description which Stegner paraphrases in the following dialogue: " 'He's not enough like George William Curtis. He never washed dishes with Margaret Fuller' " (*Angle*, p. 183)
- the details of the marriages of Lizzie and Marian (*Gentlewoman*, pp. 142, 150; cf. *Angle*, p. 193)
- the scene of Mary Hallock Foote's arrival late at night in Poughkeepsie (*Gentlewoman*, pp. 152–153; cf. *Angle*, pp. 196–7).

Mary Hallock Foote's Santa Cruz letters contain not only information useful to Stegner but also drawings of a promontory which the Footes considered buying. Susan's January 4, 1878, letter (*Angle*, p. 189) is excerpted from a lengthy undated letter by Foote, probably written in January 1878. In the first sentence of Susan's letter, Stegner adds the clause, "that we have not quite recovered our hope for the future, which we planned," and uses the clause to join Foote's opening line to a paragraph on the fifth page of Foote's letter, thus changing the meaning of the original substantially. The succeeding paragraphs of Susan's letter are excerpted a sentence or two at a time from longer passages in Foote's letter. Susan's March 4, 1878, letter (*Angle*, pp. 190–1) is developed by Stegner from a letter by Foote written on March 4, 1878. The first two paragraphs are quoted with two minor wording changes from Foote's letter. The last paragraph has been composed by Stegner from information, including three directly quoted sentences, scattered throughout the remainder of Foote's letter.

Part IV Leadville

As in the first three parts, Stegner's "Leadville" narrative conforms in broad outline to Mary Hallock Foote's account in her reminiscences of the corresponding period of her life (*Gentlewoman*, pp. 161–207). Stegner also found the following specific details and scenes in the reminiscences, many in passages which he paraphrases closely or quotes directly:

- the mounted head and the beaver skins Arthur sent to Mary from Deadwood (*Gentlewoman*, p. 161; cf. *Angle*, p. 211)
- Mary's arrival in Denver, where Arthur's eyes were scanning faces and remained "expressionless, till suddenly they change" (*Gentlewoman*, p. 169), a description which Stegner uses in the following sentence: "Then the expressionless eyes found her, and she saw them change" (*Angle*, p. 215)
- the telegram sent too late to prevent an unnecessary earlier trip by Arthur to Denver (*Gentlewoman*, p. 167; cf. *Angle*, p. 216)
- the German wife who walked over Mosquito Pass carrying household goods (*Gentlewoman*, p. 166; cf. *Angle*, p. 217)
- the dollar each cost of the logs for the Leadville cabin (*Gentlewoman*, p. 177; cf. *Angle*, p. 218)
- the lot jumper on Arthur's first cabin site (*Gentlewoman*, p. 175; cf. *Angle*, p. 219)
- Arthur's expert testimony for $100 (*Gentlewoman*, p. 164; cf. *Angle*, p. 220)
- Mary and Arthur's meeting with the former Deadwood stage driver, who calls to Arthur: " 'Hello, hello! That you, Mr. Foote? How's the Old Woman's Fork tonight!' " (*Gentlewoman*, p. 170), a scene which Stegner records with the following paraphrase of the salute by the driver: " 'Hey there, Mister Ward! How'd you like a swim in the Old Woman Ford tonight?' " (*Angle*, p. 223)
- the description of Arthur's swimming the Old Woman Fork (*Gentlewoman*, p. 151; cf. *Angle*, pp. 223–4)
- Mary and Arthur's passing the stage coming wildly down the hill toward them, with Arthur and the driver exchanging a "queer smile" (*Gentlewoman*, p. 171), a smile that Stegner gives only the driver: "And she saw the stage driver's queer, small, gritted smile" (*Angle*, p. 233)
- the passages describing the mountains of the Great Divide and the death of their horses (*Gentlewoman*, p. 171), both of which Stegner documents as quotations from Susan's reminiscences (*Angle*, pp. 234, 235)

- the sign on the shack in Leadville, "No chickens, no eggs, no keep folks—dam!" (*Gentlewoman*, p. 172), an oddity which Stegner incorporates directly into the novel: "No chickens no eggs no keep folks dam" (*Angle*, p. 236)
- Arthur as breakfast cook (*Gentlewoman*, pp. 178–179; cf. *Angle*, pp. 243–4)
- the Geological Survey maps on the wall of the cabin (*Gentlewoman*, p. 178; cf. *Angle*, p. 247)
- Arthur's placing books under Pricey's rocking chair (*Gentlewoman*, p. 204; cf. *Angle*, p. 248)
- the riding scene in which Pricey quotes Emerson:

[H]e looked up like a worshipper and said in his fine Oxford accent:

> 'O tenderly the haughty day
> Fills his blue urn with fire—

Who in Leadville could have done that but Pricey, or would have thought of doing it! (*Gentlewoman*, p. 204),

a passage which Stegner paraphrases and quotes as follows:

Then she heard Pricey say, in his fine cultivated Oxonian voice, strongly, without the trace of a stammer,

> *Oh, tenderly the haughty day*
> *Fills his blue urn with fire.*

Who but Pricey? Where but Leadville? (*Angle*, p. 249)

- a description of the Leadville society, which included Helen Hunt Jackson, Samuel Emmons, and Clarence King (*Gentlewoman*, pp. 179–81); cf. *Angle*, p. 251)

- a description of General Vinton's funeral:

At the time of General Vinton's funeral, twenty-eight graduates of well-known technical schools rode in that extraordinary and motley procession—following the son of Dr. Vinton of Trinity to a Leadville graveyard (*Gentlewoman*, p. 201),

a passage which Stegner paraphrases as follows:

The riders were of the class of young, well-born and well-trained men who had recently contributed twenty-seven graduates of top technical schools to the procession carrying General Vinton, son of Dr. Vinton of Trinity Church, to his Leadville grave (*Angle*, p. 275)

- the defense of the Adelaide by a foreman, who remarked, " 'A Winchester is mighty comprehensive' " (*Gentlewoman*, p. 205), an action and a remark which Stegner assigns to Frank Sargent, " 'But as Jack says, a Winchester is mighty comprehensive' " (*Angle,* p. 288)

- Helen Hunt Jackson's observation about Leadville that "Grass would not grow there and cats could not live," (*Gentlewoman,* p. 179), a sentence which Stegner paraphrases as follows: "Grass won't grow, cats can't live, chickens won't lay" (*Angle,* p. 308).

In Part IV, Stegner begins his creation of Frank Sargent, a character developed from several young men who worked closely with Arthur Foote and who, as Forrest G. and Margaret G. Robinson note, had an "affectionate regard" for his wife.[14] In the Leadville section of Mary Hallock Foote's reminiscences, Stegner found the beginnings of this character in Foote's descriptions of Ferdinand Van Zandt (*Gentlewoman,* pp. 199–207). Stegner also assigns to Frank Sargent the minor roles played by various other young helpers: Sam Clark, young Fisher, and Mr. Brazier, who performed the services described in Susan's Fourth of July letter (*Angle,* p. 252).[15]

Of the two letters written by Susan Burling Ward from Leadville, Stegner apparently composed the first himself, drawing on information about Ferdinand Van Zandt and Ian Price which Foote furnished in the reminiscences and on letters which briefly mention Van Zandt and his family background.[16] The second letter, however, describing the Fourth of July party is partly excerpted (including the poem from Rossiter Raymond) with some wording changes from a letter by Foote to Charley DeKay, Helena's brother, on July 8, [1879]. The second and third paragraphs and parts of the remaining two are supplied by Stegner.

Part V Michoacán

Part V of *Angle of Repose* corresponds closely in broad outline to Mary Hallock Foote's account in her reminiscences of the Footes' experience in Mexico (*Gentlewoman,* pp. 211–43). In addition to using many details from this account, Stegner paraphrases very closely two scenes: the awakening of Casa Gravenhorst (Casa Walkenhorst in *Angle of Repose*) and the departure of the engineers from Casa Gutierrez, the latter of which Mary Hallock Foote calls "the scene of scenes in Morelia" (*Gentlewoman,* p. 230). These two scenes are also described by Foote in a *Century* article, "A Provincial Capital of Mexico."[17] Mary Hallock Foote describes morning at Casa Gravenhorst in the following passage:

> Twenty rooms opened on the corridor of the Casa Gravenhorst which was open to the sky. You looked down through its vine-wreathed arches into the main court as into a church crypt, stone pillared and full of shadows and romantic sounds. A brace of young bloodhounds chained there at night wakened us at sunrise baying to be loosed; gamecocks shouted from their gallery above the rear court; Isabel, the coachman, led

out the saddlehorses and a pair of bit white carriage mules from their
stalls beneath the arches to water at a stone tank in the sunny corral. He
sat on the curb while they were drinking, and tall bamboo stems, leaning
over the pool, sprinkled the pavement and Isabel's shoulders with flickering lights and shadows. A little later, sandals shuffled past our bedroom
door and we knew they belonged to Ascensión, in a white jacket and black
trousers and scarlet sash, who would be sweeping the corridor and water-
ing the plants and giving the doves and parrot their breakfasts. When all
the life and colors of the corridor were assembled there of a morning, including Enriqueta and her white poodle (her namesake, 'Enrique'), it was
a most lovely sitting room. Enriqueta would come springing out after
lessons with a German governess whom no one ever saw, and call in a
voice singularly deep and sonorous for a child, "Enrique, mi alma!"
(*Gentlewoman*, pp. 226–7).

Stegner's paraphrase, describing Casa Walkenhorst, contains the
basic structure and details of this passage, elaborating from Foote's
description. The paraphrase, with the elaboration omitted, is as follows:

The *corridor* was an open arcade that went around all four sides of the
court, one story up. Twenty rooms opened off it. . . . Through vine-
wreathed arches she looked down into the court pillared like a church
crypt, clean and empty in the gray light except for the hounds that surged
against their chains. . . .
Now Isabel, the coachman, came into view below her, leading a string
of two white mules and three horses. . . . While they drank, . . . Isabel
sat down on the coping of the tank. . . . with the shadows of bamboo
leaves flickering over him. . . .
Then the air was full of wings, the doves came down . . . and she saw
old Ascensión, in black trousers and white jacket and scarlet sash, scatter-
ing grain. . . . He left the doves pecking and labored up the stairs with a
heavy water jar on his shoulder; and, sandals shuffling, went along the
corridor tilting a quart or two of water into each flower pot. . . . Now
out of another door burst Don Gustavo's ten-year-old daughter Enriqueta, and embraced the poodle, crying '*Enrique, mi alma!*' (*Angle*, pp.
323–4).

Stegner's paraphrase of the description of Don Pedro Gutierrez, a
part of the scene of the departure of the engineers, is even closer to Foote's
original than the paraphrase just quoted. The following passage is Foote's
description of Don Pedro:

Don Pedro, a figure for the stage, bowed over one's hand and murmured
the phrases that matched his costume; tight leather trousers embroidered
down the seams, and I wot not of togs and silver buttons and velvet em-
bossed work on his brown leather jacket, and a wonderful hat of white
beaver, with a brim like a halo, silver braided and wound around the
crown with silver cord; soft leather boots and immense silver spurs and a
serape of price folded narrow and tossed over one shoulder. When we saw
him at the breakfast in ordinary dress, he was a little dark-visaged man of

fifty who looked as if he might have sold dry goods on Sixth Avenue; but he was one of their grandees, of a family that went back to the Conquest, owner of great ranches as well as historic mines—he probably did not know (and did not wish to measure) the extent of his own lands (*Gentlewoman*, pp. 230-1).

The following passage is Stegner's paraphrase:

His tight leather trousers, belled at the bottom, were embroidered down the seams. His leather jacket was gorgeous with togs and silver buttons and embroidered frogs. His white beaver hat had a brim like a halo, and around it for a band was wound a silver cord. His boots looked as soft as gloves, his silver spurs were wheels. A serape of great price was folded narrow and tossed over one shoulder. He might have been ridiculous; instead he was close to magificent. Susan, seeing him at breakfast the morning before, had thought him the sort of little dark man of fifty who might have sold dry goods on Sixth Avenue, but she revised her opinion as she labored to catch his likeness from the *corridor*. His family went back to the Conquest, he owned great ranches and historic mines, he would have scorned to measure the extent of his lands (*Angle*, pp. 329-30).

In the same scene, Foote describes the gear furnished by Don Pedro for the trip:

About twenty-five horses and pack mules were clattering in the court and mozos were saddling and packing them with unlimited stuff piled on the pavement: hampers of fruit, cases of vintage wines, down pillows covered with silk, linen fit for the trousseau of a duchess—I saw what they called a camp bedstead—of solid brass—taken apart and strapped on a mule's back . . . (*Gentlewoman*, p. 230).

Stegner paraphrases this description as follows:

But she saw go onto those twenty-five mules. . . . hampers of fresh fruits. . . . hampers of . . . vintage wines. . . .   There were down pillows in silk covers, linen fit for the trousseau of a duchess. She saw what the Señora Gutierrez y Salarzano said was a camp bed—solid brass . . . —taken apart and lashed onto two mules (*Angle*, p. 331).

In addition to these lengthy paraphrased passages, Stegner found the following details in Foote's reminiscences:
- the Swedish engineer who recited the Frithiof Saga on shipboard (*Gentlewoman*, pp. 212-13; cf. *Angle*, p. 318)
- the "rose-colored mountain peak" of Orizaba (*Gentlewoman*, p. 213), a phrase which Stegner paraphrases as the "rosy snow-peak" (*Angle*, p. 319)
- Arthur and the Swedish engineer's filling the railroad carriage with first-class passengers (*Gentlewoman*, p. 214; cf. *Angle*, p. 319)
- the driver of the stage who "put on speed" entering towns, aided by a man with a "leather sackful" of stones who pelted the mules (*Gentlewoman*, p. 215; cf. *Angle*, p. 319)

- their arrival in Morelia at 2 a.m., after twenty-three hours on the road (*Gentlewoman*, p. 223; cf. *Angle*, p. 320)
- Emelita, clapping her hands to call the servants (*Gentlewoman*, pp. 226, 227; cf. *Angle*, p. 324)
- a description of the linen room and the saddle room:

> She took me into her linen room one day, and if I had been a true housewife, I should have fallen down and worshipped in that shrine. We were shown the saddle room also. It impressed one with the fortunes of a house that could own those museum pieces whose worth and workmanship I had not the knowledge to evaluate . . . (*Gentlewoman*, p. 228),

a description which Stegner paraphrases in the following dialogue:

> 'She showed me her linen room yesterday. . . . If I'd been a true housewife myself I'd have gone down on my knees. It's a shrine.'
> 'You ought to see the saddle room. Museum pieces' (*Angle*, p. 325).

Mary Hallock Foote described the Footes' return trip from Morelia in a *Century* article fittingly titled, "From Morelia to Mexico City on Horseback."[18] In the opening two paragraphs of this article, she describes the sharp smells retained in her Colorado riding habit and the silk mask she wore to protect her face ("Morelia," p. 643). She included these details in her reminiscences (*Gentlewoman*, p. 235). In addition to using the image of the Colorado riding habit (*Angle*, p. 347), Stegner paraphrased from the reminiscences Foote's remarks about the face mask. Foote writes:

> And Emelita saved my complexion. . . . [S]he made me a little black silk mask. . . . The sun of Mexico, she warned me, was 'muy fuerte'! (*Gentlewoman*, p. 235).

Stegner paraphrases this passage as follows:

> Through the black silk face mask that Emelita had given her as protection against the *muy fuerte* Mexican sun . . . (*Angle*, p. 350).

Stegner closes Part V with a quotation from Susan Burling Ward's third *Century* article. The article is Foote's "Morelia" article. In that article, Foote does include a paragraph describing the party's meeting with the young Indian couple. She includes a similar paragraph in the reminiscences, closing this one with captive image used by Stegner. Stegner's version paraphrases and quotes directly from Foote's originals. In the "Morelia" article, Foote describes the scene as follows:

> We met no travelers except the itinerant Indians. . . . [O]ne . . . had given his broad hat to the woman behind him and himself walked bareheaded, his coarse thatch of hair shining like shoeblacking in the sun. The woman bore the sweet burden of womanhood, a sleeping child, hanging heavily in the folds of her *rebozo* and softly swaying with her steps. Beside

her walked a straight-backed girl, with that peculiar thick aquiline nose which gives a sensuous kind of pride to the profile of these dull faces. She carried her shoes, of light sheepskin, and a rude guitar, at her back, and looked at us fixedly with her great black eyes, lifting one corner of the blue cotton headcloth she wore, folded like that of an Italian *contadina* ("Morelia," p. 646).

Foote obviously reworked this paragraph for her reminiscences:

We met no one but Indians; once it was a young man who had given his straw hat to the woman behind him and went bare-headed, his coarse thatch of hair shining like shoeblacking in the sun. She carried a sleeping child swaying heavily in the folds of her rebozo. Behind her marched one of those straight-backed girls with the peculiar thick aquiline nose which gives a sensuous look of pride to their dull profiles. She carried nothing but her shoes of light-colored sheepskin, and a rude guitar at her back, and stared at us fixedly with her great black eyes, lifting one corner of the blue cotton headcloth she wore. A. had taken my bridle, and as we passed these Indians I happened to be riding with hands clasped behind me as a rest from holding in my Rosillo, who was a much freer traveler than the broncos. I may have looked to them like a captive masked and bound, being led away to the mountains (*Gentlewoman*, p. 237).

Stegner paraphrases and quotes from the passage as follows:

'We met no one but Indians,' she writes. 'Once it was a young man who had given his straw hat to the woman behind him and went bare headed himself, his coarse thatch of hair shining like shoe blacking in the sun. She carried a sleeping child swaying heavily in the folds of her *rebozo*. With one hand, which also carried her shoes of light-colored sheepskin, she held the end of the *rebozo* across her face. In the other hand she carried a rude guitar. Over the blue cotton cloth held across her face she stared at us fixedly out of her great black eyes.

'I wondered at her look of awed curiosity, until I realized that I was riding with my hands clasped behind me, to rest them from holding in my *rosillo*, while Oliver had taken my bridle and was leading me along. I was wearing the black silk mask that Emelita had given me. To that Indian woman I must have looked like a captive, bound and masked, being led away to the mountains' (*Angle*, pp. 351–2).

Part VI On The Bough

The events in Part VI correspond to Mary Hallock Foote's account of the interlude in the Footes' lives between their return from Mexico and the beginning of Arthur's irrigation project in Idaho (*Gentlewoman*, pp. 247–73). The title of Part VI is borrowed from the following statement by Foote: "We were 'on the bough' in New York, before starting for Idaho on the longest and wildest of our schemes" (*Gentlewoman*, p. 251). In the reminiscences, Stegner also found the following details:

- Foote's not meeting Henry James because of his " 'flirtation with coffee' " (*Gentlewoman*, p. 261; cf. *Angle*, p. 355)
- her attending *Patience* with E. L. Godkin (*Gentlewoman*, p. 261; cf. *Angle*, p. 355)
- the description of the report of Arthur's irrigation company and Clarence King's remark, which Foote reports as follows:

> . . . Fellaheen in loincloths carrying 'pots' slung from a pole across their shoulders and emptying them on the land; underneath, from Psalms: 'I have removed his shoulder from the burden; his hands were delivered from the pots.' When Clarence King saw this report . . . he said, 'That quotation ought to build the canal' (*Gentlewoman*, p. 269),

a passage which Stegner paraphrases as follows:

> . . . Fellaheen in loincloths are carrying water in pots slung on a pole, and underneath the woodcut is a quotation which with great difficulty I have determined comes from Psalms: 'I have removed his shoulder from the burden; his hands were delivered from the pots.'
>
> 'I showed that to Clarence King,' Oliver said. '. . . He says that quotation alone insures us success' (*Angle*, p. 367).

In this section of the reminiscences, Foote also reports that Ferdinand Van Zandt had chased a murderer in Mexico and that some years later he shot himself (*Gentlewoman*, pp. 250–2), events which Stegner assigns to the fictional Frank Sargent in Part VIII of *Angle of Repose*.

Part VII The Canyon

With Part VII, Stegner begins to depart from some of the actual events in the Foote's lives, although he continues to draw heavily on Foote's reminiscences and letters for important details and scenes. When Mary Hallock Foote went to Idaho, she was accompanied by her sister Bessie Sherman and her husband John. The Shermans lived in the Canyon with the Footes for a time, before establishing themselves in Boise, where Bessie ran a thriving boarding house. Thus, Stegner's account of Susan Burling Ward's sister and her husband is quite different from the events in the life of Foote's sister. The two young men who worked with Arthur Foote on the irrigation project were A. J. Wiley and Harry Tompkins. Stegner's account of Wiley fits the historical account provided by Foote. Harry Tompkins, however, becomes another source for the fictional Frank Sargent. Stegner's account of Oliver and Susan Ward's life in the Boise Canyon does otherwise closely correspond to Foote's account of her life there with Arthur (*Gentlewoman*, pp. 274–308).

Foote's reminiscences are the source of the following details and scenes used by Stegner, many in passages which Stegner paraphrases closely:

- a description of the canyon camp as three-storied:

> It was a three-story place: the river and beach floor, the hill where we said we should build if ever that came to pass, and the bluffs that rose to the level of the mountain pastures (*Gentlewoman*, pp. 292–3),

a passage which Stegner paraphrases as follows:

> Eden had three stories. The upper one ran from the canyon rim up high sage slopes toward the aspen groves, pines, mountain meadows, and cold lakes and streams of the high country. The middle story was the rounding flat in the side gulch where a spring broke out and where their buildings and garden were. The lowest story was the river beach (*Angle*, p. 383)

- a description of the photograph of young Keyser, Harry Tompkins, and Arthur in the gulch (*Gentlewoman*, p. 285; cf. *Angle*, pp. 383–4)
- a description of Nelly Linton's workbox:

> . . . a gem of Victorian marquetry inlaid with ivory and ebony and satin-wood, all fitted inside with little trays and lidded boxes which Nelly had filled with an assortment of good English pins and buttons and 'reels' of cotton and silk and yards of linen tapes and bobbins enough to last for years . . . (*Gentlewoman*, p. 281).

a passage which Stegner paraphrases as follows:

> . . . a thing of marquetry inlaid with ivory and ebony and mother of pearl, fitted inside with exquisite little drawers and lidded boxes crammed with papers and pins, reels of cotton and silk, yards of linen tape and braid, bobbins, buttons, hooks and eyes (*Angle*, pp. 400–1)

- the double rainbow that spanned the river canyon when Foote's second daughter was born and the scene that ensued:

> . . . [Arthur], who did not know that he had another daughter about two minutes old, came to the door and begged them not to let me miss this welcome to our Cañon baby. . . . Bessie held the door against him and said sternly, 'She is not thinking of rainbows!' (*Gentlewoman*, p. 300),

a passage which Stegner paraphrases in the following dialogue:

> 'Sue? Sue, if you're able, look outside. There's an absolute sign, the most perfect double rainbow you ever saw.' . . .
> 'Your wife isn't interested in rainbows,' the doctor said. 'You've got a daughter three minutes old' (*Angle*, pp. 418–9)

- the quotation from Confucius: " 'I can find no flaw in the character of Yu. . . . He lived in a low mean house, but expended all his strength on the ditches and water-channels' " (*Gentlewoman*, p. 276; *Angle*, pp. 378, 429)
- John Wesley Powell's hiring Arthur to work on the Snake River

Valley surveys (*Gentlewoman*, pp. 307–308; cf. *Angle*, p. 432)

- Harry Tompkins' giving her a two volume set of Wordsworth for Christmas, which he had bound in white lambskin (*Gentlewoman*, p. 296), an event that Stegner transforms into Frank Sargent's gift to Susan on her birthday (*Angle*, p. 447).

The passage quoted from Susan Burling Ward's reminiscences on her motivation for going to Victoria is a partial quotation and partial paraphrase of the paragraph with which Mary Hallock Foote introduces her trip to Victoria. Foote writes:

> For me, since I could not 'march with my beaten man,' I preferred to march alone somewhere down to the sea level and have my children to myself for a little while and learn to know my silent boy of eleven who was to leave us in the fall. He was ready, thanks to Nelly, for the first form at St. Paul's (*Gentlewoman*, p. 309).

Stegner's verion is as follows:

> 'Since I could not march with my beaten man,' she wrote, 'I preferred to march alone somewhere down to sea level and have my children to myself for a little while and learn to know my silent boy of eleven, who if I could possibly arrange it would be leaving us for an eastern school in the fall' (*Angle*, p. 445).

Part VIII The Mesa

Part VIII departs drastically from the Foote's real life experience. After the failure of the irrigation project, Arthur Foote was forced again to take work where he could find it while Mary remained in Boise with her sister Bessie. One position was as an engineer at an onyx mine in Baja California. Eventually, Arthur became resident superintendent of the North Star mine in Grass Valley, California. Using this broad outline, Stegner creates a scenario for Oliver and Susan Burling Ward very different from Mary Hallock Foote's account in her reminiscences of her life after she returned to Boise from Victoria. It is not surprising, therefore, that Foote's reminiscences provide few details for Part VIII. One of these is Mary Hallock Foote's brief description of the house on the mesa (*Gentlewoman*, p. 324). Another is her description of looking down from the gallery in the chapel at St. Paul's and seeing her son's "whitey brown head" (*Gentlewoman*, p. 316). Stegner uses this incident as an experience that Susan Burling Ward "never had" (*Angle*, p. 529). A third is the fact that Nelly Linton started a school in Boise after they left the Canyon (*Gentlewoman*, p. 308). Stegner places the school at the mesa ranch (*Angle*, p. 531).

The letters in Part VIII are mainly created by Stegner, to suit the changes he made from the actual events in the Footes' lives to the fictional account of the Wards' lives, but Stegner also used some particularly effective passages from letters written by Mary Hallock Foote. An undated letter from Foote to Helena, containing the statement, "We have slept two nights in this house (on the Mesa)," is the source from which Stegner quoted and paraphrased the fourth and fifth paragraphs of Susan's August 16, 1889, letter (*Angle*, pp. 476-7), the paragraphs which describe the Mesa house and her desire for Augusta's visit. A letter written July 5, [1890] by Foote to Helena is the source from which Stegner quoted and paraphrased the first two paragraphs of Susan's August 16, 1889, letter (*Angle*, p. 476), the paragraphs describing what they need on the Mesa and the comparison to Almaden. This letter also contains a description of the previous day's Fourth of July celebration on which Stegner obviously drew for the Fourth of July scene in Part VIII. A letter written October 20, 1890, by Foote to Helena is the source from which Stegner quoted and paraphrased the fourth through seventh paragraphs of Susan's November 10, 1889, letter (*Angle*, pp. 480-1), the paragraphs describing the jumped claims and the poor white family. A letter written March 2, 1890, by Foote to Helena is the source from which Stegner quoted and paraphrased the first three paragraphs of Susan's March 1, 1890, letter (*Angle*, p. 484), the paragraphs about Thomas's book and her state of mind. A letter written October 2, [1890], by Foote to Helena is the source from which Stegner quoted and paraphrased the two paragraphs describing the jilting of Sedonie in Susan's June 17, 1890, letter (*Angle*, p. 487).

II

The confusion on the point of how closely the Susan Burling Ward story reflects the life story of Mary Hallock Foote was begun by Stegner's prefatory note to *Angle of Repose*: "My thanks to J. M. and her sister for the loan of their ancestors. Though I have used many details of their lives and characters, I have not hesitated to warp both personalities and events to fictional needs. This is a novel which utilizes selected facts from their real lives. It is in no sense a family history." Stegner implies here that there is some resemblance but not much between his fictional characters and the real people upon whom he based them. Forrest G. and Margaret G. Robinson, however, state that "the details of Lyman's narrative differ little from the actual experiences of Mary Hallock Foote."[19] The Robinsons' statement is more accurate than Stegner's but it implies that all the major experiences in the lives of the fictional and the real women are the same.

Stegner in fact made few changes in recording Foote's life as the life of Susan Burling Ward. The changes he made, however, are substantial ones which, as he remarks in his note, "warp" Foote's life and personality. Stegner chose to make Susan Burling Ward an adulteress, to make her responsible for the death of a child, to show her estranged from her son for ten years, and to create a terrible rift between her and her husband because of her adultery and her responsibility for the child's death. None of these negative events occurred in Mary Hallock Foote's life. She had no lover. Her younger daughter died, not by drowning, but of appendicitis in Grass Valley on May 12, 1904 (*Gentlewoman*, p. 398). She was not estranged from her son (*Gentlewoman*, pp. 315–7, 354–5, 382). The one rift in the Footes' marriage appears to have resulted from Mary's despair at Arthur's heavy drinking. She apparently went to Victoria on a trial separation as a result. She decided to return to Arthur and after that happily lived with her decision.[20] It is obviously to these changes that Rodman Paul refers in his warning that the novel "should not be regarded as a factual explanation of Mary Hallock Foote and her career" (*Gentlewoman*, p. 403). It is an appropriate warning because commentators are generally content to note simply that the novel is based on the life of Foote without pointing to these major distortions of her biography.[21]

III

The ethical issues raised by the composition of *Angle of Repose* are almost as complex as the nature of the composition itself. Does artistic license allow Stegner to pass Mary Hallock Foote's work off as his own? Does writing "fiction" allow Stegner to ignore the constraints that are in effect for other scholars who must identify passages quoted and paraphrased from another writer? By writing "fiction," is Stegner absolved from obtaining permission to quote Foote's letters when other scholars must do so? Does Stegner escape responsibility under the aegis of artistic license for sensationalizing Mary Hallock Foote's life and bringing real grief to her heirs? Scholars snicker when a colleague points to Zane Grey's uncited borrowings. What is the appropriate response to Stegner's borrowings from Mary Hallock Foote's life and work?

One possible response to these questions is that the general reading public is unaware that Stegner used either Mary Hallock Foote's life or her writings and that, therefore, no damage has been done either to her life or to her art. This response ignores the issue of the appropriateness of one writer's use of another's work as if it were his own. It also suggests that so long as people do not know that a writer has quoted and paraphrased from another writer, he is free to borrow as he pleases. This response further ignores the fact that many readers do know that Susan Burling Ward was based on Mary Hallock Foote and that consequently considerable damage has been done to her personal reputation.

Another possible response is that Stegner was writing fiction and an author does not footnote his fiction. This response ignores the fact that *Angle of Repose* is only partly fictional. In the Susan Burling Ward story, the characters, the majority of the important scenes, and all of the settings both large and small are real, pulled directly from Mary Hallock Foote's accounts in her letters, reminiscences, and essays, very frequently incorporated into *Angle of Repose* in Foote's own language. When Stegner creates dialogue, it is often based on or paraphrased from conversations or other information reported by Mary Hallock Foote. This situation is far different from one in which an author chooses, let us say, the life of Sara Bernhardt as the outline for a novel and then creates from his own imagination the characters who people the novel, the scenes in which his characters act out their roles, and the settings where they act them out. The one main character "created" by Stegner, Frank Sargent, is a compilation of the characteristics, actions, and backgrounds of several young men described by Mary Hallock Foote. Even the sensational events created by Stegner for the final part of the Susan Burling Ward story are incorporated into the actual framework of Arthur and Mary Hallock Foote's life.

Stegner himself might offer the defense that he was protecting the wishes of Foote's heirs by not identifying Mary Hallock Foote as the source of his character. This response ignores the fact that the only protection he offered was to give different names to Arthur and Mary. It also wrongly suggests that Foote's heirs fully understood and agreed to the use that Stegner made of her life and writings. In fact, the history of Stegner's involvement with Foote's papers is long and tangled. In 1954, George McMurry, a doctoral student writing a dissertation on Foote under Stegner's direction, arranged with Janet Micoleau, Mary Hallock Foote's granddaughter, and Rosamond Gilder, Helena DeKay Gilder's daughter, to house the collection of Mary's letters to Helena at the Stanford University Library. Under their agreement with the library, Miss Gilder and Mrs. Micoleau retained for the Gilder and Foote heirs permission rights for any direct quotation of the letters. In 1967, after reading McMurry's typescripts of the letters, Stegner contacted Mrs. Micoleau with his idea for using the western experience of Arthur and Mary Hallock Foote as the outline for a novel, assuring her that the Footes would be unrecognizable in the novel and that he would not quote directly from the letters. On this basis, Mrs. Micoleau gave Stegner permission to use both the letters and the reminiscences. Stegner neither asked for nor received permission from the other Foote heirs or from Miss Gilder. In 1970, when Stegner learned that Rodman Paul was editing Foote's reminiscences for publication, he revealed to Mrs. Micoleau that he had interpreted her permission very generously but he continued to assure her that her grandparents' lives were unrecognizable. After *Angle of Repose* was in print, Stegner explained to Mrs. Micoleau that he had been unable to provide a foreword explaining his use of Foote's letters and reminiscences because Mrs. Micoleau had not wanted him to use any real names! Stegner thus excused himself from any responsibility for revealing his indebtedness to Mary Hallock Foote's writings.

While Stegner did not use Foote's real name (although he used the real names of nearly all the people with whom she was associated), he used her real life in such minute detail that she is clearly recognizable in *Angle of Repose* despite his disclaimers. Because he did so, it seems reasonable to suggest that he placed himself under a moral obligation—if not an artistic one—to avoid slandering Mary Hallock Foote through Susan Burling Ward. When Stegner chose to write a novel based on the life of Foote, world literature provided him many distinguished precedents of fictionalized versions of historical figures. Unless the author indicates otherwise, readers accept the convention that the fictional portraits are the author's interpretation of what these people must have been like, based on known historical events in which they participated or on the details of their lives that are known through their recorded acts and statements. Readers who know that Stegner based his novel on the life of Mary Hallock Foote have been allowed to assume that Stegner followed the convention. Most have not been aware that Stegner deviated significantly from the historical record when he made Susan Burling Ward an adulteress and a filicide. Most have accepted these as additional factual events in Foote's life. It is a weak, theoretical defense to assert that Susan Burling Ward should be considered a fictional character apart from the real woman on whom she is based and that to confuse the two is poor literary judgment. The theoretical defense does not prevent what has actually happened in Grass Valley, California, and elsewhere. According to Mrs. Marian Coway, "People who had barely known M. H. Foote [in Grass Valley] would stop me on the street and say, in essence, 'I never knew your grandmother did *that!*' Even though some of them listened politely to denials of all these evil doings, it was only a matter of time until a man in our local book store said to my brother-in-law, 'Don't worry—there's one in every family!' "[22]

It is true that *Angle of Repose* has reawakened interest in Mary Hallock Foote and her work. It is unfortunate that many readers have accepted the novel as a valid interpretation of her life. It is doubly unfortunate that few readers have recognized how much of her work Stegner used to build his book. Her life is fascinating in its own right. Her work deserves attention for its own sake.

Notes

1. Mary Hallock Foote, *A Victorian Gentlewoman in the Far West: The Reminiscences of Mary Hallock Foote*, ed. Rodman Paul (San Marino, Cal.: The Huntington Library, 1972), p. 403. Subsequent references appear parenthetically in the text.

2. I am indebted for this discovery to Mrs. Marian Conway, Mary Hallock Foote's granddaughter, who brought the story to my attention, noting some of the resemblances to the Lyman sections of the novel.

3. Permission to quote from "The Miniature" granted by Marian F. Conway, Janet T. Micoleau, Evelyn Foote Gardiner, Agnes Swift, and Sarah R. Swift.

4. Review of *Angle of Repose*, *Saturday Review*, 54 (March 20, 1971), 29.

5. Cf. "snow-white buckskins," *Angle of Repose* (Garden City, N.Y.: Doubleday, 1971), p. 251. Subsequent references appear parenthetically in the text.

6. "The Real Thing," *Atlantic*, 227 (April 1971), 96.

7. "The Real Thing," p. 96.

8. Mary Hallock Foote wrote more than 500 letters to Helena DeKay Gilder. The correspondence is housed at Stanford University Library. Permission to quote from the letters granted by Stanford University Library, Marian F. Conway, Janet T. Micoleau, Evelyn Foote Gardiner, Agnes Swift, Sarah R. Swift, and Rosamund Gilder. I wish to thank Barbara Cragg, University of Montana, for her important assistance in my work with the letters.

9. "Wallace Stegner and John Wesley Powell: The Real—and Maimed—Western Spokesmen," *South Dakota Review*, 15 (Winter 1977–78), 44.

10. "Heroes vs. Women: Conflict and Duplicity in Stegner," *Western Humanities Review*, 31 (Spring 1977), 136.

11. Stegner uses this letter to advance the lesbianism theme in *Angle of Repose*. See Carroll Smith-Rosenberg, "The Female World of Love and Ritual: Relations Between Women in Nineteenth-Century America," *Signs*, 1 (Autumn 1975), 1–29, for a discussion which demonstrates that the language in Foote's letter is quite typical of that used between women friends in the nineteenth century.

12. *Scribner's Monthly*, 15 (February 1878), 480–93. Subsequent references appear parenthetically in the text.

13. *Scribner's Monthly*, 16 (August 1878), 449–60.

14. *Wallace Stegner* (Boston: G. K. Hall & Co., 1977), p. 154.

15. See MHF to Charley DeKay, July 8, [1879], for the description of Mr. Brazier.

16. See MHF to Helena, June 12, [1880]; June 13, [1880]; July 10, [1880].

17. *Century Magazine*, 23 (January 1882), 321–33.

18. *Century Magazine*, 23 (March 1882), 643–55. Subsequent references appear parenthetically in the text.

19. Robinson and Robinson, p. 153.

20. From Victoria, Foote wrote to Helena DeKay Gilder on April 7, [1889]: "He [Arthur] is very well now. I had a time of great anxiety about him, which was quite demoralizing—but that is over." In another letter from Victoria, written July 5, [1889], she appraised her situation for Helena: "This experiment has settled one thing in my mind. There is no use my thinking I could go anywhere with the children for their improvement and my own away from my old boy. I'm irrevocably committed to the part of an anxious wife." On December 28, [1890], after her return to Boise, she writes to Helena of the "peace" that has succeeded her "great anxiety connected with my husband."

21. See, for example, Merrill and Lorene Lewis, *Wallace Stegner* (Boise, Idaho: Boise State College, 1972), p. 36, and Audrey C. Peterson, "Narrative Voice in Wallace Stegner's *Angle of Repose*," Western American Literature, 10 (August 1975), p. 127.

22. Mrs. Marian Conway to Mary Ellen Williams, January 11, 1980.

Wallace Stegner's *Recapitulation:*
Memory as Art Form

Merrill Lewis*

It seems inevitable—now, after the fact—that Wallace Stegner would one day write *Recapitulation* (1979). A writer who always has said he believed fiction was based on personal experiences, he has also indicated on numerous occasions that Salt Lake City was imbued for him with a very special emotional and imaginative significance. In an early essay, "At Home in the Fields of the Lord," he called it his hometown, "though I adopted my home as an adolescent and abandoned it as a young man."[1] He develops the same theme in *Recapitulation*. More recently, in "The New Jerusalem," the portrait of the city he wrote for "Rocky Mountain Country" and *The Atlantic* with his son, Page Stegner, he evokes the city again—as it was for him as an adolescent in the late 1920s and early 1930s and as it is now.[2] He adopts the same strategy in *Recapitulation*. This is Stegner's Salt Lake novel.

It is also another episode in the unfinished story of Bruce Mason, last seen clearly at the end of *The Big Rock Candy Mountain* (1943) having just buried a brother, a mother, and a father, with a law degree all but in his pocket and an uncomfortable question on his mind:

> Perhaps it took several generations to make a man, perhaps it took several combinations and re-creations of his mother's gentleness and resilience, his father's enormous energy and appetite for the new, a subtle blending of masculine and feminine, selfish and selfless, stubborn and yielding, before a proper man could be fashioned.[3]

Because those sentiments seem a bit stuffy and presumptuous for a twenty-one or twenty-two year old adolescent, regardless of what he has been through in the past several years, it seems all but inevitable that Stegner would someday return to those prophetic words. And in *Recapitulation* he has. Not with a story that is really a sequel to *The Big Rock Candy Mountain,* but with what is rather a reflective reconsideration and re-creation of events narrated during the last seven or eight years

*This essay was written especially for this volume and is published here for the first time by permission of the author.

210

of that novel, the reflections of Bruce Mason himself, about himself, conducted forty-five to fifty-five years after the original events.

In *Recapitulation* Bruce Mason takes the time to relive a segment of his adolescent life—to look back through the tangled emotions of those years—to bring more order and meaning to them than they originally had and in order to show himself he is a better man than he perhaps once was. At the end of "A Field Guide to Western Birds," Joe Allston tells his wife Ruth, "I don't know whether I'm tired, or sad, or confused. Or maybe just irritated that they don't give you enough time in a single life to figure anything out."[4] Since then, Stegner's major fictional characters, Allston, Lyman Ward, and now Mason, have tried to cope with that handicap by somehow reliving and recreating another life (their own or someone else's) in order to see whether it helps them "figure things out."

Bruce Mason is merely the latest to do this. At the end of *Recapitulation* he speculates about the relative success memory has in doubling back upon experience, what comes of revisioning—and revising—one's life:

> An undocumented life had its limitations, but also its advantages. He was not bound by verifiable facts. What he liked about the past he could coat with clear plastic, and preserve it from scratching and fading, and dust. What he did not like, he could either black out or revise. Memory, sometimes a preservative, sometimes a censor's stamp, could also be an art form.[5]

Is the life richer for having been revised? Are writer and reader better off with such knowledge?

I

When Stegner read the somber story of the Blue-Winged Teal at the Banff, Alberta Symposium "Crossing Frontiers" in April, 1978, he laconically noted that he had cannibalized it and several other early short stories for *Recapitulation*. A revision of the story "Maiden in a Tower," collected in *The City of the Living* (1956), launches the novel and gives the narrative its initial motive. Bruce Mason returns one last time to Salt Lake City. The occasion, is yet another funeral, of an aunt he hardly knew, a sister of his father, who had moved to the city unpropitiously during those last trying years when the family was falling apart. The arrangements for her funeral are to be his last obligations to that past. But the house with the tower that now serves as the Merrill Funeral Home was once an apartment for one of Bruce Mason's college flames, Holly, and for a very short time, Nola Gordon, the girl he fell in love with while still attending the University of Utah.

Bruce Mason feels like a "newsreel diver" from the moment he rounds the southern edge of the Great Salt Lake and heads north, then East again, towards the city laid out along the base of the Wasatch

Range; but once he makes the connection between funeral and Holly and Nola, the reader senses that burying Aunt Margaret is incidental. There is more to bury here, and in the two shortened days he spends in the city, the arc of Mason's memories will reach back and forth across the decades since he left, across the city itself and into the mountains beyond, until all that has ever bothered him about the place and those ancient-seeming ghosts of people and events is dug-up and exposed, and then laid to rest.

"The Volunteer," the second story Stegner borrows for the novel, furnishes one of the earliest recollections of the older Bruce Mason—he is only thirteen at the time, and setting his faint hopes for escape and approval on school and his compassionate mother. The memory follows quickly upon the heels of Mason's visit to the funeral parlor and indicates that the novel is not going to just about college and girls, but about home, or the absence of home. Driven from the house on a cold autumn evening out of shame because he has inadvertently stumbled upon two of his father's speakeasy customers petting in the parlor, young Bruce later hears his mother's protest:

> Will you tell me why—just tell me why—a boy should have to stay out of part of his own house, and hang out in the kitchen like the hired girl, for fear of what he'll see if he doesn't? Is that the way a home should be? How can he grow up? How can he have any self-respect, how can he even know right from wrong, when all he sees at home is people like Lew McReady? (p. 43)

How can Bruce Mason ever know security, or be "a proper man," indeed? It is much more likely that he will know only fear, shame, disgust and repudiation.

"The Blue-Winged Teal," perhaps Stegner's best short story, furnishes the material for the climactic episode of the novel. It, too, is about shame and repudiation; but it is also about reconciliation and leave-taking. In the early morning hours of the second day of his odyssey Mason recalls the time, shortly after his mother's death, that he brought the ducks he had shot to the old, dilapidated basement pool room/diner run by his father and Maxie Schmeckebier and then reluctantly joined in the feast Schmeckebier prepared for the three of them ("with its troubled and nearly compassionate ending" the older Bruce Mason adds in the novel, p. 264). The ducks seem an offering, and the feast communion. The reader realizes that young Bruce Mason's search for a home has met with some final disaster and the search of the old Bruce Mason for young Bruce Mason has led to a change of heart.

Stegner frequently launches his longer narratives from some initial work in short fiction. *The Big Rock Candy Mountain* is the most obvious example. *All the Little Live Things* (1967) had similar beginnings. Stegner's own word "cannibalization" does not do justice to the imaginative skill by which he adapts the stories to his novelistic purposes—and in the case of *Recapitulation* invents an extended narrative that will link the materials in these different stories, and make them effective beginnings and endings.

The most important changes, from story to novel, are easy enough to identify. In the novel, Aunt Margaret is made the sister of Bo Mason, rather than the sister of Mason' mother, a change that makes Mason's dutiful trip quite different in its emotional impact on him. More significantly, Kimball Harris, the protagonist of "Maiden in a Tower, " is a happily-married family man, while the Bruce Mason of *Recapitulation* is a confirmed bachelor. Harris recalls that evening in Holly's tower apartment, when she offered herself to him ("that moment when Holly stopped playing make-believe") as a moment when prudence met imprudence in a joust and won. He had made the right choice when (somehow, he is not quite sure) he rejected her. He would sadly but undoubtedly make the same choice again. Afterwards, she had broken away, to Shanghai and the world. "He had played it the other way, not so much from choice as from yielding to pressures."[6] Because Bruce Mason of *Recapitulation* remains single, the episode in the novel seems more innocent while it establishes Bruce's cautiousness. Another difference between the versions is that in the novel version both he and Holly are people who did break away from the provinciality of the city; thus Holly's leave-taking becomes a preamble to Bruce's later break. And finally, since the character of Holly is shaped and Mason's final judgment of her made only as he *recapitulates* the action, the episode indicates just how completely everything in the past will be subject to Mason's later *re*-creation.

The brief affair with Holly is also made a preamble to the great affair of Bruce's life. The novel version introduces us to Nola. But Nola is associated with other places than the tower. Bruce's love for her involved much more than an unexpected and momentary encounter and temptation on a window seat—motivated half by curiosity, half by comic masculine role-playing. And the plea Nola makes will be the opposite of Holly's, for Nola wants Bruce to stay in Salt Lake, to settle down and get married. Holly, clinging to him and crying, pleads with him to take her away from this grubby place (p. 13). This is but an extended version of her plea to Kim Hattis in the short story.[7]

The major change between the story "The Volunteer" and the same episode in the novel is the shift in point of view from first person to third person limited, to make the episode consistent with the rest of the novel. In other words, Stegner has turned back to the point of view he used in *The Big Rock Candy Mountain* here, too. "The Blue-Winged Teal" was already written from this point of view, one that Forrest and Margaret Robinson point out is characteristic of stories about Bruce Mason, or young men of his stamp. They note, for example, that in "The Blue-Winged Teal" Henry Lederer is really a Bruce-type character, caught in a Bruce-type dilemma, but a character considerably matured beyond the earliest "Brucie" stories, capable of sympathy and tolerance and an uncharacteristic capacity "to see through another's eyes."[8]

In *Recapitulation* Stegner has also turned away from the first person narrator used in the Joe Allston novels and in *Angle of Repose*. I am not concerned here with getting involved in any controversy over which point of view is preferable for which kind of story. In my view Stegner is interested in these late novels in how each point of view can enlarge upon autobiographical material with quite different effects. Allston's acerbic voice belongs to a tradition of autobiographical writing that I associate with the late Mark Twain of the *Autobiography*. He is characteristically incisive, caustic, occasionally nasty and spiteful, opinionated and therefore unreliable—and reluctant to admit that he shows any of these qualities. Mason's voice—and the third person point of view does allow him one—may occasionally sound like Allston (as when he laces into Jack Bailey), but it belongs more to that tradition of autobiographical writing I associate with Henry Adams' *Education*. He is characteristically reflective and meditative. Allston writes from his nerve endings; Mason is more cerebral. Allston is typically concerned with what is wrong with the world and others, and why they get on his nerves. Mason's more moderate and rueful voice tries to negotiate the grievances with those closest to him. Allston wants to speak the truth; Mason wants to be understood and believed. One key to both narrative voices is the way they are self-consciously ironic. They both use irony as an elaborate and deliberate cover as well as a weapon.

The changes made in the novel to the story "The Blue-Winged Teal" consist almost entirely of additions to the end of the story that make it Bruce Mason's story—a man in his sixties rather than in his twenties or thirties, who is concerned about what he remembers and what he wants to believe he remembers, and the deeply personal motives for doing either.

II

While *Recapitulation* may appear to be a novel that moves back and forth between time past and time present like its two immediate predecessors, *Angle of Repose* (1971) and *The Spectator Bird* (1976), it is closer to the first part of *Wolf Willow* in being a remembrance of things past.[9] It juxtaposes a young Bruce Mason and an old Bruce Mason, just as *The Spectator Bird* juxtaposes an old Joe Allston and a middle-aged Joe Allston. But the journal that Joe reads his wife Ruth in *The Spectator Bird* is an "historical" document, as are the letters and journal of Lyman Ward's grandmother. For such external evidence Mason is limited to a few photographs and some letters young Bruce wrote Nola. The fact that he uses these very little, and never aggressively pursues other potential documentation, indicates how fully he accepts the authority of memory, despite its handicaps. Unlike the case in *Wolf Willow*, then, memory alone will give sufficient motive and shape to events and people.

In a sense, the novel is Mason's extended meditation on the subject of his quest—his youthful self. He and his younger self are one and yet divisible—doubles but not duplicates. As he walks down the street his first evening in the city, Mason notices that "the person who saw and the person who remembered were not the same, though they used the same eyes" (p. 19). The boy he walks with was "not so much a person as a possibility, or a bundle of possibilities." "A vessel of primary sensations undiluted by experience, wisdom, or fatigue," Bruce's character was not fully formed: "put aside, postponed, overtaken by events, he was never defined, much less fulfilled—hardly even remembered" until this moment (p. 19). Bruce is a ghost: first, in the sense that he was not a complete personality (neither fully developed or fully imagined) and, second, in the sense that he haunts his creator and older self.

The relationship between the two is immensely rich. One can point out only part of the complexity. They share a common view of women:

> Whether women have difficulty getting credit cards or not, it is not they who rocket around through empty universes hunting for a place in which to come to rest. They are themselves such a place.
> So it seemed to Bruce Mason then. So it seems to Mason now (p. 136).

The reader must note the rather ludicrous but plaintive self-pity in such an observation as well as how closely it echoes Bo Mason's sentiments in *Big Rock Candy Mountain*. Both long for the security and sense of well-being associated with the woman's world and home. But they will continue to turn away from women and home at crucial points in their lives.

On other occasions, Mason puts young Bruce down in firm, almost paternalistic fashion. As a young teenager, Bruce is "a shrimp," trying to gain favor and status however he can. He develops a "comic ferocity" to protect a strong sense of inferiority. He becomes a dude and a dandy in college, roles that Mason calls "social and imitative," motivated by a strong desire to belong (see pp. 27, 29, 77). Catching Bruce at an atypical moment paying a compliment to Olive Bramwell, "a really nice girl," Mason feels obliged to identify his more typical behavior: "Some of the bluster of his runt years clung to him. He affected the humor of belittlement and insult, he specialized in the outrageous. Hello, Double-Ugly. Hey, Repulsive, give us a kiss" (p. 82). Describing Bruce's halcyon days at the university, Mason modifies the impression again: "It would be falsifying memory to pretend that he was anything but arrogant and a prig. . . . He assumed that his happiness was the product of his own excellence" (p. 124).

But Mason has genuinely mixed feelings about the young man as well. He may be so embarrassed by one of Bruce's letters to Nola that he momentarily shrinks from "the relationship" (p. 184). But he is sometimes jealous of the life Bruce only knew—if not the girl, Nola, then "the romantic readiness, the emotions as responsive as wind chimes" (pp. 115–16). When he asks himself how Bruce could possibly have been attracted to Jack Bailey, laugh at his dirty jokes, steal radiator caps to entertain him, he concedes that it is plausible. When a female confidante whom he has invented (Mason calls her "one of those imaginary women who soothe") tells him that at least he has—in his mature years—overcome the handicaps of his youth and "outgrown" young Bruce, Mason is not so sure and replies, "Maybe. Maybe not" (p. 86). His reply to her is ambiguous, as are so many of his responses to Bruce. But certainly his own character has been shaped by Bruce's reaction to the events of those early years. He is alienated from his father yet. And he is a confirmed Stoic.

III

The novel is structured out of these somewhat random and seemingly chaotic memories. But there are two clear dramatic lines established within this seeming chaos. The first of these covers the seven or eight years of Bruce's life that begin with the episode related in "The Volunteer" and end with the events narrated in "The Blue-Winged Teal." These two episodes frame Bruce's story. In retrospect we can see that the "story" begins in what Mason calls Bruce's "runt years," where he settles it that he hates and despises his father for failing to give the family a decent home and is unreconciled to the underground existence forced upon him and his mother. It takes the reader through a series of episodes from the high school years where we see Bruce somewhat ludicrously attempting to grow up and become independent by working as a bus boy at Saltair, or joining the National Guard at Fort Douglas. Then there is the all but miraculous discovery of Bruce by Joe Mulder at the tennis club—where Bruce's mother has sent him to get him out of the house and away from books and introspection. Joe not only introduces Bruce to tennis (to Kreps and Bailey) but to the social life at the university. For five years he works at the Mulder nursery, is welcomed into the Mulder home and practically made part of the family, and, with graduation, offered a permanent job that promises a future partnership. During his last golden senior year he also falls in love with Nola, a girl with an "incomparably physical, barefoot woman's walk" (p. 202).

Nola is another of Stegner's earthy women, like Marian Catlin in *All the Little Live Things*. There is more cowboy than church in her Mormon family. She is part Indian, loves to ride horses, hates to talk books. The two are complete opposites but for a brief time seem one: Yin and Yang. Even in the midst of such a paradise, Bruce's life starts to unravel. He develops a stomach ulcer. His mother gets cancer and needs surgery. He and Nola consummate their own love during a hurried trip to her sister's wedding, down on the ranch. They plan to get married, but Bruce is offered a fellowship at law school in Minnesota. He wavers, but goes. Then catastrophe hits. Chet unexpectedly dies during Bruce's first year away. Then his mother dies, just as he is completing work on the law degree. He see Nola only on those tragic occasions that bring him back, or fitfully during a summer. Nola urges him to return or to stay; finally dirty Bailey steals her.

Framing this story line, and infusing it as well with his own presence, is Mason, with his own story. His search through the past takes place between late afternoon of one day, and morning of the next. I have called his search a meditation. At one point he calls it a pilgrimage. It is something of a Dantesque dark night of the soul. Duty has brought Mason to Salt Lake City. But once his memories have been stirred, he feels duty-bound as well to follow them where they lead him. As he finds himself drawn "through some barrier into an earlier and simpler time" (p. 30) it becomes clear that the simplicity he finds there is as much the creation of Mason's imagination as it is history. Mason is surprised that that earlier life was so innocent, but remembering it also exposes him to feelings "he thought completely outgrown"—emotions that, recollected, can move him more than emotions of his mature years.

The changes in the city mirror the changes in individual lives, changes that at once mask the past and cover it up and subsequently require an active imagination to bring it back. As the past returns, it is changed—transformed, enlarged as well as simplified. Memory infuses the place with psychic and moral energy. Mason can see the street he walks as "Anystreet, Anywhere," yet he knows it "in its special and local identity" (p. 71). Later he adds: "This was his place—first his problem, then his oyster, and now the museum or diorama where early versions of him were preserved" (p. 120). At first his journey through this, his city, seems rather casual, and not clearly motivated, and he half apologizes at one point for writing about "frivolous things" (p. 121). But as the night passes, his travels by foot, car, and imagination becomes more direct and less discreet. As his recollections become more troubled, serious, and grave, brilliant dream sequences intermesh with more rationally constructed scenes.

In the beginning he is sure how he will find Bruce, if he does succeed in finding him. He will be "rat-eyed and watchful in some corner, or gnawing his own trapped limbs in his agony to escape" (p. 30). The image is too melodramatic, but the petting scene in the front parlor with McReady and the nurse, followed by yet another parental quarrel and thirteen-year-old Brucie's protestations that he will rescue his mother from it all, does give some credence to the emotion behind the image. By the time Mason gets to the last of his memories, the one involving the blue-winged teal (his mother's favorite bird) and the duck feed, our knowledge of Bruce has changed dramatically. We owe that knowledge to Mason's willingness to expose the most awkward and painful memories of his youth, and to his critical but scrupulous eye. The knowledge prepares us for the reconciliation of son to father that does not quite seem plausible at the end of *The Big Rock Candy Mountain*. The changes are in Bruce, not his father. The Bo Mason of *Recapitulation* is largely the Bo Mason of the earlier novel. But Bruce is radically different. By uncovering Bruce's life sympathetically yet critically, Mason comes to see his father more clearly and more honestly, too. The reconciliation of the son to the father requires a reconciliation of the self with the self. Before he can put his ghosts to rest, Mason must accept what was and see clearly what remains. Mason's awakening does not come easily because he is obstinate and reluctant. When he can bring himself finally to look for the building containing Bo's pool hall, he finds it is gone. The flea-bag hotel where his father had killed himself is also gone: "downtown rehabilitation has paved over the lowest points in his life" (p. 83). He is shocked at the change, because he can still remember the place and scene so vividly—down to the bullet hole in the door. He is offended; important places should remain. He begins to realize that he also wishes his father were still alive, "so that he could return to him and settle something" (p. 84). If he could settle things with his father, he could also settle them with Joe, and Bailey, and Nola. "With all of them, dead or alive, he had binding treaties to make" (p. 84). Mason becomes, then, an ambassador, desiring to negotiate a settlement and bring some peace between them and himself.

Mason realizes this much of his awakening and this much of his changing motive in the middle of his night journey. But desiring a treaty and striking one are two different things. He had in a few months of the first years of the 1930s buried his brother, his mother, his "young love," and his "innocence." Then in a few more, his father and his youth (p. 84). "An influential part of his consciousness" would like to "leave it that way" (p. 83). But the dead will not rest in peace; or Mason is not at peace with them. As he traverses his city, his great motive becomes to bury the ghosts as well. But the ghosts are *his* ghosts, part of his world and his identity, so he must expose himself as he exposes them. Some come readily forward and submit. The case of Nola is settled quickly. Some, such as his mother, don't need to be brought back because he feels at ease with her. Some, like Joe Mulder, were such utterly decent people that they are no problem as ghosts. And Joe is still alive, so the problem there is to reconcile the living with the living and explain the forty-five years of silence. But the mysterious ones, like Nola, and the profoundly troubling ones, like Bailey and his father, are difficult to recollect and difficult to bury. They tell him the most about himself.

His loss of Nola raises the issue first. At the beginning of his adventure Mason finds the remembered past more real and more moving than the present. But later, as he prepares for bed in the Hotel Utah, he hesitates to open a box of Nola's memorabilia (which was among his aunt's last few effects) because these photographs and letters may not be consistent with what he remembers and/or imagines. Memory, he concedes, is "deceptive and self-serving." Nola may not have been "the dark mysterious desirable girl he thought he remembered." "What if he had invented her?" he asks. If Nola was not what he imagined, then what about his imagined suffering? And how can he justify his stoicism? He is "reconciled to having been a fool," but if she was not irresistable, then he is more than a fool and worse than a fool (pp. 184–85). These last observations do not surface in Mason's consciousness, but he leads the reader to the edge of them. He prefers that the story of his and Nola's love be the kind of story that justifies his actions.

The case of his father is as problematic. In the early morning hours of the second day, while he waits for the funeral, Mason again tours the city, looking for places not looked for the night before. It is equally disappointing: Fort Douglas has become a golf course, the Mulder Nursery has a face-lifting, the first house they lived in in the city is no longer there. Finally, he swings by the apartment where his mother died, and it, too, has disappeared. Once again he feels cheated, for "this was what he had been inexorably returning to—this misery, this wreck of everything" (pp. 242–43). He repeats for one last time his litany of losses—brother, money, girl, and now mother. Again, the city seems to conspire to deny him the past and the identity—the sorrow and the anger—that he so wants.

He is sure that it is all his father's fault. He has repudiated him for forty-five years ("He never had a father" [p. 141]) and he wants that repudiation justified. But memory and the past do not give him the satisfaction he so desperately wants. He is not sure now just how he did break away from his father and this, his city of early sorrow. "Did he make a brutal scene?" he asks himself. Did he say any harsh things on parting, or did he "only rehearse them sullenly, wanting to say them" (pp. 244–45)? Briefly he imagines what a scene might have been like. It is twin to that fantasy thirteen-year-old Bruce has at the end of the scene with McReady and the speakeasy, where he "whipped his father with his tongue until he cried and begged forgiveness for all his impatience and contempt" (p. 45).

As with Nola, such scenes are deceptive and self-serving. Mason had worked his whole life to "dis-create" them both (see p. 62), but memory won't let him. On the other hand, he is forced to recreate them, he is not at all sure he has the real thing. Why, he asked himself early in the novel, did he persist in seeing his father as a violent man—"his father was not always like that" (p. 49). Now, in remembering or inventing their separation, he feels even less sure of himself. "Anything he remembered about his father might be pure fiction" (p. 264). The scene he does give us—the duck-feed in the pool room—is understated and full of that "watchful, obscurely sullen silence" with which he had learned to respond to his father during his early years (see p. 140). His leave-taking, at the end of the feast, contains no rancor and involves no confrontation. When he tells his father that he is starting back to Minneapolis, "He said it like a cry, and with the feeling he might have had on letting go the hand of a companion too weak and exhausted to cling any longer to their inadequate shared driftwood in a wide cold sea" (p. 263). That gesture, following a toast by his father to "Happy days," is as far as the reconciliation goes, though it is given some permanency by the tombstone that Mason then orders for his father's grave.

IV

The character of Jack Bailey mediates this reconciliation. Mason claims that when Bruce left Salt Lake he hated Bailey as much as he hated his father (p. 23). And he establishes Bailey's peculiar kind of moral shabbiness and carelessness early in the novel: when Bailey wrecked his father's car the second time, he killed the girl who was joy riding with him. He is sent on a mission by the Mormon Church, but it is quickly aborted because he spends his time converting girls down on the beach. He next proceeds to become a haberdasher's clerk and sets the style and tone for much of the social life in Bruce's college crowd. Bruce is "snake-charmed" by Bailey's story of how he "made it" with a girl on the front porch with the girl's mother at the door. When Mason asks himself why Bruce caught "like another childhood disease the sexual morality that was properly Bailey's inheritance, not his," he can give no sure answer. He is more sure why Bailey "troubles" him now: since Bailey ended up with Nola (but for how long we are never told) his feelings are fed by jealousy or vanity. But Bailey also "demonstrated the attractiveness of amorality and self-indulgence and irresponsibility" (p. 81).

Another answer is implicit in the frequent association Mason makes between Bailey's morality and his father's. Mason finds the old pool hall as troubling a presence as Bailey (p. 81). When Bruce takes Nola home to meet his mother for the first time (she is recovering from her masectomy), they are surprised by the unexpected return of Bo from Los Angeles. He regales them with the story of a near accident on the way home and clowns around in other ways, flirting with Nola and seeking attention. Again, his father reminds him of Bailey. Nola finds that Bo's toughness reminds her of Bruce. And Bruce's reputation for clowning is well established by this time, as are his ties to Bailey (see pp. 140–43).

There is other evidence that Bruce is, in many ways, like his father. As he reads one of his letters to Nola, written from Minneapolis during a year of separation, Mason characterizes the writer as adolescent, and "mule headed" and "a digger," all qualities that remind us of his father. There is the affair with Nola at Capital Reef, when they return from her sister's wedding. Mason treats that affair with a quiet respect, but not so the broken promises that follow. The later affair in the cabin at Brighton which turned into a strip-poker party, promoted by Bailey, "a Hawthorne

Mephistopheles" (p. 222), is something else. It is a brilliant scene: by turns sordid, comic and pathetic. Mason is careful to relate the whole of it from a distance, referring to himself ruefully as "the stage manager who has revived and is directing this period piece" (p. 216) rather than participant, whereas he is both the camera eye and the actor in the Capital Reef affair. Bruce is completely implicated here. Not only does he know that Bailey is cheating at the card game, he joins in. Any further claims of innocence would be spurious. Any further attempts by Bruce, or Mason, to feel morally superior to Bo seem completely out of place. Like father, like son. The duck feed in the old pool hall is narrated in the quiet morning aftermath of the night that ends with this knowledge.

The reconciliation of Mason to his father does not involve forgiveness: after such knowledge, what forgiveness can there be? He concedes that his remembered/invented version of their parting "might be a creation of revisionism and guilt" (p. 264). It was certainly more plausible and believable, less false and histrionic than earlier imagined confrontations. He hoped there had been no "recrimination and contempt" as there had been in parting from Nola. He had never felt good about that parting. But he could "recover from a girl, who represents to some extent a choice. It is not so easy to recover from parents, who are fate" (p. 264). In his version of that leavetaking, he fully accepts his inheritance.

Notes

1. As reprinted in *The Sound of Mountain Water* (Garden City, N.Y.: Doubleday, 1969), p. 159.

2. *The Atlantic*, 241 (April 1978), 74–82.

3. *The Big Rock Candy Mountain* (New York: Duell, Sloan and Pearce, 1943), p. 515.

4. *The City of the Living* (Boston: Houghton Mifflin, 1956), p. 173.

5. *Recapitulation* (Garden City, N.Y.: Doubleday, 1979), pp. 264–65. Subsequent citations are in the text.

6. *The City of the Living*, pp. 81–82. Though the temptation Nola offers Bruce in *Recapitulation* is different from the temptation Holly offers in either the short story or novel, it is interesting to notice that at the end of the novel Bruce claims that girls represent a choice. Harris's "yielding to pressures" comes close to explaining Bruce's motive for going to graduate school rather than marrying Nola, though Stegner never make it clear just why he goes.

7. *The City of the Living*, p. 79.

8. *Wallace Stegner* (Boston: G. K. Hall, 1977), p. 81, but see their lengthy discussion of point of view in the short fiction and *The Big Rock Candy Mountain* (pp. 72–92, 117).

9. Stegner himself has drawn such a Proustian analogy in "At Home in the Fields of the Lord," *The Sound of Mountain Water*, p. 167.

INDEX